AF788849

Introductory Econometrics

Introductory Econometrics

Edited by
Piers Jackson

Larsen & Keller
www.larsen-keller.com

Introductory Econometrics
Edited by Piers Jackson
ISBN: 978-1-63549-667-3 (Hardback)

© 2018 Larsen & Keller

Larsen & Keller

Published by Larsen and Keller Education,
5 Penn Plaza,
19th Floor,
New York, NY 10001, USA

Cataloging-in-Publication Data

Introductory econometrics / edited by Piers Jackson.
p. cm.
Includes bibliographical references and index.
ISBN 978-1-63549-667-3
1. Econometrics. 2. Economics, Mathematical. I. Jackson, Piers.
HB139 .I58 2018
330.015 195--dc23

This book contains information obtained from authentic and highly regarded sources. All chapters are published with permission under the Creative Commons Attribution Share Alike License or equivalent. A wide variety of references are listed. Permissions and sources are indicated; for detailed attributions, please refer to the permissions page. Reasonable efforts have been made to publish reliable data and information, but the authors, editors and publisher cannot assume any responsibility for the vailidity of all materials or the consequences of their use.

Trademark Notice: All trademarks used herein are the property of their respective owners. The use of any trademark in this text does not vest in the author or publisher any trademark ownership rights in such trademarks, nor does the use of such trademarks imply any affiliation with or endorsement of this book by such owners.

The publisher's policy is to use permanent paper from mills that operate a sustainable forestry policy. Furthermore, the publisher ensures that the text paper and cover boards used have met acceptable environmental accreditation standards.

Printed and bound in China.

For more information regarding Larsen and Keller Education and its products, please visit the publisher's website www.larsen-keller.com

Table of Contents

Preface

Econometrics refers to particular type of statistical models that are used to test and forecast future economic trends. The models used in this subject are logit, hazard, tobit, linear regression, etc. This textbook presents the complex subject of econometrics in the most comprehensible and easy to understand language. Such selected concepts that redefine this field have been presented in it. For someone with an interest and eye for detail, the text covers the most significant topics in the field.

A foreword of all chapters of the book is provided below:

Chapter 1 - The application of statistical and mathematical methods to economics is known as econometrics. The main tool used in econometrics is multiple linear regression model. This chapter is an overview of the subject matter incorporating all the major aspects of econometrics; **Chapter 2 -** The branch of mathematics which studies probability is known as probability theory. The central topics related to the subject of probability are probability distributions, continuous random variables and stochastic processes. The other topics discusses in this section are statistical hypothesis testing, dependent and independent variables, etc. This chapter elucidates the crucial theories and principles of econometrics; **Chapter 3 -** Statistics used to describe a group of information is known as descriptive statistics. It helps in summarizing samples. Central tendency, univariate econometric modelling, univariate analysis are some of the topics discussed in the section. The aspects elucidated in this chapter are of vital importance, and provide a better understanding of statistical models; **Chapter 4 -** The process used for assessing the relationship between variables is known as regression analysis. It is mostly used for prediction and forecasting. The chapter strategically encompasses and incorporates the major components and key concepts of econometrics, providing a complete understanding.

At the end, I would like to thank all the people associated with this book devoting their precious time and providing their valuable contributions to this book. I would also like to express my gratitude to my fellow colleagues who encouraged me throughout the process.

Editor

1

An Overview of Econometrics

The application of statistical and mathematical methods to economics is known as econometrics. The main tool used in econometrics is multiple linear regression model. This chapter is an overview of the subject matter incorporating all the major aspects of econometrics.

Econometrics

Literally interpreted, econometrics means "economic measurement." Although measurement is an important part of econometrics, the scope of econometrics is much broader, as can be seen from the following quotations:

"Econometrics, the result of a certain outlook on the role of economics/ finance, consists of the application of mathematical statistics to economic data to lend empirical support to the models constructed by mathematical economics and to obtain numerical results."

"Econometrics may be defined as the quantitative analysis of actual economic phenomena based on the concurrent development of theory and observation, related by appropriate methods of inference."

"Econometrics may be defined as the social science in which the tools of economic theory, mathematics, and statistical inference are applied to the analysis of economic phenomena."

"Econometrics is concerned with the empirical determination of economic laws."

Econometrics is the application of statistical methods to economic data and is described as the branch of economics that aims to give empirical content to economic relations. More precisely, it is "the quantitative analysis of actual economic phenomena based on the concurrent development of theory and observation, related by appropriate methods of inference." An introductory economics textbook describes econometrics as allowing economists "to sift through mountains of data to extract simple relationships." The first known use of the term "econometrics" (in cognate form) was by Polish economist Paweł Ciompa in 1910. Ragnar Frisch is credited with coining the term in the sense in which it is used today.

The basic tool for econometrics is the multiple linear regression model. Econometric theory uses statistical theory and mathematical statistics to evaluate and develop econometric methods. Econometricians try to find estimators that have desirable statistical properties including unbiasedness, efficiency, and consistency. *Applied econometrics* uses theoretical econometrics and real-world data for assessing economic theories, developing econometric models, analyzing economic history, and forecasting.

Basic Models: Linear Regression

The basic tool for econometrics is the multiple linear regression model. In modern econometrics, other statistical tools are frequently used, but linear regression is still the most frequently used starting point for an analysis. Estimating a linear regression on two variables can be visualized as fitting a line through data points representing paired values of the independent and dependent variables.

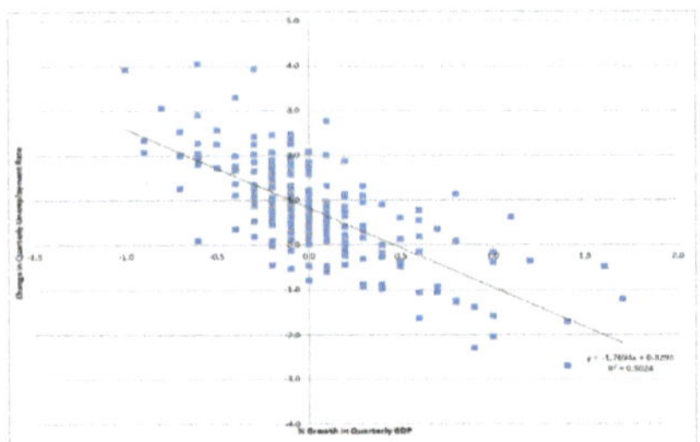

Okun's law representing the relationship between GDP growth and the unemployment rate. The fitted line is found using regression analysis.

For example, consider Okun's law, which relates GDP growth to the unemployment rate. This relationship is represented in a linear regression where the change in unemployment rate (Δ Unemployment) is a function of an intercept (β_0), a given value of GDP growth multiplied by a slope coefficient β_1 and an error term, ε:

$$\Delta \text{ Unemployment} = \beta_0 + \beta_1 \text{Growth} + \varepsilon.$$

The unknown parameters β_0 and β_1 can be estimated. Here β_1 is estimated to be −1.77 and β_0 is estimated to be 0.83. This means that if GDP growth increased by one percentage point, the unemployment rate would be predicted to drop by 1.77 points. The model could then be tested for statistical significance as to whether an increase in growth is associated with a decrease in the unemployment, as hypothesized. If the estimate of β_1 were not significantly different from 0, the test would fail to find evidence that changes in the growth rate and unemployment rate were related. The variance in a prediction of the dependent variable (unemployment) as a function of the independent variable (GDP growth) is given in polynomial least squares.

Theory

Econometric theory uses statistical theory and mathematical statistics to evaluate and develop econometric methods. Econometricians try to find estimators that have desirable statistical properties including unbiasedness, efficiency, and consistency. An estimator is unbiased if its expected value is the true value of the parameter; it is consistent if it converges to the true value as sample size gets larger, and it is efficient if the estimator has lower standard error than other unbiased estimators for a given sample size. Ordinary least squares (OLS) is often used for estimation since it provides the BLUE or "best linear unbiased estimator" (where "best" means most efficient, unbiased estimator) given the Gauss-Markov assumptions. When these assumptions are violated or other statistical properties are desired, other estimation techniques such as maximum likelihood estimation, generalized method of moments, or generalized least squares are used. Estimators that incorporate prior beliefs are advocated by those who favor Bayesian statistics over traditional, classical or "frequentist" approaches.

Methods

Applied econometrics uses theoretical econometrics and real-world data for assessing economic theories, developing econometric models, analyzing economic history, and forecasting.

Econometrics may use standard statistical models to study economic questions, but most often they are with observational data, rather than in controlled experiments. In this, the design of observational studies in econometrics is similar to the design of studies in other observational disciplines, such as astronomy, epidemiology, sociology and political science. Analysis of data from an observational study is guided by the study protocol, although exploratory data analysis may be useful for generating new hypotheses. Economics often analyzes systems of equations and inequalities, such as supply and demand hypothesized to be in equilibrium. Consequently, the field of econometrics has developed methods for identification and estimation of simultaneous-equation models. These methods are analogous to methods used in other areas of science, such as the field of system identification in systems analysis and control theory. Such methods may allow researchers to estimate models and investigate their empirical consequences, without directly manipulating the system.

One of the fundamental statistical methods used by econometricians is regression analysis. Regression methods are important in econometrics because economists typically cannot use controlled experiments. Econometricians often seek illuminating natural experiments in the absence of evidence from controlled experiments. Observational data may be subject to omitted-variable bias and a list of other problems that must be addressed using causal analysis of simultaneous-equation models.

Example

A simple example of a relationship in econometrics from the field of labor economics is:

$$\ln(\text{wage}) = \beta_0 + \beta_1(\text{years of education}) + \varepsilon.$$

This example assumes that the natural logarithm of a person's wage is a linear function of the number of years of education that person has acquired. The parameter β_1 measures the increase in the natural log of the wage attributable to one more year of education. The term ε is a random variable representing all other factors that may have direct influence on wage. The econometric goal is to estimate the parameters, β_0 and β_1 under specific assumptions about the random variable ε. For example, if ε is uncorrelated with years of education, then the equation can be estimated with ordinary least squares.

If the researcher could randomly assign people to different levels of education, the data set thus generated would allow estimation of the effect of changes in years of education on wages. In reality, those experiments cannot be conducted. Instead, the econometrician observes the years of education of and the wages paid to people who differ along many dimensions. Given this kind of data, the estimated coefficient on Years of Education in the equation above reflects both the effect of education on wages and the effect of other variables on wages, if those other variables were correlated with education. For example, people born in certain places may have higher wages and higher levels of education. Unless the econometrician controls for place of birth in the above equation, the effect of birthplace on wages may be falsely attributed to the effect of education on wages.

The most obvious way to control for birthplace is to include a measure of the effect of birthplace in the equation above. Exclusion of birthplace, together with the assumption that ϵ is uncorrelated with education produces a misspecified model. Another technique is to include in the equation additional set of measured covariates which are not instrumental variables, yet render β_1 identifiable. An overview of econometric methods used to study this problem were provided by Card (1999).

Limitations and Criticisms

Like other forms of statistical analysis, badly specified econometric models may show a spurious relationship where two variables are correlated but causally unrelated. In a study of the use of econometrics in major economics journals, McCloskey concluded that some economists report p-values (following the Fisherian tradition of tests of significance of point null-hypotheses) and neglect concerns of type II errors; some economists fail to report estimates of the size of effects (apart from statistical significance) and to discuss their economic importance. She also argues that some economists also fail to use economic reasoning for model selection, especially for deciding which variables to include in a regression.

In some cases, economic variables cannot be experimentally manipulated as treatments randomly assigned to subjects. In such cases, economists rely on observational studies, often using data sets with many strongly associated covariates, resulting in enormous numbers of models with similar explanatory ability but different covariates and regression estimates. Regarding the plurality of models compatible with observational data-sets, Edward Leamer urged that "professionals ... properly withhold belief until an inference can be shown to be adequately insensitive to the choice of assumptions".

Econometrics as a Separate Discipline

The above definition suggests that econometrics is an amalgam of economic/ finance theory, mathematical economics, economic statistics and mathematical statistics. Yet the subject deserves to be studied for the following reasons:

- Economic theory makes statements or hypotheses that are mostly qualitative in nature. For example, microeconomic theory states that, other things remaining the same, a reduction in the price of a commodity is expected to increase the quantity demanded of that commodity. Thus, economic theory postulates a negative or inverse relationship between the price and quantity demanded of a commodity. But the theory itself does not provide any numerical measure of the relationship between the two; that is, it does not tell by how much the quantity will go up or down as a result of a certain change in the price of the commodity. It is the job of the econometrician to provide such numerical estimates. Stated differently, econometrics gives empirical content to most economic theory.

- The main concern of mathematical economics is to express economic theory in mathematical form (equations) without regard to measurability or empirical verification of the theory. Econometrics, as noted previously, is mainly interested in the empirical verification of economic theory. As we shall see, the econometrician often uses the mathematical equations proposed by the mathematical economist but puts these equations in such a form that they lend themselves to empirical testing.

- Economic statistics is mainly concerned with collecting, processing, and presenting economic data in the form of charts and tables. These are the jobs of the economic statistician. It is he or she who is primarily responsible for collecting data on gross national product (GNP), employment, unemployment, prices, etc. The data thus collected constitute the raw data for econometric work. But the economic statistician does not go any further, not being concerned with using the collected data to test economic theories. Of course, one who does that becomes an econometrician.

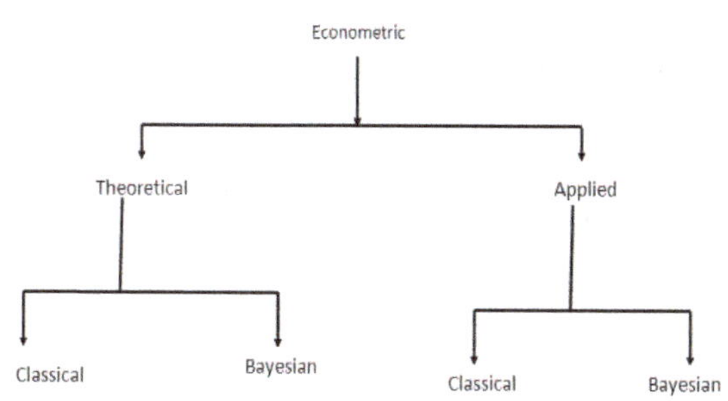

Types of Econometrics

The figure above suggests that econometrics may be divided into two broad categories: theoretical econometrics and applied econometrics. In each category, one can approach the subject in the Classical or Bayesian tradition. In this book the emphasis is on the classical approach.

- Theoretical econometrics is concerned with the development of appropriate methods for measuring economic relationships specified by econometric models. In this aspect, econometrics leans heavily on mathematical statistics. For example, one of the methods used extensively in this book is least squares. Theoretical econometrics must spell out the assumptions of this method, its properties, and what happens to these properties when one" or more of the assumptions of the method are not fulfilled.

- In applied econometrics we use the tools of theoretical econometrics to study some special field(s) of economics and business, such as the production function, investment function, demand and supply functions, portfolio theory, etc.

This chapter is concerned largely with the development of econometric methods, their assumptions, their uses, their limitations. These methods are illustrated with examples from various areas of economics and business. But this is not a book of applied econometrics in the sense that it delves deeply into any particular field of economic application. That Job is best left to books written specifically for this purpose.

Data Structure

The success of any econometric analysis ultimately depends on the availability of the appropriate data. It is therefore essential that we spend sometime discussing the nature, sources-, and limitations of the data that one may encounter in empirical analysis.

Types of Data

Four types of data may be available for empirical analysis: time series, cross-section, pooled and panel (i.e., combination of time series and cross-section) data.

- Time Series Data: A time series is a set of observations on the values that a variable takes at different times. Such data may be collected at regular time intervals, such as daily (e.g., stock prices, weather reports), weekly (e.g., money supply figures), monthly [e.g., the unemployment rate, the Consumer Price Index (CPI)], quarterly (e.g., GDP), annually (e.g., government budgets), quinquennially, that is, every 5 years (e.g., the census of manufactures), or decennially (e.g., the census of population). Sometime data are available both quarterly as well as annually, as in the case of the data on GDP and consumer expenditure. With the advent of high-speed computers, data can now be collected over an extremely short interval of time, such as the data on stock prices, which can be obtained literally continuously (the so-called real/-time quote).

- Cross-Sectional Data: Cross sectional data is a type of one dimensional data that is in context to statistics and econometrics it is data collected by observing a group of individuals at the same point of time or without regard to differences in time

- Pooled Data: Pooled data is basically a mixture of time series data and cross sectional data that is GNP of a nation for a particular year

- Panel Data: The idea of panel data comes from the surveys of individual. "Panel" means a group of individuals surveyed repeatedly overtime. Historically it is used in labour economics applications but not just confined to it.

Scaling Measures

The variables that we will generally encounter fall into four broad categories: ratio scale, interval scale, ordinal scale, and nominal scale. These are as follows:

- Ratio Scale For a variable X, taking two values, X_1 and X_2, the ratio X_1/X_2 and the distance $(X_2 - X_1)$ are meaningful quantities, Also, there is a natural ordering (ascending or descending) of the values along the scale. Hence, comparisons such as $X_2 \leq X_1$ or $X_2 \geq X_1$ are meaningful.

- Interval Scale An interval scale variable satisfies the last two properties of the ratio scale variable but not the first. Thus, the distance between two time periods, say (2000-1995) is meaningful, but not the ratio of two time periods (2000/1995).

- Ordinal Scale A variable belongs to this category only if it satisfies the third property of the ratio scale (i.e., natural ordering}. Examples are grading systems (A, B, C grades} or income class (upper, middle, lower}. For these variables the ordering exists but the distances between the categories cannot be quantified. Students of economics will recall the indifference curves between two goods, each higher indifference curve indicating higher level of utility, but one cannot quantify by how much one indifference curve is higher than the others.

- Nominal Scale Variables in this category have none of the features of the ratio scale variables. Variables such as gender (male, female} and marital status (married, unmarried, divorced, separated) simply denote categories. Question:

Over and above, econometric techniques that may be suitable for ratio scale variables may not be suitable for nominal scale variables. Therefore, it is important to bear in mind the distinctions among the four types of measurement scales discussed above.

The role of the Computer

Regression analysis, the bread-and-butter tool of econometrics, these days is unthinkable without the computer and some access to statistical software. Fortunately, several excellent regression packages are commercially available, both for the mainframe and the microcomputer, and the list is growing by the day. The most frequent used econometric/ statistical packages are ET, LIMDEP, SHAZAM, MICRO TSP, MINITAB, MATLAB, EVIEWS, SAS, SPSS, RATS, CATS, SYSTAT, STATA, MICROFIT, PCGIVE and BMD.

Scope of Econometric Modelling

Economic theory gives statements or hypothesis that are mostly qualitative in nature but econometrics gives empirical content to economic theory that is it analyses suppose the relation between two economic variables or more over a period of time for further study and development by expressing it in mathematical and equation form for computational convenience. It basically verifies economic/ finance theory.

Structure of Econometric Modelling

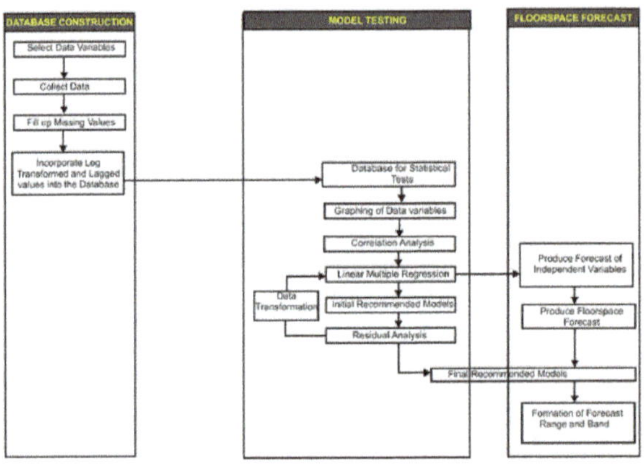

The Technical Structure of Econometric Modelling

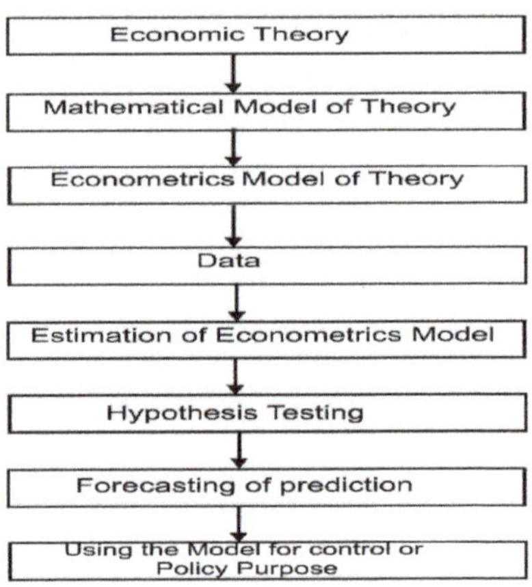

The Structure of Econometric Modelling by Regression Analysis

The basic structure of econometrics starts with the regression analysis. The following structure we need to follow to apply regression analysis to solve any real-life problems.

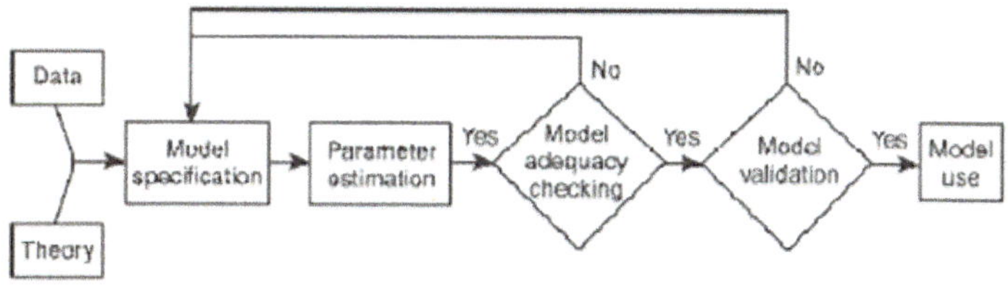

Regression model-building process

Hypothesis Testing

Such confirmation or refutation of economic theories on the basis of sample evidence is based on a branch of statistical theory known as statistical inference (hypothesis testing). The procedure of hypothesis test is as follows:

- It is the probability of observing an estimated t value greater than the critical t-value if the null hypothesis were correct.
- It measures the probability of a Type I error.
- Using a 5 percent level of significance is quite common, but it can be different if it is more important to avoid a Type I error (then maybe a 1percent significance level) or to avoid a Type 2 error.
- The level of confidence is 100 percent minus the level of significance. Thus at-test with a 5 percent level of significance can also be said to have a 95 percent level of confidence.

Hypothesis Testing has the Following Constraints

One way to test whether (β = 0 at some significance level (α) is to look whether the equivalent confidence interval (1- α) includes 0.

- If the 95% confidence interval includes zero, then we cannot reject the null hypothesis that (3 is zero at the 5% level.
- If the 95% confidence interval does not include zero, then we can reject the null hypothesis that (3 is zero at the 5% level.
- Thus, confidence intervals and two-sided t-tests give us the same results.
- It is noted that the above analysis assumes a two-sided hypothesis test. You have to check for a one-sided hypothesis test because it uses a different critical value for t than the two-sided critical value for the confidence interval.

Forecasting or Prediction

Forecasting is a systematic operational procedure for making statements about future events. There are two basic methods of forecasting

1. A "crystal ball" that can see the future,
2. Extrapolate from present information

Forecasting starts with statement that "Anything can be forecast, but not everything can be predicted."

Predict – implies inference from laws of nature, whereas

Forecast – more probabilistic

Etymology of "forecast"

- Fore – is clear, denoting "in front" or "in advance"
- Cast – dice, lots, spells, horoscopes are all cast

Casting a fly, chancing one's luck, cast about all link the notion of forecasting to gamblers and even charlatans.

In brief, forecasting is the process of making predictions about the economy. Forecasts can be carried out at a high level of aggregation - for example for GDP, inflation, unemployment or the fiscal deficit - or at a more disaggregated level, for specific sectors of the economy or even specific firms.

Methods of Economic Forecasting

1. Guessing, rules of thumb
2. Extrapolation
3. Leading indicators
4. Surveys
5. Time series models
6. Econometric forecasting models

Successful Forecasting Requires the Followings

1. There are regularities to be captured
2. The regularities are informative about the future

3. The proposed method captures those regularities, and yet
4. It excludes non-regularities

Traditional Theory of Economic Forecasting

1. The econometric model is a good representation of the economy.
2. The structure of the economy remains relatively constant.

Economists often take two tacks in building forecasting models.

Traditional, start with a theoretical model and impose it on the data in either a single equation format or structural time series approach.

More recently,

1. Understand the time series properties of the DGP (data generating process.)
2. Consider competing economic theories when specifying the variables to be used at the outset.
3. Develop evaluation criteria and model design criteria to address properties like integration, cointegration, error-correction, and model congruency.

Econometric Model for Policy Use

Econometric models are statistical models used in econometrics. An econometric model specifies the statistical relationship that is believed to hold between the various economic quantities pertaining to a particular economic phenomenon under study. An econometric model can be derived from a deterministic economic model by allowing for uncertainty, or from an economic model which itself is stochastic. However, it is also possible to use econometric models that are not tied to any specific economic theory.

We use the term "policy" in a very general sense. It includes alternative actions which might be undertaken by private businesses, governments, or family members. It could also be a drug trial.

2

Basic Concepts of Econometric Modeling

The branch of mathematics which studies probability is known as probability theory. The central topics related to the subject of probability are probability distributions, continuous random variables and stochastic processes. The other topics discusses in this section are statistical hypothesis testing, dependent and independent variables, etc. This chapter elucidates the crucial theories and principles of econometrics.

Dependent and Independent Variables

In mathematical modelling and statistical modelling, there are dependent and independent variables. The models investigate how the former depend on the latter. The dependent variables represent the output or outcome whose variation is being studied. The independent variables represent inputs or causes, i.e. potential reasons for variation. Models test or explain the effects that the independent variables have on the dependent variables. Sometimes, independent variables may be included for other reasons, such as for their potential confounding effect, without a wish to test their effect directly.

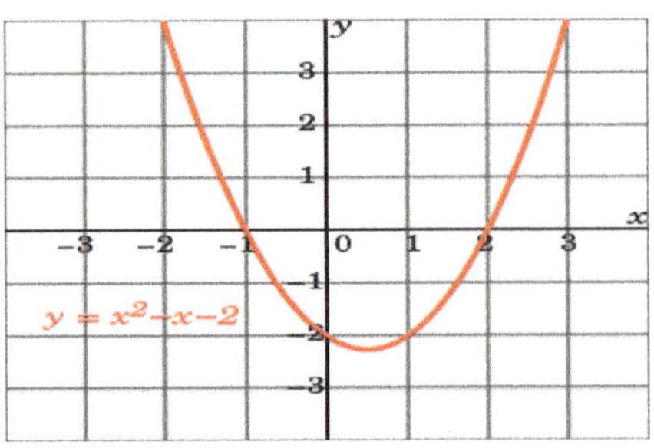

In calculus, a function is typically graphed with the horizontal axis representing the independent variable and the vertical axis representing the dependent variable. In this function, y is the dependent variable and x is the independent variable.

Mathematics

In mathematics, a function is a rule for taking an input (usually number or set of numbers) and providing an output (which is also usually a number). A symbol that stands for an arbitrary input is called an independent variable, while a symbol that stands for an arbitrary output is called a dependent variable. The most common symbol for the input is x, and the most common symbol for the output is y; the function itself is commonly written $y = f(x)$.

It is possible to have multiple independent variables and/or multiple dependent variables. For instance, in multivariable calculus, one often encounters functions of the form $z = f(x, y)$, where z is a dependent variable and x and y are independent variables. Functions with multiple outputs are often written as vector-valued functions.

In Set Theory, a function between a set X and a set Y is a subset of the Cartesian product $X \times Y$ such that every element of X appears in an ordered pair with exactly one element of Y. In this situation, a symbol representing an element of X may be called an independent variable and a symbol representing an element of Y may be called a dependent variable, such as when X is a manifold and the symbol x represents an arbitrary point in the manifold. However, many advanced textbooks do not distinguish between dependent and independent variables.

Statistics

In an experiment, the dependent variable is the event expected to change when the independent variable is manipulated.

In data mining tools (for multivariate statistics and machine learning), the depending variable is assigned a *role* as target variable (or in some tools as *label attribute*), while a dependent variable may be assigned a role as *regular variable*. Known values for the target variable are provided for the training data set and test data set, but should be predicted for other data. The target variable is used in supervised learning algorithms but not in non-supervised learning.

Modelling

In mathematical modelling, the dependent variable is studied to see if and how much it varies as the independent variables vary. In the simple stochastic linear model $y_i = a + bx_i + e_i$ the term y_i is the ith value of the dependent variable and x_i is i^{th} value of the independent variable. The term e_i is known as the "error" and contains the variability of the dependent variable not explained by the independent variable.

With multiple independent variables, the expression is: $y_i = a + bx_1 + bx_2 + ... + bx_n + e_i$, where n is the number of independent variables.

Simulation

In simulation, the dependent variable is changed in response to changes in the independent variables.

Statistics Synonyms

Depending on the context, an independent variable is sometimes called a "predictor variable", "regressor", "controlled variable", "manipulated variable", "explanatory variable", "exposure variable", "risk factor", "feature" (in machine learning and pattern recognition) or "input variable."

Depending on the context, a dependent variable is sometimes called a "response variable", "regressand", "predicted variable", "measured variable", "explained variable", "experimental variable", "responding variable", "outcome variable", "output variable" or "label".

"Explanatory variable" is preferred by some authors over "independent variable" when the quantities treated as independent variables may not be statistically independent or independently manipulable by the researcher. If the independent variable is referred to as an "explanatory variable" then the term "response variable" is preferred by some authors for the dependent variable.

"Explained variable" is preferred by some authors over "dependent variable" when the quantities treated as "dependent variables" may not be statistically dependent. If the dependent variable is referred to as an "explained variable" then the term "predictor variable" is preferred by some authors for the independent variable.

Variables may also be referred to by their form: continuous, binary/dichotomous, nominal categorical, and ordinal categorical, among others.

Other Variables

A variable may be thought to alter the dependent or independent variables, but may not actually be the focus of the experiment. So that variable will be kept constant or monitored to try to minimise its effect on the experiment. Such variables may be designated as either a "controlled variable", "control variable", or "extraneous variable".

Extraneous variables, if included in a regression as independent variables, may aid a researcher with accurate response parameter estimation, prediction, and goodness of fit, but are not of substantive interest to the hypothesis under examination. For example, in a study examining the effect of post-secondary education on lifetime earnings, some extraneous variables might be gender, ethnicity, social class, genetics, intelligence, age, and so forth. A variable is extraneous only when it can be assumed (or shown) to influence the dependent variable. If included in a regression, it can improve the fit of the model. If it is excluded from the regression and if it has a non-zero covariance with one or more of the independent variables of interest, its omission will bias the regression's result for the effect of that independent variable of interest. This effect is called confounding or omitted variable bias; in these situations, design changes and/or statistical control is necessary.

Extraneous variables are often classified into three types:

1. Subject variables, which are the characteristics of the individuals being studied that might affect their actions. These variables include age, gender, health status, mood, background, etc.

2. Blocking variables or experimental variables are characteristics of the persons conducting the experiment which might influence how a person behaves. Gender, the presence of racial discrimination, language, or other factors may qualify as such variables.

3. Situational variables are features of the environment in which the study or research was conducted, which have a bearing on the outcome of the experiment in a negative way. Included are the air temperature, level of activity, lighting, and the time of day.

In modelling, variability that is not covered by the independent variable is designated by e_i and is known as the "residual", "side effect", "error", "unexplained share", "residual variable", or "tolerance".

Examples

- Effect of fertilizer on plant growth

  In a study measuring the influence of different quantities of fertilizer on plant growth, the independent variable would be the amount of fertilizer used. The dependent variable would be the growth in height or mass of the plant. The controlled variables would be the type of plant, the type of fertilizer, the amount of sunlight the plant gets, the size of the pots, etc.

- Effect of drug dosage on symptom severity

  In a study of how different doses of a drug affect the severity of symptoms, a researcher could compare the frequency and intensity of symptoms when different doses are administered. Here the independent variable is the dose and the dependent variable is the frequency/intensity of symptoms.

- Effect of temperature on pigmentation

  In measuring the amount of color removed from beetroot samples at different temperatures, temperature is the independent variable and amount of pigment removed is the dependent variable.

Probability Theory

Probability theory is the branch of mathematics concerned with probability. Although there are several different interpretations of probability, probability theory treats the concept in a rigorous mathematical manner by expressing it through a set of axioms. Typically these axioms formalise probability in terms of a probability space, which assigns a measure taking values between 0 and 1, termed the probability measure, to a set of outcomes called the sample space. Any specified subset of these outcomes is called an event.

Central subjects in probability theory include discrete and continuous random variables, probability distributions, and stochastic processes, which provide mathematical abstractions of non-deterministic or uncertain processes or measured quantities that may either be single occurrences or evolve over time in a random fashion.

Although it is not possible to perfectly predict random events, much can be said about their behaviour. Two major results in probability theory describing such behaviour are the law of large numbers and the central limit theorem.

As a mathematical foundation for statistics, probability theory is essential to many human activities that involve quantitative analysis of data. Methods of probability theory also apply to descriptions of complex systems given only partial knowledge of their state, as in statistical mechanics. A great discovery of twentieth century physics was the probabilistic nature of physical phenomena at atomic scales, described in quantum mechanics.

History

The mathematical theory of probability has its roots in attempts to analyze games of chance by Gerolamo Cardano in the sixteenth century, and by Pierre de Fermat and Blaise Pascal in the seventeenth century (for example the "problem of points"). Christiaan Huygens published a book on the subject in 1657 and in the 19th century, Pierre Laplace completed what is today considered the classic interpretation.

Initially, probability theory mainly considered discrete events, and its methods were mainly combinatorial. Eventually, analytical considerations compelled the incorporation of continuous variables into the theory.

This culminated in modern probability theory, on foundations laid by Andrey Nikolaevich Kolmogorov. Kolmogorov combined the notion of sample space, introduced by Richard von Mises, and measure theory and presented his axiom system for probability theory in 1933. This became the mostly undisputed axiomatic basis for modern probability theory; but, alternatives exist, such as the adoption of finite rather than countable additivity by Bruno de Finetti.

Treatment

Most introductions to probability theory treat discrete probability distributions and continuous probability distributions separately. The more mathematically advanced measure theory-based treatment of probability covers the discrete, continuous, a mix of the two, and more.

Motivation

Consider an experiment that can produce a number of outcomes. The set of all outcomes is called the *sample space* of the experiment. The *power set* of the sample space (or equivalently, the event space) is formed by considering all different collections of possible results. For example, rolling an honest die produces one of six possible results. One collection of possible results corresponds to getting an odd number. Thus, the subset {1,3,5} is an element of the power set of the sample space of die rolls. These collections are called *events*. In this case, {1,3,5} is the event that the die falls on some odd number. If the results that actually occur fall in a given event, that event is said to have occurred.

Probability is a way of assigning every "event" a value between zero and one, with the requirement that the event made up of all possible results (in our example, the event {1,2,3,4,5,6}) be assigned a value of one. To qualify as a probability distribution, the assignment of values must satisfy the requirement that if you look at a collection of mutually exclusive events (events that contain no common results, e.g., the events {1,6}, {3}, and {2,4} are all mutually exclusive), the probability that any of these events occurs is given by the sum of the probabilities of the events.

The probability that any one of the events {1,6}, {3}, or {2,4} will occur is 5/6. This is the same as saying that the probability of event {1,2,3,4,6} is 5/6. This event encompasses the possibility of any number except five being rolled. The mutually exclusive event {5} has a probability of 1/6, and the event {1,2,3,4,5,6} has a probability of 1, that is, absolute certainty.

Discrete Probability Distributions

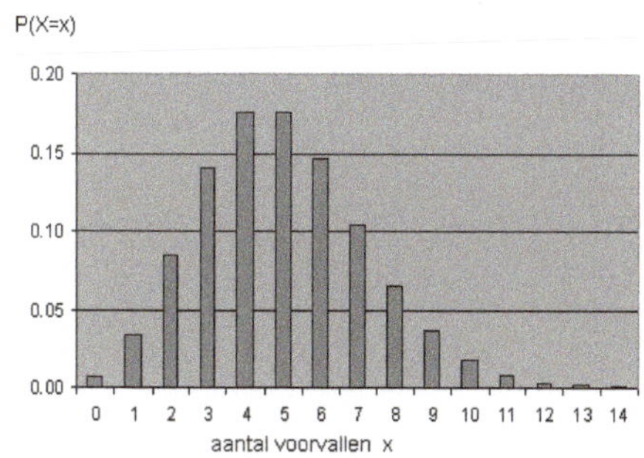

The Poisson distribution, a discrete probability distribution.

Discrete probability theory deals with events that occur in countable sample spaces.

Examples: Throwing dice, experiments with decks of cards, random walk, and tossing coins

Classical definition: Initially the probability of an event to occur was defined as number of cases favorable for the event, over the number of total outcomes possible in an equiprobable sample space.

For example, if the event is "occurrence of an even number when a die is rolled", the probability is given by $\frac{3}{6}=\frac{1}{2}$, since 3 faces out of the 6 have even numbers and each face has the same probability of appearing.

Modern definition: The modern definition starts with a finite or countable set called the sample space, which relates to the set of all *possible outcomes* in classical sense, denoted by Ω. It is then assumed that for each element $x \in \Omega$, an intrinsic "probability" value $f(x)$ is attached, which satisfies the following properties:

1. $f(x) \in [0,1]$ for all $x \in \Omega$;
2. $\sum_{x \in \Omega} f(x) = 1.$

That is, the probability function $f(x)$ lies between zero and one for every value of x in the sample space Ω, and the sum of $f(x)$ over all values x in the sample space Ω is equal to 1. An event is defined as any subset E of the sample space Ω. The probability of the event E is defined as

$$P(E) = \sum_{x \in E} f(x).$$

So, the probability of the entire sample space is 1, and the probability of the null event is 0.

The function $f(x)$ mapping a point in the sample space to the "probability" value is called a probability mass function abbreviated as pmf. The modern definition does not try to answer how probability mass functions are obtained; instead it builds a theory that assumes their existence.

Continuous Probability Distributions

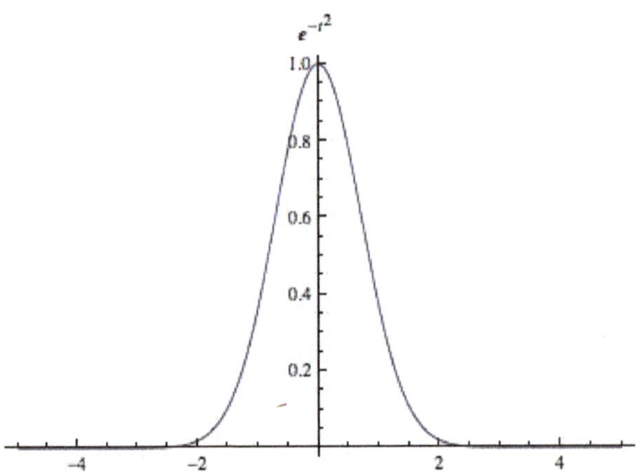

The normal distribution, a continuous probability distribution.

Continuous probability theory deals with events that occur in a continuous sample space.

Classical definition: The classical definition breaks down when confronted with the continuous case.

Modern definition: If the outcome space of a random variable *X* is the set of real numbers ($\mathbb{R}$) or a subset thereof, then a function called the cumulative distribution function (or cdf) F exists, defined by $F(x) = P(X \leq x)$. That is, *F*(*x*) returns the probability that *X* will be less than or equal to *x*.

The cdf necessarily satisfies the following properties.

1. F is a monotonically non-decreasing, right-continuous function;
2. $\lim_{x \to -\infty} F(x) = 0;$
3. $\lim_{x \to \infty} F(x) = 1.$

If F is absolutely continuous, i.e., its derivative exists and integrating the derivative gives us the cdf back again, then the random variable *X* is said to have a probability density function or pdf or simply density $f(x) = \frac{dF(x)}{dx}$.

For a set $E \subseteq \mathbb{R}$, the probability of the random variable *X* being in E is

$$P(X \in E) = \int_{x \in E} dF(x).$$

In case the probability density function exists, this can be written as

$$P(X \in E) = \int_{x \in E} f(x)dx.$$

Whereas the *pdf* exists only for continuous random variables, the *cdf* exists for all random variables (including discrete random variables) that take values in $\mathbb{R}$

These concepts can be generalized for multidimensional cases on $\mathbb{R}^n$ and other continuous sample spaces.

Measure-theoretic Probability Theory

The *raison d'être* of the measure-theoretic treatment of probability is that it unifies the discrete and the continuous cases, and makes the difference a question of which measure is used. Furthermore, it covers distributions that are neither discrete nor continuous nor mixtures of the two.

An example of such distributions could be a mix of discrete and continuous distributions—for example, a random variable that is 0 with probability 1/2, and takes a random value from a normal distribution with probability 1/2. It can still be studied to some extent by considering it to have a pdf of $(\delta[x]+\varphi(x))/2$, where $\delta[x]$ is the Dirac delta function.

Other distributions may not even be a mix, for example, the Cantor distribution has no positive probability for any single point, neither does it have a density. The modern approach to probability theory solves these problems using measure theory to define the probability space:

Given any set Ω, (also called sample space) and a σ-algebra $\mathcal{F}$ on it, a measure P defined on $\mathcal{F}$ is called a probability measure if $P(\Omega)=1$.

If $\mathcal{F}$ is the Borel σ-algebra on the set of real numbers, then there is a unique probability measure on $\mathcal{F}$ for any cdf, and vice versa. The measure corresponding to a cdf is said to be induced by the cdf. This measure coincides with the pmf for discrete variables and pdf for continuous variables, making the measure-theoretic approach free of fallacies.

The *probability* of a set E in the σ-algebra $\mathcal{F}$ is defined as

$$P(E)=\int_{\omega\in E}\mu_F(d\omega)$$

where the integration is with respect to the measure μ_F induced by F.

Along with providing better understanding and unification of discrete and continuous probabilities, measure-theoretic treatment also allows us to work on probabilities outside $\mathbb{R}^n$, as in the theory of stochastic processes. For example, to study Brownian motion, probability is defined on a space of functions.

When it's convenient to work with a dominating measure, the Radon-Nikodym theorem is used to define a density as the Radon-Nikodym derivative of the probability distribution of interest with respect to this dominating measure. Discrete densities are usually defined as this derivative with respect to a counting measure over the set of all possible outcomes. Densities for absolutely continuous distributions are usually defined as this derivative with respect to the Lebesgue measure. If a theorem can be proved in this general setting, it holds for both discrete and continuous distributions as well as others; separate proofs are not required for discrete and continuous distributions.

Classical Probability Distributions

Certain random variables occur very often in probability theory because they well describe many natural or physical processes. Their distributions therefore have gained *special importance* in probability theory. Some fundamental *discrete distributions* are the discrete uniform, Bernoulli, binomial, negative binomial, Poisson and geometric distributions. Important *continuous distributions* include the continuous uniform, normal, exponential, gamma and beta distributions.

Convergence of Random Variables

In probability theory, there are several notions of convergence for random variables. They are listed below in the order of strength, i.e., any subsequent notion of convergence in the list implies convergence according to all of the preceding notions.

Weak convergence

A sequence of random variables $X_1, X_2, \ldots,$ converges weakly to the random variable X if their respective cumulative *distribution functions* $F_1, F_2, \ldots$ converge to the cumulative distribution function F of X, wherever F is continuous. Weak convergence is also called convergence in distribution.

Most common shorthand notation: $X_n \xrightarrow{\mathcal{D}} X$

Convergence in probability

The sequence of random variables $X_1, X_2, \ldots,$ is said to converge towards the random variable X in probability if $\lim_{n\to\infty} P\left(|X_n - X| \geq \varepsilon\right) = 0$ for every $\varepsilon > 0$.

Most common shorthand notation: $X_n \xrightarrow{P} X$

Strong convergence

The sequence of random variables $X_1, X_2, \ldots,$ is said to converge towards the random variable X strongly if $P(\lim_{n\to\infty} X_n = X) = 1$. Strong convergence is also known as almost sure convergence.

Most common shorthand notation: $X_n \xrightarrow{a.s.} X$

As the names indicate, weak convergence is weaker than strong convergence. In fact, strong convergence implies convergence in probability, and convergence in probability implies weak convergence. The reverse statements are not always true.

Law of Large Numbers

Common intuition suggests that if a fair coin is tossed many times, then *roughly* half of the time it will turn up *heads*, and the other half it will turn up *tails*. Furthermore, the more often the coin is tossed, the more likely it should be that the ratio of the number of *heads* to the number of *tails* will approach unity. Modern probability theory provides a formal version of this intuitive idea, known as the law of large numbers. This law is remarkable because it is not assumed in the foundations of probability theory, but instead emerges from these foundations as a theorem. Since it links theoretically derived probabilities to their actual frequency of occurrence in the real world, the law of large numbers is considered as a pillar in the history of statistical theory and has had widespread influence.

The law of large numbers (LLN) states that the sample average

$$\bar{X}_n = \frac{1}{n}\sum_{k=1}^{n} X_k$$

of a sequence of independent and identically distributed random variables X_k converges towards their common expectation μ, provided that the expectation of $|X_k|$ is finite.

It is in the different forms of convergence of random variables that separates the *weak* and the *strong* law of large numbers

Weak law: $\bar{X}_n \xrightarrow{P} \mu$ for $n \to \infty$

Strong law: $\bar{X}_n \xrightarrow{a.s.} \mu$ for $n \to \infty$

It follows from the LLN that if an event of probability *p* is observed repeatedly during independent experiments, the ratio of the observed frequency of that event to the total number of repetitions converges towards *p*.

For example, if $Y_1, Y_2, \ldots$ are independent Bernoulli random variables taking values 1 with probability *p* and 0 with probability 1-*p*, then $E(Y_i) = p$ for all *i*, so that $\bar{Y}_n$ converges to *p* almost surely.

Central Limit Theorem

"The central limit theorem (CLT) is one of the great results of mathematics." It explains the ubiquitous occurrence of the normal distribution in nature.

The theorem states that the average of many independent and identically distributed random variables with finite variance tends towards a normal distribution *irrespective* of the distribution followed by the original random variables. Formally, let $X_1, X_2, \ldots,$ be independent random variables with mean μ and variance $\sigma^2 > 0$. Then the sequence of random variables

$$Z_n = \frac{\sum_{i=1}^{n}(X_i - \mu)}{\sigma\sqrt{n}}$$

converges in distribution to a standard normal random variable.

For some classes of random variables the classic central limit theorem works rather fast, for example the distributions with finite first, second and third moment from the exponential family; on the other hand, for some random variables of the heavy tail and fat tail variety, it works very slowly or may not work at all: in such cases one may use the Generalized Central Limit Theorem (GCLT).

Statistical Hypothesis Testing

A statistical hypothesis, sometimes called confirmatory data analysis, is a hypothesis that is testable on the basis of observing a process that is modeled via a set of random variables. A statistical hypothesis test is a method of statistical inference. Commonly, two statistical data sets are compared, or a data set obtained by sampling is compared against a synthetic data set from an idealized model. A hypothesis is proposed for the statistical relationship between the two data sets, and this is compared as an alternative to an idealized null hypothesis that proposes no relationship between two data sets. The comparison is deemed *statistically significant* if the relationship between the data sets would be an unlikely realization of the null hypothesis according to a threshold probability—the significance level. Hypothesis tests are used in determining what outcomes of a study would lead to a rejection of the null hypothesis for a pre-specified level of significance. The process of distinguishing between the null hypothesis and the alternative hypothesis is aided by identifying two conceptual types of errors (type 1 & type 2), and by specifying parametric limits on e.g. how much type 1 error will be permitted.

An alternative framework for statistical hypothesis testing is to specify a set of statistical models, one for each candidate hypothesis, and then use model selection techniques to choose the most appropriate model. The most common selection techniques are based on either Akaike information criterion or Bayes factor.

Confirmatory data analysis can be contrasted with exploratory data analysis, which may not have pre-specified hypotheses.

Variations and Sub-classes

Statistical hypothesis testing is a key technique of both frequentist inference and Bayesian inference, although the two types of inference have notable differences. Statistical hypothesis tests define a procedure that controls (fixes) the probability of incorrectly *deciding* that a default position (null hypothesis) is incorrect. The procedure is based on how likely it would be for a set of observations to occur if the null hypothesis were true. Note that this probability of making an incorrect decision is *not* the probability that the null hypothesis is true, nor whether any specific alternative hypothesis is true. This contrasts with other possible techniques of decision theory in which the null and alternative hypothesis are treated on a more equal basis.

One naïve Bayesian approach to hypothesis testing is to base decisions on the posterior probability, but this fails when comparing point and continuous hypotheses. Other approaches to decision making, such as Bayesian decision theory, attempt to balance the consequences of incorrect decisions across all possibilities, rather than concentrating on a single null hypothesis. A number of other approaches to reaching a decision based on data are available via decision theory and optimal decisions, some of which have desirable properties. Hypothesis testing, though, is a dominant approach to data analysis in many fields of science. Extensions to the theory of hypothesis testing include the study of the power of tests, i.e. the probability of correctly rejecting the null hypothesis given that it is false. Such considerations can be used for the purpose of sample size determination prior to the collection of data.

The Testing Process

In the statistics literature, statistical hypothesis testing plays a fundamental role. The usual line of reasoning is as follows:

1. There is an initial research hypothesis of which the truth is unknown.
2. The first step is to state the relevant null and alternative hypotheses. This is important, as mis-stating the hypotheses will muddy the rest of the process.
3. The second step is to consider the statistical assumptions being made about the sample in doing the test; for example, assumptions about the statistical independence or about the form of the distributions of the observations. This is equally important as invalid assumptions will mean that the results of the test are invalid.
4. Decide which test is appropriate, and state the relevant test statistic T.
5. Derive the distribution of the test statistic under the null hypothesis from the assumptions. In standard cases this will be a well-known result. For example, the test statistic might follow a Student's t distribution or a normal distribution.
6. Select a significance level (α), a probability threshold below which the null hypothesis will be rejected. Common values are 5% and 1%.
7. The distribution of the test statistic under the null hypothesis partitions the possible values of T into those for which the null hypothesis is rejected—the so-called *critical region*—and those for which it is not. The probability of the critical region is α.
8. Compute from the observations the observed value t_{obs} of the test statistic T.
9. Decide to either reject the null hypothesis in favor of the alternative or not reject it. The decision rule is to reject the null hypothesis H_0 if the observed value t_{obs} is in the critical region, and to accept or "fail to reject" the hypothesis otherwise.

An alternative process is commonly used:

1. Compute from the observations the observed value t_{obs} of the test statistic T.
2. Calculate the p-value. This is the probability, under the null hypothesis, of sampling a test statistic at least as extreme as that which was observed.

3. Reject the null hypothesis, in favor of the alternative hypothesis, if and only if the p-value is less than the significance level (the selected probability) threshold.

The two processes are equivalent. The former process was advantageous in the past when only tables of test statistics at common probability thresholds were available. It allowed a decision to be made without the calculation of a probability. It was adequate for classwork and for operational use, but it was deficient for reporting results.

The latter process relied on extensive tables or on computational support not always available. The explicit calculation of a probability is useful for reporting. The calculations are now trivially performed with appropriate software.

The difference in the two processes applied to the Radioactive suitcase example (below):

- "The Geiger-counter reading is 10. The limit is 9. Check the suitcase."
- "The Geiger-counter reading is high; 97% of safe suitcases have lower readings. The limit is 95%. Check the suitcase."

The former report is adequate, the latter gives a more detailed explanation of the data and the reason why the suitcase is being checked.

It is important to note the difference between accepting the null hypothesis and simply failing to reject it. The "fail to reject" terminology highlights the fact that the null hypothesis is assumed to be true from the start of the test; if there is a lack of evidence against it, it simply continues to be assumed true. The phrase "accept the null hypothesis" may suggest it has been proved simply because it has not been disproved, a logical fallacy known as the argument from ignorance. Unless a test with particularly high power is used, the idea of "accepting" the null hypothesis may be dangerous. Nonetheless the terminology is prevalent throughout statistics, where the meaning actually intended is well understood.

The processes described here are perfectly adequate for computation. They seriously neglect the design of experiments considerations.

It is particularly critical that appropriate sample sizes be estimated before conducting the experiment.

The phrase "test of significance" was coined by statistician Ronald Fisher.

Interpretation

If the *p*-value is less than the required significance level (equivalently, if the observed test statistic is in the critical region), then we say the null hypothesis is rejected at the given level of significance. Rejection of the null hypothesis is a conclusion. This is like a "guilty" verdict in a criminal trial: the evidence is sufficient to reject innocence, thus proving guilt. We might accept the alternative hypothesis (and the research hypothesis).

If the *p*-value is *not* less than the required significance level (equivalently, if the observed test statistic is outside the critical region), then the test has no result. The evidence is insufficient to support a conclusion. (This is like a jury that fails to reach a verdict.) The researcher typically gives extra consideration to those cases where the *p*-value is close to the significance level.

Some people find it helpful to think of the hypothesis testing framework as analogous to a mathematical proof by contradiction.

In the Lady tasting tea example (below), Fisher required the Lady to properly categorize all of the cups of tea to justify the conclusion that the result was unlikely to result from chance. He defined the critical region as that case alone. The region was defined by a probability (that the null hypothesis was correct) of less than 5%.

Whether rejection of the null hypothesis truly justifies acceptance of the research hypothesis depends on the structure of the hypotheses. Rejecting the hypothesis that a large paw print originated from a bear does not immediately prove the existence of Bigfoot. Hypothesis testing emphasizes the rejection, which is based on a probability, rather than the acceptance, which requires extra steps of logic.

"The probability of rejecting the null hypothesis is a function of five factors: whether the test is one- or two tailed, the level of significance, the standard deviation, the amount of deviation from the null hypothesis, and the number of observations." These factors are a source of criticism; factors under the control of the experimenter/analyst give the results an appearance of subjectivity.

Use and Importance

Statistics are helpful in analyzing most collections of data. This is equally true of hypothesis testing which can justify conclusions even when no scientific theory exists. In the Lady tasting tea example, it was "obvious" that no difference existed between (milk poured into tea) and (tea poured into milk). The data contradicted the "obvious".

Real world applications of hypothesis testing include:

- Testing whether more men than women suffer from nightmares
- Establishing authorship of documents
- Evaluating the effect of the full moon on behavior
- Determining the range at which a bat can detect an insect by echo

- Deciding whether hospital carpeting results in more infections
- Selecting the best means to stop smoking
- Checking whether bumper stickers reflect car owner behavior
- Testing the claims of handwriting analysts

Statistical hypothesis testing plays an important role in the whole of statistics and in statistical inference. For example, Lehmann (1992) in a review of the fundamental paper by Neyman and Pearson (1933) says: "Nevertheless, despite their shortcomings, the new paradigm formulated in the 1933 paper, and the many developments carried out within its framework continue to play a central role in both the theory and practice of statistics and can be expected to do so in the foreseeable future".

Significance testing has been the favored statistical tool in some experimental social sciences (over 90% of articles in the *Journal of Applied Psychology* during the early 1990s). Other fields have favored the estimation of parameters (e.g., effect size). Significance testing is used as a substitute for the traditional comparison of predicted value and experimental result at the core of the scientific method. When theory is only capable of predicting the sign of a relationship, a directional (one-sided) hypothesis test can be configured so that only a statistically significant result supports theory. This form of theory appraisal is the most heavily criticized application of hypothesis testing.

Cautions

"If the government required statistical procedures to carry warning labels like those on drugs, most inference methods would have long labels indeed." This caution applies to hypothesis tests and alternatives to them.

The successful hypothesis test is associated with a probability and a type-I error rate. The conclusion *might* be wrong.

The conclusion of the test is only as solid as the sample upon which it is based. The design of the experiment is critical. A number of unexpected effects have been observed including:

- The clever Hans effect. A horse appeared to be capable of doing simple arithmetic.
- The Hawthorne effect. Industrial workers were more productive in better illumination, and most productive in worse.
- The placebo effect. Pills with no medically active ingredients were remarkably effective.

A statistical analysis of misleading data produces misleading conclusions. The issue of data quality can be more subtle. In forecasting for example, there is no agreement on a measure of forecast accuracy. In the absence of a consensus measurement, no decision based on measurements will be without controversy.

The book *How to Lie with Statistics* is the most popular book on statistics ever published. It does not much consider hypothesis testing, but its cautions are applicable, including: Many claims are made on the basis of samples too small to convince. If a report does not mention sample size, be doubtful.

Hypothesis testing acts as a filter of statistical conclusions; only those results meeting a probability threshold are publishable. Economics also acts as a publication filter; only those results favorable to the author and funding source may be submitted for publication. The impact of filtering on publication is termed publication bias. A related problem is that of multiple testing (sometimes linked to data mining), in which a variety of tests for a variety of possible effects are applied to a single data set and only those yielding a significant result are reported. These are often dealt with by using multiplicity correction procedures that control the family wise error rate (FWER) or the false discovery rate (FDR).

Those making critical decisions based on the results of a hypothesis test are prudent to look at the details rather than the conclusion alone. In the physical sciences most results are fully accepted only when independently confirmed. The general advice concerning statistics is, "Figures never lie, but liars figure" (anonymous).

Examples

Lady Tasting Tea

In a famous example of hypothesis testing, known as the *Lady tasting tea*, Dr. Muriel Bristol, a female colleague of Fisher claimed to be able to tell whether the tea or the milk was added first to a cup. Fisher proposed to give her eight cups, four of each variety, in random order. One could then ask what the probability was for her getting the number she got correct, but just by chance. The null hypothesis was that the Lady had no such ability. The test statistic was a simple count of the number of successes in selecting the 4 cups. The critical region was the single case of 4 successes of 4 possible based on a conventional probability criterion ($< 5\%$; 1 of 70 $\approx 1.4\%$). Fisher asserted that no alternative hypothesis was (ever) required. The lady correctly identified every cup, which would be considered a statistically significant result.

Courtroom Trial

A statistical test procedure is comparable to a criminal trial; a defendant is considered not guilty as long as his or her guilt is not proven. The prosecutor tries to prove the guilt of the defendant. Only when there is enough charging evidence the defendant is convicted.

In the start of the procedure, there are two hypotheses H_0 : "the defendant is not guilty", and H_1 : "the defendant is guilty". The first one, H_0, is called the *null hypothesis*, and is for the time being accepted. The second one, H_1, is called the *alternative hypothesis*. It is the alternative hypothesis that one hopes to support.

The hypothesis of innocence is only rejected when an error is very unlikely, because one doesn't want to convict an innocent defendant. Such an error is called *error of the first kind* (i.e., the conviction of an innocent person), and the occurrence of this error is controlled to be rare. As a consequence of this asymmetric behaviour, the *error of the second kind* (acquitting a person who committed the crime), is often rather large.

	H_0 is true Truly not guilty	**H_1 is true Truly guilty**
Accept null hypothesis Acquittal	Right decision	Wrong decision Type II Error
Reject null hypothesis Conviction	Wrong decision Type I Error	Right decision

A criminal trial can be regarded as either or both of two decision processes: guilty vs not guilty or evidence vs a threshold ("beyond a reasonable doubt"). In one view, the defendant is judged; in the other view the performance of the prosecution (which bears the burden of proof) is judged. A hypothesis test can be regarded as either a judgment of a hypothesis or as a judgment of evidence.

Philosopher's Beans

The following example was produced by a philosopher describing scientific methods generations before hypothesis testing was formalized and popularized.

Few beans of this handful are white. Most beans in this bag are white. Therefore: Probably, these beans were taken from another bag. This is an hypothetical inference.

The beans in the bag are the population. The handful are the sample. The null hypothesis is that the sample originated from the population. The criterion for rejecting the null-hypothesis is the "obvious" difference in appearance (an informal difference in the mean). The interesting result is that consideration of a real population and a real sample produced an imaginary bag. The philosopher was considering logic rather than probability. To be a real statistical hypothesis test, this example requires the formalities of a probability calculation and a comparison of that probability to a standard.

A simple generalization of the example considers a mixed bag of beans and a handful that contain either very few or very many white beans. The generalization considers both extremes. It requires more calculations and more comparisons to arrive at a formal answer, but the core philosophy is unchanged; If the composition of the handful is greatly different from that of the bag, then the sample probably originated from another bag. The original example is termed a one-sided or a one-tailed test while the generalization is termed a two-sided or two-tailed test.

The statement also relies on the inference that the sampling was random. If someone had been picking through the bag to find white beans, then it would explain why the handful had so many white beans, and also explain why the number of white beans in the bag was depleted (although the bag is probably intended to be assumed much larger than one's hand).

Clairvoyant Card Game

A person (the subject) is tested for clairvoyance. He is shown the reverse of a randomly chosen playing card 25 times and asked which of the four suits it belongs to. The number of hits, or correct answers, is called X.

As we try to find evidence of his clairvoyance, for the time being the null hypothesis is that the person is not clairvoyant. The alternative is, of course: the person is (more or less) clairvoyant.

If the null hypothesis is valid, the only thing the test person can do is guess. For every card, the probability (relative frequency) of any single suit appearing is 1/4. If the alternative is valid, the test subject will predict the suit correctly with probability greater than 1/4. We will call the probability of guessing correctly p. The hypotheses, then, are:

- null hypothesis : $H_0 : p = \frac{1}{4}$ (just guessing)

and

- alternative hypothesis :$H_1 : p > \frac{1}{4}$ (true clairvoyant).

When the test subject correctly predicts all 25 cards, we will consider him clairvoyant, and reject the null hypothesis. Thus also with 24 or 23 hits. With only 5 or 6 hits, on the other hand, there is no cause to consider him so. But what about 12 hits, or 17 hits? What is the critical number, c, of hits, at which point we consider the subject to be clairvoyant? How do we determine the critical value c? It is obvious that with the choice c=25 (i.e. we only accept clairvoyance when all cards are predicted correctly) we're more critical than with c=10. In the first case almost no test subjects will be recognized to be clairvoyant, in the second case, a certain number will pass the test. In practice, one decides how critical one will be. That is, one decides how often one accepts an error of the first kind – a false positive, or Type I error. With $c = 25$ the probability of such an error is:

$$P(\textit{reject } H_0 \mid H_0 \textit{ is valid}) = P(X = 25 \mid p = \tfrac{1}{4}) = \left(\tfrac{1}{4}\right)^{25} \approx 10^{-15},$$

and hence, very small. The probability of a false positive is the probability of randomly guessing correctly all 25 times.

Being less critical, with c=10, gives:

$$P(reject\ H_0 \mid H_0\ is\ valid) = P(X \geq 10 \mid p = \tfrac{1}{4}) = \sum_{k=10}^{25} P(X = k \mid p = \tfrac{1}{4}) \approx 0.07.$$

Thus, $c = 10$ yields a much greater probability of false positive.

Before the test is actually performed, the maximum acceptable probability of a Type I error (α) is determined. Typically, values in the range of 1% to 5% are selected. (If the maximum acceptable error rate is zero, an infinite number of correct guesses is required.) Depending on this Type 1 error rate, the critical value c is calculated. For example, if we select an error rate of 1%, c is calculated thus:

$$P(reject\ H_0 \mid H_0\ is\ valid) = P(X \geq c \mid p = \tfrac{1}{4}) \leq 0.01.$$

From all the numbers c, with this property, we choose the smallest, in order to minimize the probability of a Type II error, a false negative. For the above example, we select: $c = 13$.

Radioactive Suitcase

As an example, consider determining whether a suitcase contains some radioactive material. Placed under a Geiger counter, it produces 10 counts per minute. The null hypothesis is that no radioactive material is in the suitcase and that all measured counts are due to ambient radioactivity typical of the surrounding air and harmless objects. We can then calculate how likely it is that we would observe 10 counts per minute if the null hypothesis were true. If the null hypothesis predicts (say) on average 9 counts per minute, then according to the Poisson distribution typical for radioactive decay there is about 41% chance of recording 10 or more counts. Thus we can say that the suitcase is compatible with the null hypothesis (this does not guarantee that there is no radioactive material, just that we don't have enough evidence to suggest there is). On the other hand, if the null hypothesis predicts 3 counts per minute (for which the Poisson distribution predicts only 0.1% chance of recording 10 or more counts) then the suitcase is not compatible with the null hypothesis, and there are likely other factors responsible to produce the measurements.

The test does not directly assert the presence of radioactive material. A *successful* test asserts that the claim of no radioactive material present is unlikely given the reading (and therefore ...). The double negative (disproving the null hypothesis) of the method is confusing, but using a counter-example to disprove is standard mathematical practice. The attraction of the method is its practicality. We know (from experience) the expected range of counts with only ambient radioactivity present, so we can say that a measurement is *unusually* large. Statistics just formalizes the intuitive by using numbers instead of adjectives. We probably do not know the characteristics of the radioactive suitcases; We just assume that they produce larger readings.

To slightly formalize intuition: Radioactivity is suspected if the Geiger-count with the suitcase is among or exceeds the greatest (5% or 1%) of the Geiger-counts made with ambient radiation alone. This makes no assumptions about the distribution of counts. Many ambient radiation observations are required to obtain good probability estimates for rare events.

The test described here is more fully the null-hypothesis statistical significance test. The null hypothesis represents what we would believe by default, before seeing any evidence. Statistical significance is a possible finding of the test, declared when the observed sample is unlikely to have occurred by chance if the null hypothesis were true. The name of the test describes its formulation and its possible outcome. One characteristic of the test is its crisp decision: to reject or not reject the null hypothesis. A calculated value is compared to a threshold, which is determined from the tolerable risk of error.

Definition of Terms

The following definitions are mainly based on the exposition in the book by Lehmann and Romano:

Statistical hypothesis

A statement about the parameters describing a population (not a sample).

Statistic

A value calculated from a sample, often to summarize the sample for comparison purposes.

Simple hypothesis

Any hypothesis which specifies the population distribution completely.

Composite hypothesis

Any hypothesis which does *not* specify the population distribution completely.

Null hypothesis (H_0)

A simple hypothesis associated with a contradiction to a theory one would like to prove.

Alternative hypothesis (H_1)

A hypothesis (often composite) associated with a theory one would like to prove.

Statistical test

A procedure whose inputs are samples and whose result is a hypothesis.

Region of acceptance

The set of values of the test statistic for which we fail to reject the null hypothesis.

Region of rejection / Critical region

The set of values of the test statistic for which the null hypothesis is rejected.

Critical value

The threshold value delimiting the regions of acceptance and rejection for the test statistic.

Power of a test ($1 - \beta$)

The test's probability of correctly rejecting the null hypothesis. The complement of the false negative rate, β. Power is termed sensitivity in biostatistics. ("This is a sensitive test. Because the result is negative, we can confidently say that the patient does not have the condition.") See sensitivity and specificity and Type I and type II errors for exhaustive definitions.

Size

For simple hypotheses, this is the test's probability of *incorrectly* rejecting the null hypothesis. The false positive rate. For composite hypotheses this is the supremum of the probability of rejecting the null hypothesis over all cases covered by the null hypothesis. The complement of the false positive rate is termed specificity in biostatistics. ("This is a specific test. Because the result is positive, we can confidently say that the patient has the condition.") See sensitivity and specificity and Type I and type II errors for exhaustive definitions.

Significance Level of a Test (α)

It is the upper bound imposed on the size of a test. Its value is chosen by the statistician prior to looking at the data or choosing any particular test to be used. It is the maximum exposure to erroneously rejecting H_0 he/she is ready to accept. Testing H_0 at significance level α means testing H_0 with a test whose size does not exceed α. In most cases, one uses tests whose size is equal to the significance level.

p-value

The probability, assuming the null hypothesis is true, of observing a result at least as extreme as the test statistic.

Statistical significance test

A predecessor to the statistical hypothesis test. An experimental result was said to be statistically significant if a sample was sufficiently inconsistent with the (null) hypothesis. This was variously considered common sense, a pragmatic heuristic for identifying meaningful experimental results, a convention establishing a threshold of statistical evidence or a method for drawing conclusions from data. The statistical hypothesis test added mathematical rigor and philosophical consistency to the concept by making the alternative hypothesis explicit. The term is loosely used to describe the modern version which is now part of statistical hypothesis testing.

Conservative test

A test is conservative if, when constructed for a given nominal significance level, the true probability of *incorrectly* rejecting the null hypothesis is never greater than the nominal level.

Exact test

A test in which the significance level or critical value can be computed exactly, i.e., without any approximation. In some contexts this term is restricted to tests applied to categorical data and to permutation tests, in which computations are carried out by complete enumeration of all possible outcomes and their probabilities.

A statistical hypothesis test compares a test statistic (z or t for examples) to a threshold. The test statistic (the formula found in the table below) is based on optimality. For a fixed level of Type I error rate, use of these statistics minimizes Type II error rates (equivalent to maximizing power). The following terms describe tests in terms of such optimality:

Most powerful test

For a given *size* or *significance level*, the test with the greatest power (probability of rejection) for a given value of the parameter(s) being tested, contained in the alternative hypothesis.

Uniformly most powerful test (UMP)

A test with the greatest *power* for all values of the parameter(s) being tested, contained in the alternative hypothesis.

Common Test Statistics

One-sample tests are appropriate when a sample is being compared to the population from a hypothesis. The population characteristics are known from theory or are calculated from the population.

Two-sample tests are appropriate for comparing two samples, typically experimental and control samples from a scientifically controlled experiment.

Paired tests are appropriate for comparing two samples where it is impossible to control important variables. Rather than comparing two sets, members are paired between samples so the difference between the members becomes the sample. Typically the mean of the differences is then compared to zero. The common example scenario for when a paired difference test is appropriate is when a single set of test subjects has something applied to them and the test is intended to check for an effect.

Z-tests are appropriate for comparing means under stringent conditions regarding normality and a known standard deviation.

A *t*-test is appropriate for comparing means under relaxed conditions (less is assumed).

Tests of proportions are analogous to tests of means (the 50% proportion).

Chi-squared tests use the same calculations and the same probability distribution for different applications:

- Chi-squared tests for variance are used to determine whether a normal population has a specified variance. The null hypothesis is that it does.
- Chi-squared tests of independence are used for deciding whether two variables are associated or are independent. The variables are categorical rather than numeric. It can be used to decide whether left-handedness is correlated with libertarian politics (or not). The null hypothesis is that the variables are independent. The numbers used in the calculation are the observed and expected frequencies of occurrence (from contingency tables).
- Chi-squared goodness of fit tests are used to determine the adequacy of curves fit to data. The null hypothesis is that the curve fit is adequate. It is common to determine curve shapes to minimize the mean square error, so it is appropriate that the goodness-of-fit calculation sums the squared errors.

F-tests (analysis of variance, ANOVA) are commonly used when deciding whether groupings of data by category are meaningful. If the variance of test scores of the left-handed in a class is much smaller than the variance of the whole class, then it may be useful to study lefties as a group. The null hypothesis is that two variances are the same – so the proposed grouping is not meaningful.

In the table below, the symbols used are defined at the bottom of the table. Many other tests can be found in other articles. Proofs exist that the test statistics are appropriate.

Name	Formula	Assumptions or notes
One-sample z-test	$z = \frac{\bar{x} - \mu_0}{(\sigma / \sqrt{n})}$	(Normal population or $n > 30$) and σ known. (z is the distance from the mean in relation to the standard deviation of the mean). For non-normal distributions it is possible to calculate a minimum proportion of a population that falls within k standard deviations for any k.
Two-sample z-test	$z = \frac{(\bar{x}_1 - \bar{x}_2) - d_0}{\sqrt{\frac{\sigma_1^2}{n_1} + \frac{\sigma_2^2}{n_2}}}$	Normal population and independent observations and σ_1 and σ_2 are known
One-sample *t*-test	$t = \frac{\bar{x} - \mu_0}{(s / \sqrt{n})}$, $df = n - 1$	(Normal population or $n > 30$) and σ unknown
Paired *t*-test	$t = \frac{\bar{d} - d_0}{(s_d / \sqrt{n})}$, $df = n - 1$	(Normal population of differences or $n > 30$) and unknown or small sample size $n < 30$
Two-sample pooled *t*-test, equal variances	$t = \frac{(\bar{x}_1 - \bar{x}_2) - d_0}{s_p \sqrt{\frac{1}{n_1} + \frac{1}{n_2}}}$, $s_p^2 = \frac{(n_1 - 1)s_1^2 + (n_2 - 1)s_2^2}{n_1 + n_2 - 2}$, $df = n_1 + n_2 - 2$	(Normal populations or $n_1 + n_2 > 40$) and independent observations and $\sigma_1 = \sigma_2$ unknown
Two-sample unpooled *t*-test, unequal variances (Welch's *t*-test)	$t = \frac{(\bar{x}_1 - \bar{x}_2) - d_0}{\sqrt{\frac{s_1^2}{n_1} + \frac{s_2^2}{n_2}}}$, $df = \frac{\left(\frac{s_1^2}{n_1} + \frac{s_2^2}{n_2}\right)^2}{\frac{\left(\frac{s_1^2}{n_1}\right)^2}{n_1 - 1} + \frac{\left(\frac{s_2^2}{n_2}\right)^2}{n_2 - 1}}$	(Normal populations or $n_1 + n_2 > 40$) and independent observations and $\sigma_1 \neq \sigma_2$ both unknown

One-proportion z-test	$z = \frac{\hat{p}-p_0}{\sqrt{p_0(1-p_0)}}\sqrt{n}$	$n\,p_o > 10$ and $n\,(1 - p_o) > 10$ and it is a SRS (Simple Random Sample).
Two-proportion z-test, pooled for $H_0: p_1 = p_2$	$z = \frac{(\hat{p}_1-\hat{p}_2)}{\sqrt{\hat{p}(1-\hat{p})(\frac{1}{n_1}+\frac{1}{n_2})}}$ $\hat{p} = \frac{x_1+x_2}{n_1+n_2}$	$n_1 p_1 > 5$ and $n_1(1 - p_1) > 5$ and $n_2 p_2 > 5$ and $n_2(1 - p_2) > 5$ and independent observations.
Two-proportion z-test, unpooled for $\lvert d_0 \rvert > 0$	$z = \frac{(\hat{p}_1-\hat{p}_2)-d_0}{\sqrt{\frac{\hat{p}_1(1-\hat{p}_1)}{n_1}+\frac{\hat{p}_2(1-\hat{p}_2)}{n_2}}}$	$n_1 p_1 > 5$ and $n_1(1 - p_1) > 5$ and $n_2 p_2 > 5$ and $n_2(1 - p_2) > 5$ and independent observations.
Chi-squared test for variance	$\chi^2 = (n-1)\frac{s^2}{\sigma_0^2}$	Normal population
Chi-squared test for goodness of fit	$\chi^2 = \sum^{k} \frac{(\text{observed}-\text{expected})^2}{\text{expected}}$	$df = k - 1 -$ *# parameters estimated*, and one of these must hold. • All expected counts are at least 5. • All expected counts are > 1 and no more than 20% of expected counts are less than 5
Two-sample F test for equality of variances	$F = \frac{s_1^2}{s_2^2}$	Normal populations Arrange so $s_1^2 \geq s_2^2$ and reject H_0 for $F > F(\alpha/2, n_1-1, n_2-1)$
Regression *t*-test of $H_0: R^2 = 0.$	$t = \sqrt{\frac{R^2(n-k-1^*)}{1-R^2}}$	Reject H_0 for $t > t(\alpha/2, n-k-1^*)$ *Subtract 1 for intercept; *k* terms contain independent variables.

In general, the subscript 0 indicates a value taken from the null hypothesis, H_0, which should be used as much as possible in constructing its test statistic. ... *Definitions of other symbols:*

- α, the probability of Type I error (rejecting a null hypothesis when it is in fact true)
- n = sample size
- n_1 = sample 1 size
- n_2 = sample 2 size
- $\overline{x}$ = sample mean
- s^2 = sample variance
- s_1 = sample 1 standard deviation
- s_2 = sample 2 standard deviation
- t = t statistic
- $\hat{p} = x/n$ = sample proportion, unless specified otherwise
- p_0 = hypothesized population proportion
- p_1 = proportion 1
- p_2 = proportion 2

- μ_0 = hypothesized population mean
- μ_1 = population 1 mean
- μ_2 = population 2 mean
- σ = population standard deviation
- σ^2 = population variance
- s = sample standard deviation
- $\sum^k$ = sum (of k numbers)
- df = degrees of freedom
- $\bar{d}$ = sample mean of differences
- d_0 = hypothesized population mean difference
- s_d = standard deviation of differences
- χ^2 = Chi-squared statistic
- d_p = hypothesized difference in proportion
- $\min\{n_1, n_2\}$ = minimum of n_1 and n_2
- $x_1 = n_1 p_1$
- $x_2 = n_2 p_2$
- F = F statistic

Origins and Early Controversy

Significance testing is largely the product of Karl Pearson (p-value, Pearson's chi-squared test), William Sealy Gosset (Student's t-distribution), and Ronald Fisher ("null hypothesis", analysis of variance, "significance test"), while hypothesis testing was developed by Jerzy Neyman and Egon Pearson (son of Karl). Ronald Fisher began his life in statistics as a Bayesian (Zabell 1992), but Fisher soon grew disenchanted with the subjectivity involved (namely use of the principle of indifference when determining prior probabilities), and sought to provide a more "objective" approach to inductive inference.

Fisher was an agricultural statistician who emphasized rigorous experimental design and methods to extract a result from few samples assuming Gaussian distributions. Neyman (who teamed with the younger Pearson) emphasized mathematical rigor and methods to obtain more results from many samples and a wider range of distributions. Modern hypothesis testing is an inconsistent hybrid of the Fisher vs Neyman/Pearson formulation, methods and terminology developed in the early 20th century. While hypothesis testing was popularized early in the 20th century, evidence of its use can be found much earlier. In the 1770s Laplace considered the statistics of almost half a million births. The statistics showed an excess of boys compared to girls. He concluded by calculation of a p-value that the excess was a real, but unexplained, effect.

Fisher popularized the "significance test". He required a null-hypothesis (corresponding to a population frequency distribution) and a sample. His (now familiar) calculations determined whether to reject the null-hypothesis or not. Significance testing did not utilize an alternative hypothesis so there was no concept of a Type II error.

The p-value was devised as an informal, but objective, index meant to help a researcher determine (based on other knowledge) whether to modify future experiments or strengthen one's faith in the null hypothesis. Hypothesis testing (and Type I/II errors) was devised by Neyman and Pearson as a more objective alternative to Fisher's p-value, also meant to determine researcher behaviour, but without requiring any inductive inference by the researcher.

Neyman & Pearson considered a different problem (which they called "hypothesis testing"). They initially considered two simple hypotheses (both with frequency distributions). They calculated two probabilities and typically selected the hypothesis associated with the higher probability (the hypothesis more likely to have generated the sample). Their method always selected a hypothesis. It also allowed the calculation of both types of error probabilities.

Fisher and Neyman/Pearson clashed bitterly. Neyman/Pearson considered their formulation to be an improved generalization of significance testing.(The defining paper was abstract. Mathematicians have generalized and refined the theory for decades.) Fisher thought that it was not applicable to scientific research because often, during the course of the experiment, it is discovered that the initial assumptions about the null hypothesis are questionable due to unexpected sources of error. He believed that the use of rigid reject/accept decisions based on models formulated before data is collected was incompatible with this common scenario faced by scientists and attempts to apply this method to scientific research would lead to mass confusion.

The dispute between Fisher and Neyman–Pearson was waged on philosophical grounds, characterized by a philosopher as a dispute over the proper role of models in statistical inference.

Events intervened: Neyman accepted a position in the western hemisphere, breaking his partnership with Pearson and separating disputants (who had occupied the same building) by much of the planetary diameter. World War II provided an intermission in the debate. The dispute between Fisher and Neyman terminated (unresolved after 27 years) with Fisher's death in 1962. Neyman wrote a well-regarded eulogy. Some of Neyman's later publications reported p-values and significance levels.

The modern version of hypothesis testing is a hybrid of the two approaches that resulted from confusion by writers of statistical textbooks (as predicted by Fisher) beginning in the 1940s. (But signal detection, for example, still uses the Neyman/Pearson formulation.) Great conceptual differences and many caveats in addition to those mentioned above were ignored. Neyman and Pearson provided the stronger terminology, the more rigorous mathematics and the more consistent philosophy, but the subject taught today in introductory statistics has more similarities with Fisher's method than theirs. This history explains the inconsistent terminology (example: the null hypothesis is never accepted, but there is a region of acceptance).

Sometime around 1940, in an apparent effort to provide researchers with a "non-controversial" way to have their cake and eat it too, the authors of statistical text books began anonymously combining these two strategies by using the p-value in place of the test statistic (or data) to test against the Neyman–Pearson "significance level". Thus, researchers were encouraged to infer the strength of their data against some null hypothesis using p-values, while also thinking they are retaining the post-data collection objectivity provided by hypothesis testing. It then became customary for the null hypothesis, which was originally some realistic research hypothesis, to be used almost solely as a strawman "nil" hypothesis (one where a treatment has no effect, regardless of the context).

A Comparison Between Fisherian, Frequentist (Neyman–Pearson)

Fisher's null hypothesis testing	Neyman–Pearson decision theory
1. Set up a statistical null hypothesis. The null need not be a nil hypothesis (i.e., zero difference).	1. Set up two statistical hypotheses, H1 and H2, and decide about α, β, and sample size before the experiment, based on subjective cost-benefit considerations. These define a rejection region for each hypothesis.
2. Report the exact level of significance (e.g., p = 0.051 or p = 0.049). Do not use a conventional 5% level, and do not talk about accepting or rejecting hypotheses. If the result is "not significant", draw no conclusions and make no decisions, but suspend judgement until further data is available.	2. If the data falls into the rejection region of H1, accept H2; otherwise accept H1. Note that accepting a hypothesis does not mean that you believe in it, but only that you act as if it were true.
3. Use this procedure only if little is known about the problem at hand, and only to draw provisional conclusions in the context of an attempt to understand the experimental situation.	3. The usefulness of the procedure is limited among others to situations where you have a disjunction of hypotheses (e.g., either μ1 = 8 or μ2 = 10 is true) and where you can make meaningful cost-benefit trade-offs for choosing alpha and beta.

Early Choices of Null Hypothesis

Paul Meehl has argued that the epistemological importance of the choice of null hypothesis has gone largely unacknowledged. When the null hypothesis is predicted by theory, a more precise experiment will be a more severe test of the underlying theory. When the null hypothesis defaults to "no difference" or "no effect", a more precise experiment is a less severe test of the theory that motivated performing the experiment. An examination of the origins of the latter practice may therefore be useful:

1778: Pierre Laplace compares the birthrates of boys and girls in multiple European cities. He states: "it is natural to conclude that these possibilities are very nearly in the same ratio". Thus Laplace's null hypothesis that the birthrates of boys and girls should be equal given "conventional wisdom".

1900: Karl Pearson develops the chi squared test to determine "whether a given form of frequency curve will effectively describe the samples drawn from a given population."

Thus the null hypothesis is that a population is described by some distribution predicted by theory. He uses as an example the numbers of five and sixes in the Weldon dice throw data.

1904: Karl Pearson develops the concept of "contingency" in order to determine whether outcomes are independent of a given categorical factor. Here the null hypothesis is by default that two things are unrelated (e.g. scar formation and death rates from smallpox). The null hypothesis in this case is no longer predicted by theory or conventional wisdom, but is instead the principle of indifference that lead Fisher and others to dismiss the use of "inverse probabilities".

Null Hypothesis Statistical Significance Testing

An example of Neyman–Pearson hypothesis testing can be made by a change to the radioactive suitcase example. If the "suitcase" is actually a shielded container for the transportation of radioactive material, then a test might be used to select among three hypotheses: no radioactive source present, one present, two (all) present. The test could be required for safety, with actions required in each case. The Neyman–Pearson lemma of hypothesis testing says that a good criterion for the selection of hypotheses is the ratio of their probabilities (a likelihood ratio). A simple method of solution is to select the hypothesis with the highest probability for the Geiger counts observed. The typical result matches intuition: few counts imply no source, many counts imply two sources and intermediate counts imply one source.

Neyman–Pearson theory can accommodate both prior probabilities and the costs of actions resulting from decisions. The former allows each test to consider the results of earlier tests (unlike Fisher's significance tests). The latter allows the consideration of economic issues (for example) as well as probabilities. A likelihood ratio remains a good criterion for selecting among hypotheses.

The two forms of hypothesis testing are based on different problem formulations. The original test is analogous to a true/false question; the Neyman–Pearson test is more like multiple choice. In the view of Tukey the former produces a conclusion on the basis of only strong evidence while the latter produces a decision on the basis of available evidence. While the two tests seem quite different both mathematically and philosophically, later developments lead to the opposite claim. Consider many tiny radioactive sources. The hypotheses become 0,1,2,3... grains of radioactive sand. There is little distinction between none or some radiation (Fisher) and 0 grains of radioactive sand versus all of the alternatives (Neyman–Pearson). The major Neyman–Pearson paper of 1933 also considered composite hypotheses (ones whose distribution includes an unknown parameter). An example proved the optimality of the (Student's) *t*-test, "there can be no better test for the hypothesis under consideration" (p 321). Neyman–Pearson theory was proving the optimality of Fisherian methods from its inception.

Fisher's significance testing has proven a popular flexible statistical tool in application with little mathematical growth potential. Neyman–Pearson hypothesis testing is claimed as a pillar of mathematical statistics, creating a new paradigm for the field. It also stimulated new applications in statistical process control, detection theory, decision theory and game theory. Both formulations have been successful, but the successes have been of a different character.

The dispute over formulations is unresolved. Science primarily uses Fisher's (slightly modified) formulation as taught in introductory statistics. Statisticians study Neyman–Pearson theory in graduate school. Mathematicians are proud of uniting the formulations. Philosophers consider them separately. Learned opinions deem the formulations variously competitive (Fisher vs Neyman), incompatible or complementary. The dispute has become more complex since Bayesian inference has achieved respectability.

The terminology is inconsistent. Hypothesis testing can mean any mixture of two formulations that both changed with time. Any discussion of significance testing vs hypothesis testing is doubly vulnerable to confusion.

Fisher thought that hypothesis testing was a useful strategy for performing industrial quality control, however, he strongly disagreed that hypothesis testing could be useful for scientists. Hypothesis testing provides a means of finding test statistics used in significance testing. The concept of power is useful in explaining the consequences of adjusting the significance level and is heavily used in sample size determination. The two methods remain philosophically distinct. They usually (but *not always*) produce the same mathematical answer. The preferred answer is context dependent. While the existing merger of Fisher and Neyman–Pearson theories has been heavily criticized, modifying the merger to achieve Bayesian goals has been considered.

Criticism

Criticism of statistical hypothesis testing fills volumes citing 300–400 primary references. Much of the criticism can be summarized by the following issues:

- The interpretation of a *p*-value is dependent upon stopping rule and definition of multiple comparison. The former often changes during the course of a study and the latter is unavoidably ambiguous. (i.e. "p values depend on both the (data) observed and on the other possible (data) that might have been observed but weren't").
- Confusion resulting (in part) from combining the methods of Fisher and Neyman–Pearson which are conceptually distinct.
- Emphasis on statistical significance to the exclusion of estimation and confirmation by repeated experiments.

- Rigidly requiring statistical significance as a criterion for publication, resulting in publication bias. Most of the criticism is indirect. Rather than being wrong, statistical hypothesis testing is misunderstood, overused and misused.
- When used to detect whether a difference exists between groups, a paradox arises. As improvements are made to experimental design (e.g., increased precision of measurement and sample size), the test becomes more lenient. Unless one accepts the absurd assumption that all sources of noise in the data cancel out completely, the chance of finding statistical significance in either direction approaches 100%.
- Layers of philosophical concerns. The probability of statistical significance is a function of decisions made by experimenters/analysts. If the decisions are based on convention they are termed arbitrary or mindless while those not so based may be termed subjective. To minimize type II errors, large samples are recommended. In psychology practically all null hypotheses are claimed to be false for sufficiently large samples so "...it is usually nonsensical to perform an experiment with the *sole* aim of rejecting the null hypothesis.". "Statistically significant findings are often misleading" in psychology. Statistical significance does not imply practical significance and correlation does not imply causation. Casting doubt on the null hypothesis is thus far from directly supporting the research hypothesis.
- "It does not tell us what we want to know".

Critics and supporters are largely in factual agreement regarding the characteristics of null hypothesis significance testing (NHST): While it can provide critical information, it is *inadequate as the sole tool for statistical analysis. Successfully rejecting the null hypothesis may offer no support for the research hypothesis.* The continuing controversy concerns the selection of the best statistical practices for the near-term future given the (often poor) existing practices. Critics would prefer to ban NHST completely, forcing a complete departure from those practices, while supporters suggest a less absolute change.

Controversy over significance testing, and its effects on publication bias in particular, has produced several results. The American Psychological Association has strengthened its statistical reporting requirements after review, medical journal publishers have recognized the obligation to publish some results that are not statistically significant to combat publication bias and a journal (*Journal of Articles in Support of the Null Hypothesis*) has been created to publish such results exclusively. Textbooks have added some cautions and increased coverage of the tools necessary to estimate the size of the sample required to produce significant results. Major organizations have not abandoned use of significance tests although some have discussed doing so.

Alternatives

The numerous criticisms of significance testing do not lead to a single alternative. A unifying position of critics is that statistics should not lead to a conclusion or a decision but to a probability or to an estimated value with a confidence interval rather than to an accept-reject decision regarding a particular hypothesis. It is unlikely that the controversy surrounding significance testing will be resolved in the near future. Its supposed flaws and unpopularity do not eliminate the need for an objective and transparent means of reaching conclusions regarding studies that produce statistical results. Critics have not unified around an alternative. Other forms of reporting confidence or uncertainty could probably grow in popularity. One strong critic of significance testing suggested a list of reporting alternatives: effect sizes for importance, prediction intervals for confidence, replications and extensions for replicability, meta-analyses for generality. None of these suggested alternatives produces a conclusion/decision. Lehmann said that hypothesis testing theory can be presented in terms of conclusions/decisions, probabilities, or confidence intervals. "The distinction between the ... approaches is largely one of reporting and interpretation."

On one "alternative" there is no disagreement: Fisher himself said, "In relation to the test of significance, we may say that a phenomenon is experimentally demonstrable when we know how to conduct an experiment which will rarely fail to give us a statistically significant result." Cohen, an influential critic of significance testing, concurred, "... don't look for a magic alternative to NHST *[null hypothesis significance testing]* ... It doesn't exist." "... given the problems of statistical induction, we must finally rely, as have the older sciences, on replication." The "alternative" to significance testing is repeated testing. The easiest way to decrease statistical uncertainty is by obtaining more data, whether by increased sample size or by repeated tests. Nickerson claimed to have never seen the publication of a literally replicated experiment in psychology. An indirect approach to replication is meta-analysis.

Bayesian inference is one proposed alternative to significance testing. (Nickerson cited 10 sources suggesting it, including Rozeboom (1960)). For example, Bayesian parameter estimation can provide rich information about the data from which researchers can draw inferences, while using uncertain priors that exert only minimal influence on the results when enough data is available. Psychologist John K. Kruschke has suggested Bayesian estimation as an alternative for the *t*-test. Alternatively two competing models/hypothesis can be compared using Bayes factors. Bayesian methods could be criticized for requiring information that is seldom available in the cases where significance testing is most heavily used. Neither the prior probabilities nor the probability distribution of the test statistic under the alternative hypothesis are often available in the social sciences.

Advocates of a Bayesian approach sometimes claim that the goal of a researcher is most often to objectively assess the probability that a hypothesis is true based on the data they have collected. Neither Fisher's significance testing, nor Neyman–Pearson hypothesis testing can provide this information, and do not claim to. The probability a hypothesis is true can only be derived from use of Bayes' Theorem, which was unsatisfactory to both the Fisher and Neyman–Pearson camps due to the explicit use of subjectivity in the form of the prior probability. Fisher's strategy is to sidestep this with the p-value (an objective *index* based on the data alone) followed by *inductive inference*, while Neyman–Pearson devised their approach of *inductive behaviour*.

Philosophy

Hypothesis testing and philosophy intersect. Inferential statistics, which includes hypothesis testing, is applied probability. Both probability and its application are intertwined with philosophy. Philosopher [[tyr]] wrote, "All knowledge degenerates into probability." Competing practical definitions of probability reflect philosophical differences. The most common application of hypothesis testing is in the scientific interpretation of experimental data, which is naturally studied by the philosophy of science.

Fisher and Neyman opposed the subjectivity of probability. Their views contributed to the objective definitions. The core of their historical disagreement was philosophical.

Many of the philosophical criticisms of hypothesis testing are discussed by statisticians in other contexts, particularly correlation does not imply causation and the design of experiments. Hypothesis testing is of continuing interest to philosophers.

Education

Statistics is increasingly being taught in schools with hypothesis testing being one of the elements taught. Many conclusions reported in the popular press (political opinion polls to medical studies) are based on statistics. An informed public should understand the limitations of statistical conclusions and many college fields of study require a course in statistics for the same reason. An introductory college statistics class places much emphasis on hypothesis testing – perhaps half of the course. Such fields as literature and divinity now include findings based on statistical analysis. An introductory statistics class teaches hypothesis testing as a cookbook process. Hypothesis testing is also taught at the postgraduate level. Statisticians learn how to create good statistical test procedures (like *z*, Student's *t*, *F* and chi-squared). Statistical hypothesis testing is considered a mature area within statistics, but a limited amount of development continues.

The cookbook method of teaching introductory statistics leaves no time for history, philosophy or controversy. Hypothesis testing has been taught as received unified method. Surveys showed that graduates of the class were filled with philosophical misconceptions (on all aspects of statistical inference) that persisted among instructors. While the problem was addressed more than a decade ago, and calls for educational reform continue, students still graduate from statistics classes holding fundamental misconceptions about hypothesis testing. Ideas for improving the teaching of hypothesis testing include encouraging students to search for statistical errors in published papers, teaching the history of statistics and emphasizing the controversy in a generally dry subject.

Hypothesis Testing

Hypothesis testing typically begins with some theory, claim or ascertain about a particular parameter of a population. The procedure to test the hypothesis is to formulate the null hypothesis and alternative hypothesis. This can be defined as follows:

- Null hypothesis: It is a statement regarding the value(s) of unknown parameter(s). Typically will imply no association between explanatory and response variables in our applications (will always contain an equality). In other words, we ascertain that it hold as true unless we have sufficient statistical evidence to conclude otherwise. In short, it is a claim about population parameters.
- Alternative hypothesis: The statement contradictory to the null hypothesis (will always contain an inequality).

For example,

Chuck sees that his investment strategy produces higher average returns than simply buying and holding a stock. The null hypothesis claims that there is no difference between the two average returns, and Chuck has to believe this until he proves otherwise. Refuting the null hypothesis would require showing statistical significance, which can be found using a variety of tests. If Chuck conducts one of these tests and proves that the difference between his returns and the buyand-hold returns is significant, he can then refute the null hypothesis.

H_0: Tomato plants do not exhibit a higher rate of growth when planted in compost rather than soil.

H_1: Tomato plants exhibit a higher rate of growth when planted in compost rather than in soil.

It is important to carefully select the wording of the null, and ensure that it is as specific as possible. For example, the researcher might postulate a null hypothesis:

H_0: Tomato plants show no difference in growth rates when planted in compost rather than soil.

There is a major flaw with this null hypothesis. If the plants actually grow more slowly in compost than in soil, an impasse is reached. H_1 is not supported, but neither is H_0, because there is a difference in growth rates.

If the null is rejected, with no alternative, the experiment may be invalid. This is the reason why science uses a battery of deductive and inductive processes to ensure that there are no flaws in the hypotheses. There is a major flaw with this null hypothesis. If the plants actually grow more slowly in compost than in soil, an impasse is reached. H_1 is not supported, but neither is H_0, because there is a difference in growth rates. If the null is rejected, with no alternative, the experiment may be invalid.

This is the reason why science uses a battery of deductive and inductive processes to ensure that there are no flaws in the hypotheses. Many scientists neglect the null, assuming that it is merely the opposite of the alternative, but it is good practice to spend a little time creating a sound hypothesis.

Null Hypothesis

Ronald Fisher

Jerzy Neyman

In inferential statistics, the term "null hypothesis" is a general statement or default position that there is no relationship between two measured phenomena, or no association among groups. Rejecting or disproving the null hypothesis—and thus concluding that there are grounds for believing that there *is* a relationship between two phenomena (e.g. that a potential treatment has a measurable effect)—is a central task in the modern practice of science; the field of statistics gives precise criteria for rejecting a null hypothesis.

The null hypothesis is generally assumed to be true until evidence indicates otherwise. In statistics, it is often denoted H_0 (read "H-nought", "H-null", or "H-zero").

The concept of a null hypothesis is used differently in two approaches to statistical inference. In the significance testing approach of Ronald Fisher, a null hypothesis is rejected if the observed data are significantly unlikely to have occurred if the null hypothesis were true. In this case the null hypothesis is rejected and an alternative hypothesis is accepted in its place. If the data are consistent with the null hypothesis, then the null hypothesis is not rejected. In neither case is the null hypothesis or its alternative proven; the null hypothesis is tested with data and a decision is made based on how likely or unlikely the data are. This is analogous to a criminal trial, in which the defendant is assumed to be innocent (null is not rejected) until proven guilty (null is rejected) beyond a reasonable doubt (to a statistically significant degree).

In the hypothesis testing approach of Jerzy Neyman and Egon Pearson, a null hypothesis is contrasted with an alternative hypothesis and the two hypotheses are distinguished on the basis of data, with certain error rates.

Proponents of each approach criticize the other approach. Nowadays, though, a hybrid approach is widely practiced and presented in textbooks. The hybrid is in turn criticized as incorrect and incoherent.

Statistical inference can be done without a null hypothesis, by specifying a statistical model corresponding to each candidate hypothesis and using model selection techniques to choose the most appropriate model. (The most common selection techniques are based on either Akaike information criterion or Bayes factor.)

Principle

Hypothesis testing requires constructing a statistical model of what the data would look like given that chance or random processes alone were responsible for the results. The hypothesis that chance alone is responsible for the results is called the *null hypothesis*. The model of the result of the random process is called the *distribution under the null hypothesis*. The obtained results are then compared with the distribution under the null hypothesis, and the likelihood of finding the obtained results is thereby determined.

Hypothesis testing works by collecting data and measuring how likely the particular set of data is, assuming the null hypothesis is true, when the study is on a randomly selected representative sample. The null hypothesis assumes no relationship between variables in the population from which the sample is selected.

If the data-set of a randomly selected representative sample is very unlikely relative to the null hypothesis (defined as being part of a class of sets of data that only rarely will be observed), the experimenter rejects the null hypothesis concluding it (probably) is false. This class of data-sets is usually specified via a test statistic which is designed to measure the extent of apparent departure from the null hypothesis. The procedure works by assessing whether the observed departure measured by the test statistic is larger than a value defined so that the probability of occurrence of a more extreme value is small under the null hypothesis (usually in less than either 5% or 1% of similar data-sets in which the null hypothesis does hold).

If the data do not contradict the null hypothesis, then only a weak conclusion can be made: namely, that the observed data set provides no strong evidence against the null hypothesis. In this case, because the null hypothesis could be true or false, in some contexts this is interpreted as meaning that the data give insufficient evidence to make any conclusion; in other contexts it is interpreted as meaning that there is no evidence to support changing from a currently useful regime to a different one.

For instance, a certain drug may reduce the chance of having a heart attack. Possible null hypotheses are "this drug does not reduce the chances of having a heart attack" or "this drug has no effect on the chances of having a heart attack". The test of the hypothesis consists of administering the drug to half of the people in a study group as a controlled experiment. If the data show a statistically significant change in the people receiving the drug, the null hypothesis is rejected.

Basic Definitions

The *null hypothesis* and the *alternate hypothesis* are terms used in statistical tests, which are formal methods of reaching conclusions or making decisions on the basis of data. The hypotheses are conjectures about a statistical model of the population, which are based on a sample of the population. The tests are core elements of statistical inference, heavily used in the interpretation of scientific experimental data, to separate scientific claims from statistical noise.

"The statement being tested in a test of [statistical] significance is called the null hypothesis. The test of significance is designed to assess the strength of the evidence against the null hypothesis. Usually, the null hypothesis is a statement of 'no effect' or 'no difference'." It is often symbolized as H_0.

The statement that is hoped or expected to be true instead of the null hypothesis is the alternative hypothesis. Symbols include H_1 and H_a.

Statistical significance test: "Very roughly, the procedure for deciding goes like this: Take a random sample from the population. If the sample data are consistent with the null hypothesis, then do not reject the null hypothesis; if the sample data are inconsistent with the null hypothesis, then reject the null hypothesis and conclude that the alternative hypothesis is true."

The following sections add context and nuance to the basic definitions.

Example

Given the test scores of two random samples of men and women, does one group differ from the other? A possible null hypothesis is that the mean male score is the same as the mean female score:

$$H_0: \mu_1 = \mu_2$$

where

H_0 = the null hypothesis,

μ_1 = the mean of population 1, and

μ_2 = the mean of population 2.

A stronger null hypothesis is that the two samples are drawn from the same population, such that the variances and shapes of the distributions are also equal.

Terminology

Simple hypothesis

> Any hypothesis which specifies the population distribution completely. For such a hypothesis the sampling distribution of any statistic is a function of the sample size alone.

Composite hypothesis

> Any hypothesis which does *not* specify the population distribution completely. Example: A hypothesis specifying a normal distribution with a specified mean and an unspecified variance.

The simple/composite distinction was made by Neyman and Pearson.

Exact hypothesis

> Any hypothesis that specifies an exact parameter value. Example: $\mu = 100$. Synonym: point hypothesis.

Inexact hypothesis

> Those specifying a parameter range or interval. Examples: $\mu \leq 100$; $95 \leq \mu \leq 105$.

Fisher required an exact null hypothesis for testing.

A one-tailed hypothesis (AKA one-sided test) is an inexact hypothesis in which the value of a parameter is specified as being either:

- above or equal to a certain value, or
- below or equal to a certain value.

A one-tailed hypothesis is said to have directionality.

Fisher's original (Lady tasting tea) example was a one-tailed test. The null hypothesis was asymmetric. The odds of guessing all cups correctly was the same as guessing all cups incorrectly, but Fisher noted that only guessing correctly was compatible with the Lady's claim.

Goals of Null Hypothesis Tests

Statistical tests can be significance tests or hypothesis tests. There are many types of significance tests for one, two or more samples, for means, variances and proportions, paired or unpaired data, for different distributions, for large and small samples; all have null hypotheses. There are also at least four goals of null hypotheses for significance tests:

- Technical null hypotheses are used to verify statistical assumptions. For example, the residuals between the data and a statistical model cannot be distinguished from random noise. If true, there is no justification for complicating the model.
- Scientific null assumptions are used to directly advance a theory. For example, the angular momentum of the universe is zero. If not true, the theory of the early universe may need revision.
- Null hypotheses of homogeneity are used to verify that multiple experiments are producing consistent results. For example, the effect of a medication on the elderly is consistent with that of the general adult population. If true, this strengthens the general effectiveness conclusion and simplifies recommendations for use.
- Null hypotheses that assert the equality of effect of two or more alternative treatments, for example, a drug and a placebo, are used to reduce scientific claims based on statistical noise. This is the most popular null hypothesis; It is so popular that many statements about significant testing assume such null hypotheses.

Rejection of the null hypothesis is *not necessarily* the real goal of a significance tester. An adequate statistical model may be associated with a failure to reject the null; The model is adjusted until the null is not rejected. The numerous uses of significance testing were well known to Fisher who discussed many in his book written a decade before defining the null hypothesis.

A statistical significance test shares much mathematics with a confidence interval. They are mutually illuminating. A result is often significant when there is confidence in the sign of a relationship (the interval does not include 0). Whenever the sign of a relationship is important, statistical significance is a worthy goal. This also reveals weaknesses of significance testing: A result can be significant without a good estimate of the strength of a relationship; Significance can be a modest goal. A weak relationship can also achieve significance with enough data. Reporting both significance and confidence intervals is commonly recommended.

The varied uses of significance tests reduce the number of generalizations that can be made about all applications.

Choice of the Null Hypothesis

The choice of the null hypothesis is associated with sparse and inconsistent advice. Fisher mentioned few constraints on the choice and stated that many null hypotheses should be considered and that many tests are possible for each. The variety of applications and the diversity of goals suggests that the choice can be complicated. In many applications the formulation of the test is traditional. A familiarity with the range of tests available may suggest a particular null hypothesis and test. Formulating the null hypothesis is not automated (though the calculations of significance testing usually are). Sir David Cox has said, "How [the] translation from subject-matter problem to statistical model is done is often the most critical part of an analysis".

A statistical significance test is intended to test a hypothesis. If the hypothesis summarizes a set of data, there is no value in testing the hypothesis on that set of data. Example: If a study of last year's weather reports indicates that rain in a region falls primarily on weekends, it is only valid to test that null hypothesis on weather reports from any *other* year. Testing hypotheses suggested by the data is circular reasoning that proves nothing; It is a special limitation on the choice of the null hypothesis.

A routine procedure is as follows: Start from the scientific hypothesis. Translate this to a statistical alternative hypothesis and proceed: "Because H_a expresses the effect that we wish to find evidence for, we often begin with H_a and then set up H_0 as the statement that the hoped-for effect is not present." This advice is *reversed* for modeling applications where we hope not to find evidence against the null.

A complex case example is as follows: The gold standard in clinical research is the randomised placebo controlled double blind clinical trial. But testing a new drug against a (medically ineffective) placebo may be unethical for a serious illness. Testing a new drug against an older medically effective drug raises fundamental philosophical issues regarding the goal of the test and the motivation of the experimenters.

The standard "no difference" null hypothesis may reward the pharmaceutical company for gathering inadequate data. "Difference" is a better null hypothesis in this case, but statistical significance is not an adequate criterion for reaching a nuanced conclusion which requires a good numeric estimate of the drug's effectiveness. A "minor" or "simple" proposed change in the null hypothesis ((new vs old) rather than (new vs placebo)) can have a dramatic effect on the utility of a test for complex non-statistical reasons.

Directionality

The choice of null hypothesis (H_0) and consideration of directionality.

Tailedness of the Null-hypothesis Test

Consider the question of whether a tossed coin is fair (i.e. that on average it lands heads up 50% of the time) and an experiment where you toss the coin 5 times. A possible result of the experiment that we consider here is 5 heads. Let outcomes be considered unlikely with respect to an assumed distribution if their probability is lower than a significance threshold of 0.05.

A potential null hypothesis implying a one-tail test is "this coin is not biased toward heads". Beware that, in this context, the word "tail" takes two meanings: either as outcome of a single toss, or as region of extremal values in a probability distribution.

Indeed, with a fair coin the probability of this experiment outcome is $1/2^5=0.031$, which would be even lower if the coin were biased in favour of tails. Therefore, the observations are not likely enough for the null hypothesis to hold, and the test refutes it. Since the coin is ostensibly neither fair nor biased toward tails, the conclusion of the experiment is that the coin is biased towards heads.

Alternatively, a null hypothesis implying a two-tailed test is "this coin is fair". This one null hypothesis could be examined by looking out for either too many tails or too many heads in the experiments. The outcomes that would tend to refuse this null hypothesis are those with a large number of heads or a large number of tails, and our experiment with 5 heads would seem to belong to this class.

However, the probability of 5 tosses of the same kind, irrespective of whether these are head or tails, is twice as much as that of the 5-head occurrence singly considered. Hence, under this two-tailed null hypothesis, the observation receives a probability value of 0.061. Hence again, with the same significance threshold used for the one-tailed test (0.05), the same outcome is not statistically significant. Therefore, the two-tailed null hypothesis will be preserved in this case, not supporting the conclusion that the coin is biased towards heads reached with the single-tailed null hypothesis.

This example illustrates that the conclusion reached from a statistical test may depend on the precise formulation of the null and alternative hypotheses.

Discussion

Fisher said, "the null hypothesis must be exact, that is free of vagueness and ambiguity, because it must supply the basis of the 'problem of distribution,' of which the test of significance is the solution", implying a more restrictive domain for H_0. According to this view, the null hypothesis must be numerically exact—it must state that a particular quantity or difference is equal to a particular number. In classical science, it is most typically the statement that there is *no effect* of a particular treatment; in observations, it is typically that there is *no difference* between the value of a particular measured variable and that of a prediction.

Most statisticians believe that it is valid to state direction as a part of null hypothesis, or as part of a null hypothesis/alternative hypothesis pair. However, the results are not a full description of all the results of an experiment, merely a single result tailored to one particular purpose. For example, consider an H_0 that claims the population mean for a new treatment is an improvement on a well-established treatment with population mean = 10 (known from long experience), with the one-tailed alternative being that the new treatment's mean > 10. If the sample evidence obtained through x-bar equals −200 and the corresponding t-test statistic equals −50, the conclusion from the test would be that there is no evidence that the new treatmnent is better than the existing one: it would not report that it is markedly worse, but that is not what this particular test is looking for. To overcome any possible ambiguity in reporting the result of the test of a null hypothesis, it is best to indicate whether the test was two-sided and, if one-sided, to include the direction of the effect being tested.

The statistical theory required to deal with the simple cases of directionality dealt with here, and more complicated ones, makes use of the concept of an unbiased test.

The directionality of hypotheses is not always obvious. The explicit null hypothesis of Fisher's Lady tasting tea example was that the Lady had no such ability, which led to a symmetric probability distribution. The one-tailed nature of the test resulted from the one-tailed alternate hypothesis (a term not used by Fisher). The null hypothesis became implicitly one-tailed. The logical negation of the Lady's one-tailed claim was also one-tailed. (Claim: Ability > 0; Stated null: Ability = 0; Implicit null: Ability ≤ 0).

Pure arguments over the use of one-tailed tests are complicated by the variety of tests. Some tests (for instance the χ^2 goodness of fit test) are inherently one-tailed. Some probability distributions are asymmetric. The traditional tests of 3 or more groups are two-tailed.

Advice concerning the use of one-tailed hypotheses has been inconsistent and accepted practice varies among fields. The greatest objection to one-tailed hypotheses is their potential subjectivity. A non-significant result can sometimes be converted to a significant result by the use of a one-tailed hypothesis (as the fair coin test, at the whim of the analyst). The flip side of the argument: One-sided tests are less likely to ignore a real effect. One-tailed tests can suppress the publication of data that differs in sign from predictions. Objectivity was a goal of the developers of statistical tests.

It is a common practice to use a one-tailed hypotheses by default. However, "If you do not have a specific direction firmly in mind in advance, use a two-sided alternative. Moreover, some users of statistics argue that we should *always* work with the two-sided alternative."

One alternative to this advice is to use three-outcome tests. It eliminates the issues surrounding directionality of hypotheses by testing twice, once in each direction and combining the results to produce three possible outcomes. Variations on this approach have a history, being suggested perhaps 10 times since 1950.

Disagreements over one-tailed tests flow from the philosophy of science. While Fisher was willing to ignore the unlikely case of the Lady guessing all cups of tea incorrectly (which may have been appropriate for the circumstances), medicine believes that a proposed treatment that kills patients is significant in every sense and should be reported and perhaps explained. Poor statistical reporting practices have contributed to disagreements over one-tailed tests. Statistical significance resulting from two-tailed tests is insensitive to the sign of the relationship; Reporting significance alone is inadequate. "The treatment has an effect" is the uninformative result of a two-tailed test. "The treatment has a beneficial effect" is the more informative result of a one-tailed test. "The treatment has an effect, reducing the average length of hospitalization by 1.5 days" is the most informative report, combining a two-tailed significance test result with a numeric estimate of the relationship between treatment and effect. Explicitly reporting a numeric result eliminates a philosophical advantage of a one-tailed test. An underlying issue is the appropriate form of an experimental science without numeric predictive theories: A model of numeric results is more informative than a model of effect signs (positive, negative or unknown) which is more informative than a model of simple significance (non-zero or unknown); in the absence of numeric theory signs may suffice.

History of Statistical Tests

The history of the null and alternative hypotheses is embedded in the history of statistical tests.

- Before 1925: There are occasional transient traces of statistical tests for centuries in the past, which provide early examples of null hypotheses. In the late 19th century statistical significance was defined. In the early 20th century important probability distributions were defined. Gossett and Pearson worked on specific cases of significance testing.

- 1925: Fisher published the first edition of Statistical Methods for Research Workers which defined the statistical significance test and made it a mainstream method of analysis for much of experimental science. The text was devoid of proofs and weak on explanations, but it was filled with real examples. It placed statistical practice in the sciences well in advance of published statistical theory.

- 1933: In a series of papers (published over a decade starting in 1928) Neyman & Pearson defined the statistical hypothesis test as a proposed improvement on Fisher's test. The papers provided much of the terminology for statistical tests including *alternative hypothesis* and H_0 as a hypothesis to be tested using observational data (with H_1, H_2... as alternatives). Neyman did not use the term null hypothesis in later writings about his method.

- 1935: Fisher published the first edition of the book "The Design of Experiments" which introduced the null hypothesis (by example rather than by definition) and carefully explained the rationale for significance tests in the context of the interpretation of experimental results.

- Following: Fisher and Neyman quarreled over the relative merits of their competing formulations until Fisher's death in 1962. Career changes and World War II ended the partnership of Neyman and Pearson. The formulations were merged by relatively anonymous textbook writers, experimenters (journal editors) and mathematical statisticians without input from the principals. The subject today combines much of the terminology and explanatory power of Neyman & Pearson with the scientific philosophy and calculations provided by Fisher. Whether statistical testing is properly one subject or two remains a source of disagreement. Sample of two: One text refers to the subject as hypothesis testing (with no mention of significance testing in the index) while another says significance testing (with a section on inference as a decision). Fisher developed significance testing as a flexible tool for researchers to weigh their evidence. Instead testing has become institutionalized. Statistical significance has become a rigidly defined and enforced criterion for the publication of experimental results in many scientific journals. In some fields significance testing has become the dominant and nearly exclusive form of statistical analysis. As a consequence the limitations of the tests have been exhaustively studied. Books have been filled with the collected criticism of significance testing.

Alternative Hypothesis

In statistical hypothesis testing, the alternative hypothesis (or maintained hypothesis or research hypothesis) and the null hypothesis are the two rival hypotheses which are compared by a statistical hypothesis test.

In the domain of science two rival hypotheses can be compared by explanatory power and predictive power.

Example

An example might be where water quality in a stream has been observed over many years; and a test is made of the null hypothesis that: "there is no change in quality between the first and second halves of the data", against the alternative hypothesis that "the quality is poorer in the second half of the record".

History

The concept of an alternative hypothesis in testing was devised by Jerzy Neyman and Egon Pearson, and it is used in the Neyman–Pearson lemma. It forms a major component in modern statistical hypothesis testing. However it was not part of Ronald Fisher's formulation of statistical hypothesis testing, and he opposed its use. In Fisher's approach to testing, the central idea is to assess whether the observed dataset could have resulted from chance if the null hypothesis were assumed to hold, notionally without preconceptions about what other model might hold. Modern statistical hypothesis testing accommodates this type of test since the alternative hypothesis can be just the negation of the null hypothesis.

Types of Alternative Hypothesis

In the case of a scalar parameter, there are four principal types of alternative hypothesis:

- *Point.* Point alternative hypotheses occur when the hypothesis test is framed so that the population distribution under the alternative hypothesis is a fully defined distribution, with no unknown parameters; such hypotheses are usually of no practical interest but are fundamental to theoretical considerations of statistical inference and are the basis of the Neyman–Pearson lemma.

- *One-tailed directional.* A one-tailed directional alternative hypothesis is concerned with the region of rejection for only one tail of the sampling distribution.

- *Two-tailed directional.* A two-tailed directional alternative hypothesis is concerned with both regions of rejection of the sampling distribution.

- *Non-directional.* A non-directional alternative hypothesis is not concerned with either region of rejection, but, rather, it is only concerned that null hypothesis is not true.

Steps for Hypothesis Testing

The basic process of hypothesis testing starts with the following steps:

Step 1: Problem statement

Step 2: Choose the probability level of significance (α) Also determine whether the hypothesis test is one-tailed or two-tailed

Step 3: Having information (data)

Step 4: Compute test statistic

Step 5: Compare with tabulated statistic

Step 6: Making the decision

If the sample statistic is close to the population parameter, you have insufficient evidence to reject the null hypothesis. If the sample statistic is highly different from the population parameter, you have sufficient evidence to reject the null hypothesis.

The procedure to conclude the process depends upon sampling distribution and test statistics, as mentioned above. In fact, sampling distribution test statistics will classify the region of rejection and region of non-rejection. If test statistics falls into the region of non-rejection, we cannot reject the null hypothesis. On the contrary, if the test statistics falls into the rejection region, one can reject the null hypothesis.

The instance can be shown below:

Level of significance, or significance level, refers to a criterion of judgment upon which a decision is made regarding the value stated in a null hypothesis. The criterion is based on the probability of obtaining a statistic measured in a sample if the value stated in the null hypothesis were true. In behavioral science, the criterion or level of significance is typically set at 5%. When the probability of obtaining a sample mean is less than 5% if the null hypothesis were true, then we reject the value stated in the null hypothesis.

The rejection region is also called the critical region. The rejection region is the region beyond a critical value in a hypothesis test. When the value of a test statistic is in the rejection region, we decide to reject the null hypothesis; otherwise, we retain the null hypothesis.

To determine the critical region, you must choose a size for the test – the probability of a Type I error – the probability that you reject a true maintained hypothesis. What size you choose is your own choice. It is common to have sizes of 0.01, 0.05 or 0.10. In fact in reporting regression results, generally one reports whether the observed t-statistic is in a 10%, or 5% or 1% critical region. Note that if the observed t-statistic is in the 1% region, it is certainly in the 5% and 10%.

In most cases, we report significance rather than stating 'we reject the maintained hypothesis at the 5% level'. We state 'the coefficient is statistically significant at 5%'. The meaning is the same – namely that the reported T-statistic is in the 5% critical region. You would report significant at 1% and it is understood that it is also significant at 5% and 10%.

Below is a plot of the density of a T-distribution for 10 degrees of freedom. For 10 degrees of freedom there is 2.5% of the distribution below – 2.228 and 2.5% of the distribution above 2.228. The blue area shows a two sided critical region 5% test.

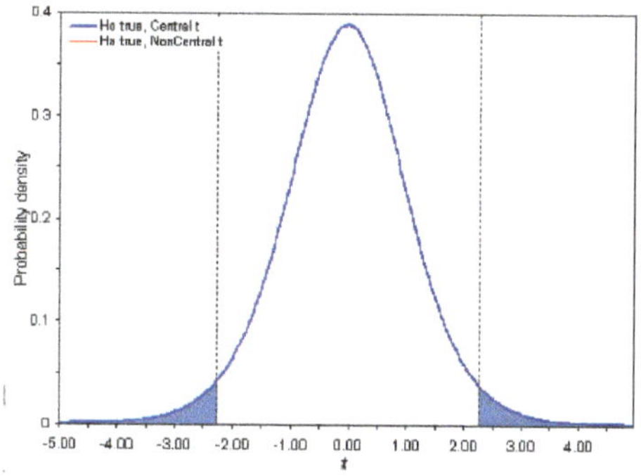

Type I and Type II Error

In statistical hypothesis testing, a type I error is the incorrect rejection of a true null hypothesis (a "false positive"), while a type II error is incorrectly retaining a false null hypothesis (a "false negative"). More simply stated, a type I error is detecting an effect that is not present, while a type II error is the failure to detect an effect that is present.

Definition

In statistics, a null hypothesis is a statement that one seeks to nullify with evidence to the contrary. Most commonly it is a statement that the phenomenon being studied produces no effect or makes no difference. An example of a null hypothesis is the statement "This diet has no effect on people's weight." Usually, an experimenter frames a null hypothesis with the intent of rejecting it: that is, intending to run an experiment which produces data that shows that the phenomenon under study does make a difference. In some cases there is a specific alternative hypothesis that is opposed to the null hypothesis, in other cases the alternative hypothesis is not explicitly stated, or is simply "the null hypothesis is false" – in either event, this is a binary judgment, but the interpretation differs and is a matter of significant dispute in statistics.

A type I error (or error of the first kind) is the incorrect rejection of a true null hypothesis. Usually a type I error leads one to conclude that a supposed effect or relationship exists when in fact it doesn't. Examples of type I errors include a test that shows a patient to have a disease when in fact the patient does not have the disease, a fire alarm going on indicating a fire when in fact there is no fire, or an experiment indicating that a medical treatment should cure a disease when in fact it does not.

A type II error (or error of the second kind) is the failure to reject a false null hypothesis. Examples of type II errors would be a blood test failing to detect the disease it was designed to detect, in a patient who really has the disease; a fire breaking out and the fire alarm does not ring; or a clinical trial of a medical treatment failing to show that the treatment works when really it does.

In terms of false positives and false negatives, a positive result corresponds to rejecting the null hypothesis, while a negative result corresponds to failing to reject the null hypothesis.

When comparing two means, concluding the means were different when in reality they were not different would be a Type I error; concluding the means were not different when in reality they were different would be a Type II error. Various extensions have been suggested as "Type III errors", though none have wide use.

All statistical hypothesis tests have a probability of making type I and type II errors. For example, all blood tests for a disease will falsely detect the disease in some proportion of people who don't have it, and will fail to detect the disease in some proportion of people who do have it. A test's probability of making a type I error is denoted by α. A test's probability of making a type II error is denoted by β. These error rates are traded off against each other: for any given sample set, the effort to reduce one type of error generally results in increasing the other type of error. For a given test, the only way to reduce both error rates is to increase the sample size, and this may not be feasible.

These terms are also used in a more general way by social scientists and others to refer to flaws in reasoning. This article is specifically devoted to the statistical meanings of those terms and the technical issues of the statistical errors that those terms describe.

Statistical Test Theory

In statistical test theory, the notion of statistical error is an integral part of hypothesis testing. The test requires an unambiguous statement of a null hypothesis, which usually corresponds to a default "state of nature", for example "this person is healthy", "this accused is not guilty" or "this product is not broken". An alternative hypothesis is the negation of null hypothesis, for example, "this person is not healthy", "this accused is guilty" or "this product is broken". The result of the test may be negative, relative to the null hypothesis (not healthy, guilty, broken) or positive (healthy, not guilty, not broken). If the result of the test corresponds with reality, then a correct decision has been made. However, if the result of the test does not correspond with reality, then an error has occurred. Due to the statistical nature of a test, the result is never, except in very rare cases, free of error. Two types of error are distinguished: type I error and type II error.

Type I Error

A type I error occurs when the null hypothesis (H_0) is true, but is rejected. It is asserting something that is absent, a false hit. A type I error may be likened to a so-called *false positive* (a result that indicates that a given condition is present when it actually is not present).

The type I error rate or significance level is the probability of rejecting the null hypothesis given that it is true. It is denoted by the Greek letter α (alpha) and is also called the alpha level. Often, the significance level is set to 0.05 (5%), implying that it is acceptable to have a 5% probability of incorrectly rejecting the null hypothesis.

Type II Error

A type II error occurs when the null hypothesis is false, but erroneously fails to be rejected. It is failing to assert what is present, a miss. A type II error may be compared with a so-called *false negative* (where an actual 'hit' was disregarded by the test and seen as a 'miss') in a test checking for a single condition with a definitive result of true or false. A Type II error is committed when we fail to believe a truth. In terms of folk tales, an investigator may fail to see the wolf ("failing to raise an alarm"). Again, H_0: no wolf.

The rate of the type II error is denoted by the Greek letter β (beta) and related to the power of a test (which equals 1−β).

Table of Error Types

Tabularised relations between truth/falseness of the null hypothesis and outcomes of the test:

Table of error types		**Null hypothesis (H_0) is**	
		True	**False**
Decision About Null Hypothesis (H_0)	**Reject**	Type I error (False Positive)	Correct inference (True Positive)
	Fail to reject	Correct inference (True Negative)	Type II error (False Negative)

Examples

Example 1

Hypothesis: "Adding water to toothpaste protects against cavities."

Null hypothesis (H_o): "Adding water to toothpaste has no effect on cavities."

This null hypothesis is tested against experimental data with a view to nullifying it with evidence to the contrary.

A type I error occurs when detecting an effect (adding water to toothpaste protects against cavities) that is not present. The null hypothesis is true (i.e., it is true that adding water to toothpaste has no effect on cavities), but this null hypothesis is rejected based on bad experimental data.

Example 2

Hypothesis: "Adding fluoride to toothpaste protects against cavities."

Null hypothesis (H_o): "Adding fluoride to toothpaste has no effect on cavities."

This null hypothesis is tested against experimental data with a view to nullifying it with evidence to the contrary.

A type II error occurs when failing to detect an effect (adding fluoride to toothpaste protects against cavities) that is present. The null hypothesis is false (i.e., adding fluoride is actually effective against cavities), but the experimental data is such that the null hypothesis cannot be rejected.

Example 3

Hypothesis: "The evidence produced before the court proves that this man is guilty."

Null hypothesis (H_o): "This man is innocent."

A type I error occurs when convicting an innocent person (a miscarriage of justice). A type II error occurs when letting a guilty person go free (an error of impunity).

A positive correct outcome occurs when convicting a guilty person. A negative correct outcome occurs when letting an innocent person go free.

Example 4

Hypothesis: "A patient's symptoms improve after treatment A more rapidly than after a placebo treatment."

Null hypothesis (H_o): "A patient's symptoms after treatment A are indistinguishable from a placebo."

A Type I error would falsely indicate that treatment A is more effective than the placebo, whereas a Type II error would be a failure to demonstrate that treatment A is more effective than placebo even though it actually is more effective.

Etymology

In 1928, Jerzy Neyman (1894–1981) and Egon Pearson (1895–1980), both eminent statisticians, discussed the problems associated with "*deciding whether or not a particular sample may be judged as likely to have been randomly drawn from a certain population*"[p. 1]: and, as Florence Nightingale David remarked, "*it is necessary to remember the adjective 'random' [in the term 'random sample'] should apply to the method of drawing the sample and not to the sample itself*".

They identified "*two sources of error*", namely:

(a) the error of rejecting a hypothesis that should have been accepted, and

(b) the error of accepting a hypothesis that should have been rejected.

In 1930, they elaborated on these *two sources of error*, remarking that:

> *...in testing hypotheses two considerations must be kept in view, (1) we must be able to reduce the chance of rejecting a true hypothesis to as low a value as desired; (2) the test must be so devised that it will reject the hypothesis tested when it is likely to be false.*

In 1933, they observed that these "*problems are rarely presented in such a form that we can discriminate with certainty between the true and false hypothesis*". They also noted that, in deciding whether to accept or reject a particular hypothesis amongst a "*set of alternative hypotheses*", H_1, H_2, . . ., it was easy to make an error:

> *...[and] these errors will be of two kinds:*
>
> *(I) we reject H_0 [i.e., the hypothesis to be tested] when it is true,*
>
> *(II) we accept H_0 when some alternative hypothesis H_A* or *H_1 is true.* (There are various notations for the alternative).

In all of the papers co-written by Neyman and Pearson the expression H_0 always signifies "the hypothesis to be tested".

In the same paper they call these *two sources of error*, errors of type I and errors of type II respectively.

Related Terms

Null Hypothesis

It is standard practice for statisticians to conduct tests in order to determine whether or not a "*speculative hypothesis*" concerning the observed phenomena of the world (or its inhabitants) can be supported. The results of such testing determine whether a particular set of results agrees reasonably (or does not agree) with the speculated hypothesis.

On the basis that it is always assumed, by *statistical convention*, that the speculated hypothesis is wrong, and the so-called "*null hypothesis*" that the observed phenomena simply occur by chance (and that, as a consequence, the speculated agent has no effect) – the test will determine whether this hypothesis is right or wrong. This is why the hypothesis under test is often called the null hypothesis (most likely, coined by Fisher (1935, p. 19)), because it is *this* hypothesis that is to be either nullified or not nullified by the test. When the null hypothesis is nullified, it is possible to conclude that data support the "*alternative hypothesis*" (which is the original speculated one).

The consistent application by statisticians of Neyman and Pearson's convention of representing "*the hypothesis to be tested*" (or "*the hypothesis to be nullified*") with the expression H_0 has led to circumstances where many understand the term "*the null hypothesis*" as meaning "*the nil hypothesis*" – a statement that the results in question have arisen through chance. This is not necessarily the case – the key restriction, as per Fisher (1966), is that "*the null hypothesis must be exact, that is free from vagueness and ambiguity, because it must supply the basis of the 'problem of distribution,' of which the test of significance is the solution.*" As a consequence of this, in experimental science the null hypothesis is generally a statement that a particular treatment has *no effect*; in observational science, it is that there is *no difference* between the value of a particular measured variable, and that of an experimental prediction.

Statistical Significance

The extent to which the test in question shows that the "speculated hypothesis" has (or has not) been nullified is called its significance level; and the higher the significance level, the less likely it is that the phenomena in question could have been produced by chance alone. British statistician Sir Ronald Aylmer Fisher (1890–1962) stressed that the "null hypothesis":

... is never proved or established, but is possibly disproved, in the course of experimentation. Every experiment may be said to exist only in order to give the facts a chance of disproving the null hypothesis.

Application Domains

Statistical tests always involve a trade-off between:

1. the acceptable level of false positives (in which a non-match is declared to be a match) and
2. the acceptable level of false negatives (in which an actual match is not detected).

A threshold value can be varied to make the test more restrictive or more sensitive, with the more restrictive tests increasing the risk of rejecting true positives, and the more sensitive tests increasing the risk of accepting false positives.

Inventory Control

An automated inventory control system that rejects high-quality goods of a consignment commits a type I error, while a system that accepts low-quality goods commits a type II error.

Computers

The notions of false positives and false negatives have a wide currency in the realm of computers and computer applications, as follows.

Computer Security

Security vulnerabilities are an important consideration in the task of keeping computer data safe, while maintaining access to that data for appropriate users. Moulton (1983), stresses the importance of:

- avoiding the type I errors (or false positives) that classify *authorized users* as *imposters*.
- avoiding the type II errors (or false negatives) that classify *imposters* as *authorized users*.

Spam Filtering

A false positive occurs when spam filtering or spam blocking techniques wrongly classify a legitimate email message as spam and, as a result, interferes with its delivery. While most anti-spam tactics can block or filter a high percentage of unwanted emails, doing so without creating significant false-positive results is a much more demanding task.

A false negative occurs when a spam email is not detected as spam, but is classified as *non-spam*. A low number of false negatives is an indicator of the efficiency of spam filtering.

Malware

The term "false positive" is also used when antivirus software wrongly classifies an innocuous file as a virus. The incorrect detection may be due to heuristics or to an incorrect virus signature in a database. Similar problems can occur with antitrojan or antispyware software.

Optical Character Recognition

Detection algorithms of all kinds often create false positives. Optical character recognition (OCR) software may detect an "a" where there are only some dots that *appear* to be an "a" to the algorithm being used.

Security Screening

False positives are routinely found every day in airport security screening, which are ultimately visual inspection systems. The installed security alarms are intended to prevent weapons being brought onto aircraft; yet they are often set to such high sensitivity that they alarm many times a day for minor items, such as keys, belt buckles, loose change, mobile phones, and tacks in shoes.

The ratio of false positives (identifying an innocent traveller as a terrorist) to true positives (detecting a would-be terrorist) is, therefore, very high; and because almost every alarm is a false positive, the positive predictive value of these screening tests is very low.

The relative cost of false results determines the likelihood that test creators allow these events to occur. As the cost of a false negative in this scenario is extremely high (not detecting a bomb being brought onto a plane could result in hundreds of deaths) whilst the cost of a false positive is relatively low (a reasonably simple further inspection) the most appropriate test is one with a low statistical specificity but high statistical sensitivity (one that allows a high rate of false positives in return for minimal false negatives).

Biometrics

Biometric matching, such as for fingerprint recognition, facial recognition or iris recognition, is susceptible to type I and type II errors. The null hypothesis is that the input *does* identify someone in the searched list of people, so:

- the probability of type I errors is called the "false reject rate" (FRR) or false non-match rate (FNMR),
- while the probability of type II errors is called the "false accept rate" (FAR) or false match rate (FMR).

If the system is designed to rarely match suspects then the probability of type II errors can be called the "false alarm rate". On the other hand, if the system is used for validation (and acceptance is the norm) then the FAR is a measure of system security, while the FRR measures user inconvenience level.

Medical Screening

In the practice of medicine, there is a significant difference between the applications of *screening* and *testing*.

- *Screening* involves relatively *cheap* tests that are given to large populations, none of whom manifest any clinical indication of disease (e.g., Pap smears).
- *Testing* involves far more *expensive*, often invasive, procedures that are given only to those who manifest some clinical indication of disease, and are most often applied to confirm a suspected diagnosis.

For example, most states in the USA require newborns to be screened for phenylketonuria and hypothyroidism, among other congenital disorders. Although they display a high rate of false positives, the screening tests are considered valuable because they greatly increase the likelihood of detecting these disorders at a far earlier stage.

The simple blood tests used to *screen* possible blood donors for HIV and hepatitis have a significant rate of false positives; however, physicians use much more expensive and far more precise *tests* to determine whether a person is actually infected with either of these viruses.

Perhaps the most widely discussed false positives in medical screening come from the breast cancer screening procedure mammography. The US rate of false positive mammograms is up to 15%, the highest in world. One consequence of the high false positive rate in the US is that, in any 10-year period, half of the American women screened receive a false positive mammogram. False positive mammograms are costly, with over $100 million spent annually in the U.S. on follow-up testing and treatment. They also cause women unneeded anxiety. As a result of the high false positive rate in the US, as many as 90–95% of women who get a positive mammogram do *not* have the condition. The lowest rate in the world is in the Netherlands, 1%. The lowest rates are generally in Northern Europe where mammography films are read twice and a high threshold for additional testing is set (the high threshold decreases the power of the test).

The ideal population screening test would be cheap, easy to administer, and produce *zero* false-negatives, if possible. Such tests usually produce more false-positives, which can subsequently be sorted out by more sophisticated (and expensive) testing.

Medical Testing

False negatives and false positives are significant issues in medical testing. False negatives may provide a falsely reassuring message to patients and physicians that disease is absent, when it is actually present. This sometimes leads to inappropriate or inadequate treatment of both the patient and their disease. A common example is relying on cardiac stress tests to detect coronary atherosclerosis, even though cardiac stress tests are known to only detect limitations of coronary artery blood flow due to advanced stenosis.

False negatives produce serious and counter-intuitive problems, especially when the condition being searched for is common. If a test with a *false negative rate* of only 10%, is used to test a population with a *true occurrence rate* of 70%, many of the negatives detected by the test will be false.

False positives can also produce serious and counter-intuitive problems when the condition being searched for is rare, as in screening. If a test has a *false positive rate* of one in ten thousand, but only one in a million samples (or people) is a *true positive*, most of the positives detected by that test will be false. The probability that an observed positive result is a false positive may be calculated using Bayes' theorem.

Paranormal Investigation

The notion of a false positive is common in cases of paranormal or ghost phenomena seen in images and such, when there is another plausible explanation. When observing a photograph, recording, or some other evidence that appears to have a paranormal origin – in this usage, a false positive is a disproven piece of media "evidence" (image, movie, audio recording, etc.) that actually has a natural explanation.

Basics of Hypothesis Testing

Test statistic: Quantity based on sample data and null hypothesis used to test between null and alternative hypotheses.

Rejection region: Values of the test statistic for which we reject the null in favour of the alternative hypothesis.

Power of test: Probability a test rejects H_0

H_0 True: Power = P (Type I error) = a

H_0 False: Power = 1-P (Type II error) = 1-b

Types of test: There are three in nature

Left-tailed Tests: $H_0 : \mu = k; H_1 : \mu < k$

Right-tailed Tests: $H_0 : \mu = k; H_1 : \mu > k$

Two-tailed Tests: $H_0 : \mu = k; H_1 : \mu \neq k$

Type I Error

In a hypothesis test, a type I error occurs when the null hypothesis is rejected when it is in fact true; that is, H_0 is wrongly rejected.

For example, in a clinical trial of a new drug, the null hypothesis might be that the new drug is no better, on average, than the current drug; i.e. H_0: there is no difference between the two drugs on average.

A type I error would occur if we concluded that the two drugs produced different effects when in fact there was no difference between them.

Type II Error

In a hypothesis test, a type II error occurs when the null hypothesis H_0, is not rejected when it is in fact false. For example, in a clinical trial of a new drug, the null hypothesis might be that the new drug is no better, on average, than the current drug; i.e.

H_0: there is no difference between the two drugs on average.

A type II error would occur if it was concluded that the two drugs produced the same effect, i.e. there is no difference between the two drugs on average, when in fact they produced different ones.

P-Value

The probability value (p-value) of a statistical hypothesis test is the probability of getting a value of the test statistic as extreme as or more extreme than that observed by chance alone, if the null hypothesis H_0, is true. It is the probability of wrongly rejecting the null hypothesis if it is in fact true. It is equal to the significance level of the test for which we would only just reject the null hypothesis. The p-value is compared with the actual significance level of our test and, if it is smaller, the result is significant. That is, if the null hypothesis were to be rejected at the 5% significance level, this would be reported as "$p < 0.05$".

Small p-values suggest that the null hypothesis is unlikely to be true. The smaller it is, the more convincing is the rejection of the null hypothesis. It indicates the strength of evidence for say, rejecting the null hypothesis H_0, rather than simply concluding "Reject H_0' or "Do not reject H_0".

Power of the Test

The power of a statistical hypothesis test measures the test's ability to reject the null hypothesis when it is actually false - that is, to make a correct decision. In other words, the power of a hypothesis test is the probability of not committing a type II error. It is calculated by subtracting the probability of a type II error from 1, usually expressed as:

Power = 1 – P (type II error) = $(1-\beta)$

The maximum power a test can have is 1, the minimum is 0. Ideally we want a test to have high power, close to 1.

One-sided Test

A one-sided test is a statistical hypothesis test in which the values for which we can reject the null hypothesis, H_0 are located entirely in one tail of the probability distribution. In other words, the critical region for a one-sided test is the set of values less than the critical value of the test, or the set of values greater than the critical value of the test. A one-sided test is also referred to as a one-tailed test of significance. The choice between a one-sided and a two-sided test is determined by the purpose of the investigation or prior reasons for using a one-sided test. For instance, Suppose we wanted to test a manufacturer's claim that there are, on average, 50 matches in a box. We could set up the following hypotheses

$$H0: \mu = 50 \text{ against } H1: \mu < 50 \text{ or } H1: \mu > 50$$

Either of these two alternative hypotheses would lead to a one-sided test. Presumably, we would want to test the null hypothesis against the first alternative hypothesis since it would be useful to know if there is likely to be less than 50 matches, on average, in a box (no one would complain if they get the correct number of matches in a box or more).

Two-Sided Test

A two-sided test is a statistical hypothesis test in which the values for which we can reject the null hypothesis, H_0 are located in both tails of the probability distribution. In other words, the critical region for a two-sided test is the set of values less than a first critical value of the test and the set of values greater than a second critical value of the test. A two-sided test is also referred to as a two-tailed test of significance. The choice between a one-sided test and a two-sided test is determined by the purpose of the investigation or prior reasons for using a one-sided test. For instance,

Suppose we wanted to test a manufacturer's claim that there are, on average, 50 matches in a box. We could set up the following hypotheses

$$H_0: \mu = 50 \text{ against}$$

$$H_1: \mu < 50 \text{ or } H_1: \mu > 50$$

Either of these two alternative hypotheses would lead to a one-sided test. Presumably, we would want to test the null hypothesis against the first alternative hypothesis since it would be useful to know if there is likely to be less than 50 matches, on average, in a box (no one would complain if they get the correct number of matches in a box or more).

One Sample t-test

A one sample t-test is a hypothesis test for answering questions about the mean where the data are a random sample of independent observations from an underlying normal distribution

$N(\mu, \sigma^2)$ where σ^2 is unknown.

The null hypothesis for the one sample t-test is:

$H0: \mu = \mu_0$ where μ_0 is known.

That is, the sample has been drawn from a population of given mean and unknown variance (which therefore has to be estimated from the sample).

Two Sample t-tests

A two sample t-test is a hypothesis test for answering questions about the mean where the data are collected from two random samples of independent observations, each from an underlying normal distribution:

$N(\mu_i, \sigma_i^2)$ where i =1,2

When carrying out a two sample t-test, it is usual to assume that the variances for the two populations are equal, i.e.

$$\sigma_1^2 - \sigma_2^2 - \sigma^2$$

The null hypothesis for the two sample t-test is:

That is, the two samples have both been drawn from the same population. This null hypothesis is tested against one of the following alternative hypotheses, depending on the question posed.

$$H1: \mu_1 \neq \mu_2$$

$$H1: \mu_1 > \mu_2$$

$$H1: \mu_1 < \mu_2$$

The Path Digram for Hypothesis Testing

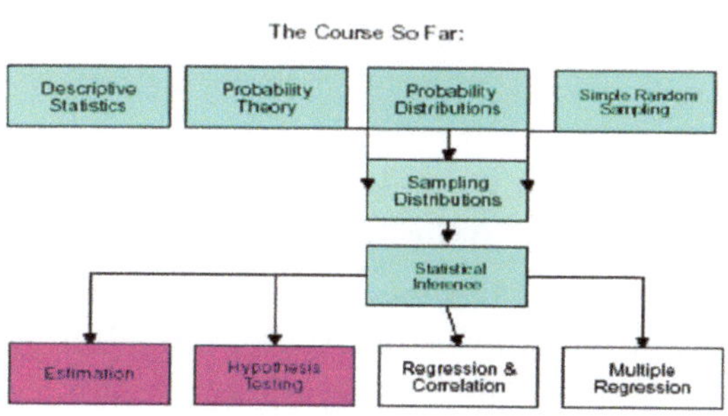

Test Statistics for Hypothesis Testing

There are four test statistics through which we can test the hypothesis. These include

- Z- Statistics

$$z = \frac{\bar{x} - \mu_{\bar{x}}}{\sigma_{\bar{x}}} = \frac{\bar{x} - \mu}{\sigma / \sqrt{n}}$$

- χ^2 - Statistics

$$\chi^2 = \sum \frac{(O - E)^2}{E}$$

χ^2 = the test statistic $\sum$ = the sum of

O = Observed frequencies E = Expected frequencies

- t- Statistics

$$t = \frac{\bar{x} - \mu}{\left(\frac{s}{\sqrt{n}}\right)}$$

Degrees of freedom d.f. = n – 1

- F- Statistics

$$F = \frac{s_1^2}{s_2^2}$$

Where s_1^2 is the variance of the first group and s_2^2 is the variance of the second group

A test statistic is a quantity calculated from the sampled value of a statistic, which is then used to calculate a p-value for a test of hypothesis.

$$\text{Test Statistics} = \left[(\text{Estimate From Data}) - (\text{Parameter Value Assu min g } H_0 \text{ Is True})\right] / SE(\text{Estimate})$$

The Sample Problems

Two teams of workers assemble automobile engines at a manufacturing plant in Michigan. A random sample of 145 assemblies from team 1 shows 15 unacceptable assemblies. A similar random sample of 125 assemblies from team 2 shows 8 unacceptable assemblies. Construct a 90% confidence interval for the difference between the proportions of unacceptable assemblies generated by the two teams.

Solutions

$$n_1 = 145, \hat{P}_1 = 0.1034, n_2 = 125, \hat{P}_2 = 0.0640, z - \text{multiple} = 1.645$$

$$SE\left(\hat{P}_1 - \hat{P}_2\right) = \sqrt{\frac{\hat{P}_1\left(1-\hat{P}_1\right)}{n_1} + \frac{\hat{P}_2\left(1-\hat{P}_2\right)}{n_2}} = 0.0334$$

$$\left(\hat{P}_1 - \hat{P}_2\right) \pm Z \cdot SE\left(\hat{P}_1 - \hat{P}_2\right) = 0.0394 \pm 0.0549$$

Lower limit = -0.0155, and Upper limit = 0.0943

The Sample Problems

Assuming that the variances of the four underlying populations are indeed equal, can you reject at the 10% significance level that the mean starting salary is the same for each of the given business majors? Explain why or why not.

Solution

One Way ANOVA table

Source of variation	SS	df	MS	F	p-value
Between groups	140927283.143	3	46975761.048	12.677	0.0001
Within groups	77820292.857	21	3705728.231		
Total variation	218747576.000	24			

$$H_0 : \mu_1 = \mu_2 = \mu_3 = \mu_4$$

H_α : At least two population means are unequal.

The ANOVA table indicates definite mean difference, even at the 1% level (since the p-value is less than .01). Even if the test is not perfectly valid (because of unequal variances), we can still be pretty confident that the means are not all equal.

The Sample Problems

The CEO of a software company is committed to expanding the proportion of highly qualified women in the organization's staff of salespersons. He claims that the proportion of women in similar sales positions across the country in 1999 is less than 45%. Hoping to find support for his claim, he directs his assistant to collect a random sample of salespersons employed by his company, which is thought to be representative of sales staffs of competing organizations in the industry. The collected random sample of size 50 showed that only 18 were women. Test this CEO's claim at the α =.05 significance level and report the p-value. Do you find statistical support for his hypothesis that the proportion of women in similar sales positions across the country is less than 40%?

Solution

$$H_0 : P \geq 0.45 ; \qquad H_\alpha : P < 0.45$$

Test statistic: Z =-1.279 and P-value = 0.10

There is not enough evidence to support this claim. The P-value is large (0.10).

The Sample Problems

Units	Price	County	Size	Elevation	Sewer	Date	Flood	Distance
1	4.5	1	138.4	10	3000	-103	0	0.3
2	10.6	1	52	4	0	-103	0	2.5
3	1.7	0	16.1	0	2640	-98	1	10.3
4	5	0	1695.2	1	3500	-93	0	14
5	5	0	845	1	1000	-92	1	14
6	3.3	1	6.9	2	10000	-86	0	0
7	5.7	1	105.9	4	0	-68	0	0
8	6.2	1	56.6	4	0	-64	0	0
9	19.4	1	51.4	20	1300	-63	0	1.2
10	3.2	1	22.1	0	6000	-62	0	0
11	4.7	1	22.1	0	6000	-61	0	0
12	6.9	1	27.7	3	4500	-60	0	0
13	8.1	1	18.6	5	5000	-59	0	0.5
14	11.6	1	69.9	8	0	-59	0	4.4
15	19.3	1	145.7	10	0	-59	0	4.2
16	11.7	1	77.2	9	0	-59	0	4.5
17	13.3	1	26.2	8	0	-59	0	4.7
18	15.1	1	102.3	6	0	-59	0	4.9
19	12.4	1	49.5	11	0	-59	0	4.6
20	15.3	1	12.2	8	0	-59	0	5
21	12.2	0	320.6	0	4000	-54	0	16.5
22	18.1	1	9.9	5	0	-54	0	5.2
23	16.8	1	15.3	2	0	-53	0	5.5
24	5.9	0	55.2	0	1320	-49	1	11.9
25	4	0	116.2	2	900	-45	1	5.5
26	37.2	0	15	5	0	-39	0	7.2
27	18.2	0	23.4	5	4420	-39	0	5.5
28	15.1	0	132.8	2	2640	-35	0	10.2
29	22.9	0	12	5	3400	-16	0	5.5
30	15.2	0	67	2	900	-5	1	5.5
31	21.9	0	30.8	2	900	-4	0	5.5

$$\text{Price} = \beta_1 + \beta_2 \cdot \text{country} + \beta_3 \cdot \text{size} + \beta_4 \cdot \text{Elevation} + \beta_5 \cdot \text{Sewer} + \beta_6 \cdot \text{date} + \beta_7 \cdot \text{flood} + \beta_8 \cdot \text{distance} + u$$

Solutions

Two parts:

Dependent Variable: Price

Independent variables: country, size, Elevation, Sewer, date, flood, distance

Objectives:

With respect to Parameters:

If β_2 is found to be statistically significant then, we can say that country affects price;

If β_3 is found to be statistically significant then, we can say that size affects price;

If β_4 is found to be statistically significant then, we can say that Elevation affects price;

If β_5 is found to be statistically significant then, we can say that Sewer affects price;

If β_6 is found to be statistically significant then, we can say that date affects price;

If β_7 is found to be statistically significant then, we can say that flood affects price;

If β_8 is found to be statistically significant then, we can say that distance affects price;

So, we look for the significance of β_2, β_3, β_4, β_5, β_6, β_7 and β_8

With Respect to Overall Fit

R_2 and Adjusted R_2

Tests

Specification test: Coefficients of parameters (t-test)

Goodness fit test: Model summary and ANOVA (F-test)

Coefficients[a]

Model		Unstandardized Coefficients		Standardized Coefficients	t	Sig.
		B	Std. Error	Beta		
1	(Constant)	23.643	3.829		6.174	.000
	Country	-8.789	3.652	-.564	-2.407	.025
	Size	-.006	.004	-.256	-1.726	.098
	Elevation	.519	.239	.293	2.177	.040

	Sewer	.000	.000	-.308	-2.296	.031
	Date	.085	.049	.270	1.749	.094
	Flood	-12.015	2.989	-.582	-4.020	.001
	Distance	.186	.340	.109	.547	.589

Model Summary				
Model	R	R Square	Adjusted R Square	Std. Error of the Estimate
1	.864a	.747	.670	4.43148

ANOVA[b]						
Model		Sum of Squares	df	Mean Square	F	Sig.
1	Regression	1333.822	7	190.546	9.703	.000a
	Residual	451.675	23	19.638		
	Total	1785.497	30			

References

- Hubbard, R.; Parsa, A. R.; Luthy, M. R. (1997). "The Spread of Statistical Significance Testing in Psychology: The Case of the Journal of Applied Psychology". Theory and Psychology. 7 (4): 545–554. doi:10.1177/0959354397074006
- A. Kolmogoroff (1933). Grundbegriffe der Wahrscheinlichkeitsrechnung. ISBN 978-3-642-49888-6. doi:10.1007/978-3-642-49888-6
- C. S. Peirce (August 1878). "Illustrations of the Logic of Science VI: Deduction, Induction, and Hypothesis". Popular Science Monthly. 13. Retrieved March 30, 2012
- Neyman, Jerzy (1967). "RA Fisher (1890—1962): An Appreciation.". Science. 156.3781: 1456–1460. doi:10.1126/science.156.3781.1456
- Fisher, R (1955). "Statistical Methods and Scientific Induction" (PDF). Journal of the Royal Statistical Society, Series B. 17 (1): 69–78
- Olav Kallenberg; Probabilistic Symmetries and Invariance Principles. Springer -Verlag, New York (2005). 510 pp. ISBN 0-387-25115-4
- Shermer, Michael (2002). The Skeptic Encyclopedia of Pseudoscience 2 volume set. ABC-CLIO. p. 455. ISBN 1-57607-653-9. Retrieved 10 January 2011
- Loftus, G R (1991). "On the Tyranny of Hypothesis Testing in the Social Sciences" (PDF). Contemporary Psychology. 36 (2): 102–105. doi:10.1037/029395
- Lehmann, E. L. (December 1993). "The Fisher, Neyman–Pearson Theories of Testing Hypotheses: One Theory or Two?". Journal of the American Statistical Association. 88 (424): 1242–1249
- Burnham, K. P.; Anderson, D. R. (2002). Model Selection and Multimodel Inference: A Practical Information-Theoretic Approach (2nd ed.). Springer-Verlag. ISBN 0-387-95364-7
- Meehl, P (1990). "Appraising and Amending Theories: The Strategy of Lakatosian Defense and Two Principles That Warrant It" (PDF). Psychological Inquiry. 1 (2): 108–141. doi:10.1207/s15327965pli0102_1

- Gigerenzer, G (November 2004). "Mindless statistics". The Journal of Socio-Economics. 33 (5): 587–606. doi:10.1016/j.socec.2004.09.033
- Hinkelmann, Klaus and Kempthorne, Oscar (2008). Design and Analysis of Experiments. I and II (Second ed.). Wiley. ISBN 978-0-470-38551-7
- Loveland, Jennifer L. (2011). Mathematical Justification of Introductory Hypothesis Tests and Development of Reference Materials (M.Sc. (Mathematics)). Utah State University. Retrieved April 30, 2013
- Zabell, S (1989). "R. A. Fisher on the History of Inverse Probability". Statistical Science. 4 (3): 247–256. JSTOR 2245634. doi:10.1214/ss/1177012488
- Cornfield, Jerome (1976). "Recent Methodological Contributions to Clinical Trials" (PDF). American Journal of Epidemiology. 104 (4): 408–421
- Moore, David (2003). Introduction to the Practice of Statistics. New York: W.H. Freeman and Co. p. 426. ISBN 9780716796572
- Kruschke, J K (July 9, 2012). "Bayesian Estimation Supersedes the T Test". Journal of Experimental Psychology: General. 142: 573–603. doi:10.1037/a0029146
- Aldrich, John. "Earliest Known Uses of Some of the Words of Probability & Statistics". Retrieved 30 June 2014. Last update 12 march 2003. From Jeff Miller
- Stigler, Stephen M. (August 1996). "The History of Statistics in 1933". Statistical Science. 11 (3): 244–252. JSTOR 2246117. doi:10.1214/ss/1032280216

3

Statistical Analysis of Econometric Modeling

Statistics used to describe a group of information is known as descriptive statistics. It helps in summarizing samples. Central tendency, univariate econometric modelling, univariate analysis are some of the topics discussed in the section. The aspects elucidated in this chapter are of vital importance, and provide a better understanding of statistical models.

Descriptive Statistics

Descriptive statistics are statistics that quantitatively describe or summarize features of a collection of information. Descriptive statistics are distinguished from inferential statistics (or inductive statistics), in that descriptive statistics aim to summarize a sample, rather than use the data to learn about the population that the sample of data is thought to represent. This generally means that descriptive statistics, unlike inferential statistics, are not developed on the basis of probability theory. Even when a data analysis draws its main conclusions using inferential statistics, descriptive statistics are generally also presented. For example, in papers reporting on human subjects, typically a table is included giving the overall sample size, sample sizes in important subgroups (e.g., for each treatment or exposure group), and demographic or clinical characteristics such as the average age, the proportion of subjects of each sex, the proportion of subjects with related comorbidities etc.

Some measures that are commonly used to describe a data set are measures of central tendency and measures of variability or dispersion. Measures of central tendency include the mean, median and mode, while measures of variability include the standard deviation (or variance), the minimum and maximum values of the variables, kurtosis and skewness.

Use in Statistical Analysis

Descriptive statistics provide simple summaries about the sample and about the observations that have been made. Such summaries may be either quantitative, i.e. summary statistics, or visual, i.e. simple-to-understand graphs. These summaries may either form the basis of the initial description of the data as part of a more extensive statistical analysis, or they may be sufficient in and of themselves for a particular investigation.

For example, the shooting percentage in basketball is a descriptive statistic that summarizes the performance of a player or a team. This number is the number of shots made divided by the number of shots taken. For example, a player who shoots 33% is making approximately one shot in every three. The percentage summarizes or describes multiple discrete events. Consider also the grade point average. This single number describes the general performance of a student across the range of their course experiences.

The use of descriptive and summary statistics has an extensive history and, indeed, the simple tabulation of populations and of economic data was the first way the topic of statistics appeared. More recently, a collection of summarisation techniques has been formulated under the heading of exploratory data analysis: an example of such a technique is the box plot.

In the business world, descriptive statistics provides a useful summary of many types of data. For example, investors and brokers may use a historical account of return behavior by performing empirical and analytical analyses on their investments in order to make better investing decisions in the future.

Univariate Analysis

Univariate analysis involves describing the distribution of a single variable, including its central tendency (including the mean, median, and mode) and dispersion (including the range and quartiles of the data-set, and measures of spread such as the variance and standard deviation). The shape of the distribution may also be described via indices such as skewness and kurtosis. Characteristics of a variable's distribution may also be depicted in graphical or tabular format, including histograms and stem-and-leaf display.

Bivariate and Multivariate Analysis

When a sample consists of more than one variable, descriptive statistics may be used to describe the relationship between pairs of variables. In this case, descriptive statistics include:

- Cross-tabulations and contingency tables
- Graphical representation via scatterplots
- Quantitative measures of dependence
- Descriptions of conditional distributions

The main reason for differentiating univariate and bivariate analysis is that bivariate analysis is not only simple descriptive analysis, but also it describes the relationship between two different variables. Quantitative measures of dependence include correlation (such as Pearson's r when both variables are continuous, or Spearman's rho if one or both are not) and covariance (which reflects the scale variables are measured on).

The slope, in regression analysis, also reflects the relationship between variables. The unstandardised slope indicates the unit change in the criterion variable for a one unit change in the predictor. The standardised slope indicates this change in standardised (z-score) units. Highly skewed data are often transformed by taking logarithms. Use of logarithms makes graphs more symmetrical and look more similar to the normal distribution, making them easier to interpret intuitively.

Central Tendency

In statistics, a central tendency (or measure of central tendency) is a central or typical value for a probability distribution. It may also be called a center or location of the distribution. Colloquially, measures of central tendency are often called *averages*. The term *central tendency* dates from the late 1920s.

The most common measures of central tendency are the arithmetic mean, the median and the mode. A central tendency can be calculated for either a finite set of values or for a theoretical distribution, such as the normal distribution. Occasionally authors use central tendency to denote "the tendency of quantitative data to cluster around some central value."

The central tendency of a distribution is typically contrasted with its *dispersion* or *variability*; dispersion and central tendency are the often characterized properties of distributions. Analysts may judge whether data has a strong or a weak central tendency based on its dispersion.

Measures of Central Tendency

The following may be applied to one-dimensional data. Depending on the circumstances, it may be appropriate to transform the data before calculating a central tendency. Examples are squaring the values or taking logarithms. Whether a transformation is appropriate and what it should be, depend heavily on the data being analyzed.

- Arithmetic mean (or simply, mean) – the sum of all measurements divided by the number of observations in the data set.
- Median – the middle value that separates the higher half from the lower half of the data set. The median and the mode are the only measures of central tendency that can be used for ordinal data, in which values are ranked relative to each other but are not measured absolutely.
- Mode – the most frequent value in the data set. This is the only central tendency measure that can be used with nominal data, which have purely qualitative category assignments.

- Geometric mean – the *n*th root of the product of the data values, where there are *n* of these. This measure is valid only for data that are measured absolutely on a strictly positive scale.
- Harmonic mean – the reciprocal of the arithmetic mean of the reciprocals of the data values. This measure too is valid only for data that are measured absolutely on a strictly positive scale.
- Weighted arithmetic mean – an arithmetic mean that incorporates weighting to certain data elements.
- Truncated mean (or trimmed mean) – the arithmetic mean of data values after a certain number or proportion of the highest and lowest data values have been discarded.
    - Interquartile mean – a truncated mean based on data within the interquartile range.
- Midrange – the arithmetic mean of the maximum and minimum values of a data set.
- Midhinge – the arithmetic mean of the two quartiles.
- Trimean – the weighted arithmetic mean of the median and two quartiles.
- Winsorized mean – an arithmetic mean in which extreme values are replaced by values closer to the median.

Any of the above may be applied to each dimension of multi-dimensional data, but the results may not be invariant to rotations of the multi-dimensional space. In addition, there is the

- Geometric median - which minimizes the sum of distances to the data points. This is the same as the median when applied to one-dimensional data, but it is not the same as taking the median of each dimension independently. It is not invariant to different rescaling of the different dimensions.

The Quadratic mean (often known as the root mean square) is useful in engineering, but is not often used in statistics. This is because it is not a good indicator of the center of the distribution when the distribution includes negative values.

Solutions to Variational Problems

Several measures of central tendency can be characterized as solving a variational problem, in the sense of the calculus of variations, namely minimizing variation from the center. That is, given a measure of statistical dispersion, one asks for a measure of central tendency that minimizes variation: such that variation from the center is minimal among all choices of center. In a quip, "dispersion precedes location". In the sense of L^p spaces, the correspondence is:

L^p	dispersion	central tendency
L^1	average absolute deviation	median
L^2	standard deviation	mean
L^∞	maximum deviation	midrange

Thus standard deviation about the mean is lower than standard deviation about any other point, and the maximum deviation about the midrange is lower than the maximum deviation about any other point. The uniqueness of this characterization of mean follows from convex optimization. Indeed, for a given (fixed) data set x, the function

$$f_2(c) = \| x - c \|_2$$

represents the dispersion about a constant value c relative to the L^2 norm. Because the function f_2 is a strictly convex coercive function, the minimizer exists and is unique.

Note that the median in this sense is not in general unique, and in fact any point between the two central points of a discrete distribution minimizes average absolute deviation. The dispersion in the L^1 norm, given by

$$f_1(c) = \| x - c \|_1$$

is not *strictly* convex, whereas strict convexity is needed to ensure uniqueness of the minimizer. In spite of this, the minimizer is unique for the L^∞ norm.

Relationships Between the Mean, Median and Mode

For unimodal distributions the following bounds are known and are sharp:

$$\frac{|\theta - \mu|}{\sigma} \le \sqrt{3},$$

$$\frac{|\nu - \mu|}{\sigma} \le \sqrt{0.6},$$

$$\frac{|\theta - \nu|}{\sigma} \le \sqrt{3},$$

where μ is the mean, ν is the median, θ is the mode, and σ is the standard deviation.

For every distribution,

$$\frac{|\nu - \mu|}{\sigma} \le 1.$$

Univariate Econometric Modelling

The beginning of econometric modelling starts with two variables, where there is proper classification of dependent variable and independent variable. The basic objective here is to fit the data as per the availability of theory. However, the necessary requirement of any model building is to know the descriptive of the variable information (i.e. otherwise called as descriptive statistics). It gives the structure of model building; otherwise there is chance of misspecification of the mathematical/ statistical form of the model.

Descriptive statistics is the discipline of quantitatively describing the main features of a collection of data. They are distinguished from inferential statistics (or inductive statistics), in that descriptive statistics aim to summarize a data set, rather than use the data to learn about the population that the data are thought to represent.

Descriptive statistics are used to present quantitative descriptions in a manageable form. In a research study, we may have lots of measures. Or we may measure a large number of people on any measure. Descriptive statistics help us to simplify large amounts of data in a sensible way. Each descriptive statistic reduces lots of data into a simpler summary.

Usually, it is analyzed/ described in various forms. But in the present context, we stress on three aspects such as central tendency, dispersion and skewness and kurtosis. The detail discussions of these statistics are as follows:

Measures of Central Tendency

The objective of central tendency is to find out a single figure that describes the entire picture. There are three widely used measures of central tendency such as mean, median and mode. The brief discussions of these three are as follows:

Mean: the arithmetic mean (or the average, simple mean) is computed by summing all numbers in an array of numbers (x_i) and then dividing by the number of observations (n) in the array.

Mean = summation x_i /n, the sum is over all i's.

The mean uses all of the observations, and each observation affects the mean. Even though the mean is sensitive to extreme values; i.e., extremely large or small data can cause the mean to be pulled toward the extreme data; it is still the most widely used measure of location. This is due to the fact that the mean has valuable mathematical properties that make it convenient for use with inferential statistical analysis. For example, the sum of the deviations of the numbers in a set of data from the mean is zero, and the sum of the squared deviations of the numbers in a set of data from the mean is the minimum value.

Median: the median is the middle value in an ordered array of observations. If there is an even number of observations in the array, the median is the average of the two middle numbers. If there is an odd number of data in the array, the median is the middle number. The median is often used to summarize the distribution of an outcome. If the distribution is skewed, the median and the interquartile range (iqr) may be better than other measures to indicate where the observed data are concentrated. Generally, the median provides a better measure of location than the mean when there are some extremely large or small observations; i.e., when the data are skewed to the right or to the left. For this reason, median income is used as the measure of location for the U.S. household income. Note that if the median is less than the mean, the data set is skewed to the right. If the median is greater than the mean, the data set is skewed to the left.

Mode: the mode is the most frequently occurring value in a set of observations. Why use the mode? The classic example is the shirt/shoe manufacturer who wants to decide what sizes to introduce. Data may have two modes. In this case, we say the data are bimodal, and sets of observations with more than two modes are referred to as multimodal. Note that the mode is not a helpful measure of location, because there can be more than one mode or even no mode.

When the mean and the median are known, it is possible to estimate the mode for the unimodal distribution using the other two averages as follows:

mode = 3(median) - 2(mean)

The pair of statistical measures, skewness and kurtosis, are two measuring tools, which are used in selecting a distribution(s) to fit your data. To make an inference with respect to the population distribution, you may first compute skewness and kurtosis from your random sample from the entire population.

Dispersion

Dispersion refers to the spread of the values around the central tendency. Like central tendency, we have several tolls to measure the dispersion. These are as follows:

- The range
- The quartile deviation
- The mean deviation
- The standard deviation and variance
- The relative measures of dispersion are:

Out of all measures, standard deviation is a widely used measure of variation. It is a useful measure when your data distribution is very close to a normal curve. In this situation, the mean is the best measure of central tendency, and the standard deviation is the best measure of dispersion.

$$\text{Population Standard Deviation} = \sigma = \sqrt{\sigma^2} = \sqrt{\frac{\sum(x-\mu)^2}{N}}$$

$$\text{Sample Standard Deviation} = s = \sqrt{s^2} = \sqrt{\frac{\sum(x-\bar{x})^2}{n-1}}$$

The coefficient of variation measures variability in relation to the mean (or average) and is used to compare the relative dispersion in one type of data with the relative dispersion in another type of data. The data to be compared may be in the same units, in different units, with the same mean, or with different means. The coefficient of variation is a calculation built on other calculations -- the standard deviation and the mean -- as follows:

Statistical Dispersion

In statistics, dispersion (also called variability, scatter, or spread) is the extent to which a distribution is stretched or squeezed. Common examples of measures of statistical dispersion are the variance, standard deviation, and interquartile range.

Dispersion is contrasted with location or central tendency, and together they are the most used properties of distributions.

Measures of Statistical Dispersion

A measure of statistical dispersion is a nonnegative real number that is zero if all the data are the same and increases as the data become more diverse.

Most measures of dispersion have the same units as the quantity being measured. In other words, if the measurements are in metres or seconds, so is the measure of dispersion. Examples of dispersion measures include:

- Standard deviation
- Interquartile range (IQR)
- Range
- Mean absolute difference (also known as Gini mean absolute difference)
- Median absolute deviation (MAD)
- Average absolute deviation (or simply called average deviation)
- Distance standard deviation

These are frequently used (together with scale factors) as estimators of scale parameters, in which capacity they are called estimates of scale. Robust measures of scale are those unaffected by a small number of outliers, and include the IQR and MAD.

All the above measures of statistical dispersion have the useful property that they are location-invariant and linear in scale. This means that if a random variable X has a dispersion of S_X then a linear transformation $Y = aX + b$ for real a and b should have dispersion $S_Y = |a|S_X$, where $|a|$is the absolute value of a, that is, ignores a preceding negative sign –.

Other measures of dispersion are dimensionless. In other words, they have no units even if the variable itself has units. These include:

- Coefficient of variation
- Quartile coefficient of dispersion
- Relative mean difference, equal to twice the Gini coefficient
- Entropy: While the entropy of a discrete variable is location-invariant and scale-independent, and therefore not a measure of dispersion in the above sense, the entropy of a continuous variable is location invariant and additive in scale: If Hz is the entropy of continuous variable z and $y=ax+b$, then $Hy=Hx+log(a)$.

There are other measures of dispersion:

- Variance (the square of the standard deviation) – location-invariant but not linear in scale.
- Variance-to-mean ratio – mostly used for count data when the term coefficient of dispersion is used and when this ratio is dimensionless, as count data are themselves dimensionless, not otherwise.

Some measures of dispersion have specialized purposes, among them the Allan variance and the Hadamard variance.

For categorical variables, it is less common to measure dispersion by a single number. One measure that does so is the discrete entropy.

Sources of Statistical Dispersion

In the physical sciences, such variability may result from random measurement errors: instrument measurements are often not perfectly precise, i.e., reproducible, and there is additional inter-rater variability in interpreting and reporting the measured results. One may assume that the quantity being measured is stable, and that the variation between measurements is due to observational error. A system of a large number of particles is characterized by the mean values of a relatively few number of macroscopic quantities such as temperature, energy, and density. The standard deviation is an important measure in Fluctuation theory, which explains many physical phenomena, including why the sky is blue.

In the biological sciences, the quantity being measured is seldom unchanging and stable, and the variation observed might additionally be *intrinsic* to the phenomenon: It may be due to *inter-individual variability*, that is, distinct members of a population differing from each other. Also, it may be due to *intra-individual variability*, that is, one and the same subject differing in tests taken at different times or in other differing conditions. Such types of variability are also seen in the arena of manufactured products; even there, the meticulous scientist finds variation.

In economics, finance, and other disciplines, regression analysis attempts to explain the dispersion of a dependent variable, generally measured by its variance, using one or more independent variables each of which itself has positive dispersion. The fraction of variance explained is called the coefficient of determination.

A Partial Ordering of Dispersion

A mean-preserving spread (MPS) is a change from one probability distribution A to another probability distribution B, where B is formed by spreading out one or more portions of A's probability density function while leaving the mean (the expected value) unchanged. The concept of a mean-preserving spread provides a partial ordering of probability distributions according to their dispersions: of two probability distributions, one may be ranked as having more dispersion than the other, or alternatively neither may be ranked as having more dispersion.

Range (Statistics)

In statistics, the range of a set of data is the difference between the largest and smallest values.

However, in descriptive statistics, this concept of range has a more complex meaning. The range is the size of the smallest interval which contains all the data and provides an indication of statistical dispersion. It is measured in the same units as the data. Since it only depends on two of the observations, it is most useful in representing the dispersion of small data sets.

Independent Identically Distributed Continuous Random Variables

For n independent and identically distributed continuous random variables $X_1, X_2, ..., X_n$ with cumulative distribution function $G(x)$ and probability density function $g(x)$. Let T denote the range of a sample of size n from a population with distribution function $G(x)$.

Distribution

The range has cumulative distribution function

$$F(t) = n\int_{-\infty}^{\infty} g(x)[G(x+t) - G(x)]^{n-1} dx.$$

Gumbel notes that the "beauty of this formula is completely marred by the facts that, in general, we cannot express $G(x + t)$ by $G(x)$, and that the numerical integration is lengthy and tiresome."

If the distribution of each X_i is limited to the right (or left) then the asymptotic distribution of the range is equal to the asymptotic distribution of the largest (smallest) value. For more general distributions the asymptotic distribution can be expressed as a Bessel function.

Moments

The mean range is given by

$$n\int_0^1 x(G)[G^{n-1} - (1-G)^{n-1}]dG$$

where $x(G)$ is the inverse function. In the case where each of the X_i has a standard normal distribution, the mean range is given by

$$\int_{-\infty}^{\infty} (1-(1-\Phi(x))^n - \Phi(x)^n)dx.$$

Independent Nonidentically Distributed Continuous Random Variables

For n nonidentically distributed independent continuous random variables X_1, X_2, ..., X_n with cumulative distribution functions $G_1(x)$, $G_2(x)$, ..., $G_n(x)$ and probability density functions $g_1(x)$, $g_2(x)$, ..., $g_n(x)$, the range has cumulative distribution function

$$F(t) = \sum_{i=1}^{n} \int_{-\infty}^{\infty} g_i(x) \prod_{j=1, j\neq i}^{n} [G_j(x+t) - G_j(x)]dx.$$

Independent Identically Distributed Discrete Random Variables

For n independent and identically distributed discrete random variables X_1, X_2, ..., X_n with cumulative distribution function $G(x)$ and probability mass function $g(x)$ the range of the X_i is the range of a sample of size n from a population with distribution function $G(x)$. We can assume without loss of generality that the support of each X_i is $\{1,2,3,...,N\}$ where N is a positive integer or infinity.

Distribution

The range has probability mass function

$$f(t)=\begin{cases}\sum_{x=1}^{N}[g(x)]^n & t=0\\ \sum_{x=1}^{N-t}\begin{pmatrix}[G(x+t)-G(x-1)]^n\\ -[G(x+t)-G(x)]^n\\ -[G(x+t-1)-G(x-1)]^n\\ +[G(x+t-1)-G(x)]^n\end{pmatrix} & t=1,2,3\ldots,N-1.\end{cases}$$

Example

If we suppose that $g(x) = 1/N$, the discrete uniform distribution for all x, then we find

$$f(t)=\begin{cases}\frac{1}{N^{n-1}} & t=0\\ \sum_{x=1}^{N-t}\left([\frac{t+1}{N}]^n-2[\frac{t}{N}]^n+[\frac{t-1}{N}]^n\right) & t=1,2,3\ldots,N-1.\end{cases}$$

Related Quantities

The range is a simple function of the sample maximum and minimum and these are specific examples of order statistics. In particular, the range is a linear function of order statistics, which brings it into the scope of L-estimation.

Interquartile Range

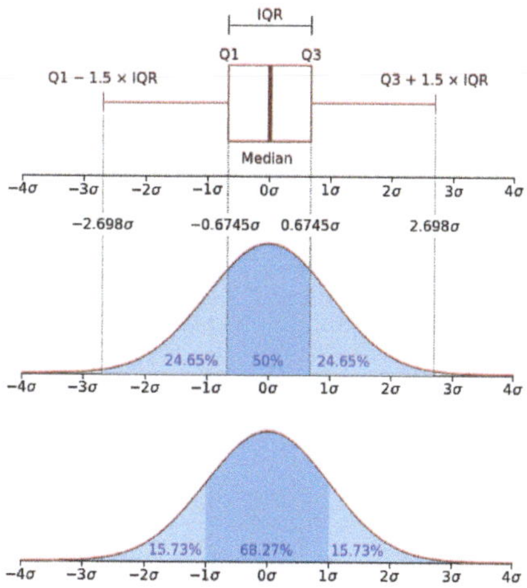

Boxplot (with an interquartile range) and a probability density function (pdf) of a Normal $N(0,\sigma^2)$ Population

In descriptive statistics, the interquartile range (IQR), also called the midspread or middle 50%, or technically H-spread, is a measure of statistical dispersion, being equal to the difference between 75th and 25th percentiles, or between upper and lower quartiles, IQR $= Q_3 - Q_1$. In other words, the IQR is the 1st quartile subtracted from the 3rd quartile; these quartiles can be clearly seen on a box plot on the data. It is a trimmed estimator, defined as the 25% trimmed range, and is the most significant basic robust measure of scale.

The interquartile range (IQR) is a measure of variability, based on dividing a data set into quartiles. Quartiles divide a rank-ordered data set into four equal parts. The values that separate parts are called the first, second, and third quartiles; and they are denoted by Q1, Q2, and Q3, respectively.

Use

Unlike total range, the interquartile range has a breakdown point of 25%, and is thus often preferred to the total range.

The IQR is used to build box plots, simple graphical representations of a probability distribution.

For a symmetric distribution (where the median equals the midhinge, the average of the first and third quartiles), half the IQR equals the median absolute deviation (MAD). By

The median is the corresponding measure of central tendency.

The IQR can be used to identify outliers.

The quartile deviation or semi-interquartile range is defined as half the IQR.

Examples

Data Set in a Table

The following table has 13 rows, and follows the rules for the odd number of entries.

<table>
<tr><th>i</th><th>x[i]</th><th>Median</th><th>Quartile</th></tr>
<tr><td>1</td><td>7</td><td rowspan="13">Q2=87
(median of
whole table)</td><td rowspan="7">Q1=31
(median of
upper half,
from row 1 to7)</td></tr>
<tr><td>2</td><td>7</td></tr>
<tr><td>3</td><td>21</td></tr>
<tr><td>4</td><td>31</td></tr>
<tr><td>5</td><td>47</td></tr>
<tr><td>6</td><td>75</td></tr>
<tr><td>7</td><td>87</td></tr>
<tr><td>8</td><td>115</td><td rowspan="6">Q3=119
(median of
lower half,
from row 7 to 13)</td></tr>
<tr><td>9</td><td>116</td></tr>
<tr><td>10</td><td>119</td></tr>
<tr><td>11</td><td>119</td></tr>
<tr><td>12</td><td>155</td></tr>
<tr><td>13</td><td>177</td></tr>
</table>

For the data in this table the interquartile range is $IQR = Q_3 - Q_1 = 119 - 31 = 88$.

```
                                +-----+-+
    o           *       |-------|     | |---|
                                +-----+-+

+---+---+---+---+---+---+---+---+---+---+---+---+   number line
0   1   2   3   4   5   6   7   8   9   10  11  12
```

For the data set in this box plot:

- lower (first) quartile $Q_1 = 7$
- median (second quartile) $Q_2 = 8.5$
- upper (third) quartile $Q_3 = 9$
- interquartile range, $\text{IQR} = Q_3 - Q_1 = 2$

Distributions

The interquartile range of a continuous distribution can be calculated by integrating the probability density function (which yields the cumulative distribution function—any other means of calculating the CDF will also work). The lower quartile, Q_1, is a number such that integral of the PDF from $-\infty$ to Q_1 equals 0.25, while the upper quartile, Q_3, is such a number that the integral from $-\infty$ to Q_3 equals 0.75; in terms of the CDF, the quartiles can be defined as follows:

$$Q_1 = \text{CDF}^{-1}(0.25),$$

$$Q_3 = \text{CDF}^{-1}(0.75),$$

where CDF^{-1} is the quantile function.

The interquartile range and median of some common distributions are shown below

Distribution	Median	IQR
Normal	μ	$2\,\Phi^{-1}(0.75)\sigma \approx 1.349\sigma \approx (27/20)\sigma$
Laplace	μ	$2b\ln(2) \approx 1.386b$
Cauchy	μ	2γ

Interquartile Range test for Normality of Distribution

The IQR, mean, and standard deviation of a population *P* can be used in a simple test of whether or not *P* is normally distributed, or Gaussian. If *P* is normally distributed, then the standard score of the first quartile, z_1, is -0.67, and the standard score of the third quartile, z_3, is +0.67. Given *mean* = *X* and *standard deviation* = σ for *P*, if *P* is normally distributed, the first quartile

$$Q_1 = (\sigma z_1) + X$$

and the third quartile

$$Q_3 = (\sigma z_3) + X$$

If the actual values of the first or third quartiles differ substantially from the calculated values, *P* is not normally distributed. However, a normal distribution can be trivially perturbed to maintain its Q1 and Q2 std. scores at 0.67 and -0.67 and not be normally distributed (so the above test would produce a false positive). A better test of normality, such as Q-Q plot would be indicated here.

Outliers

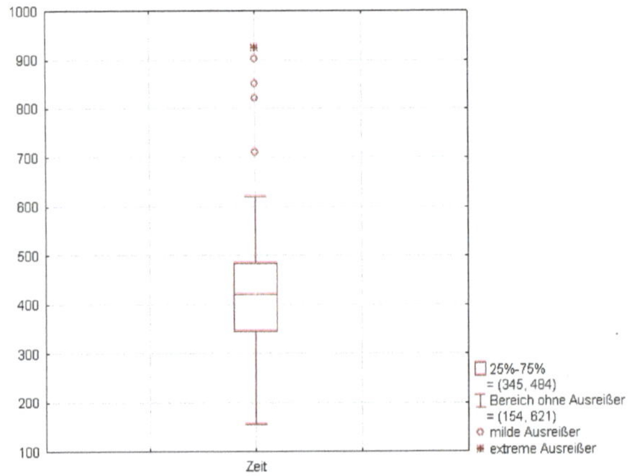

Box-and-whisker plot with four close and one far away extreme values, defined as outliers above Q3 + 1.5 IQR and Q3 + 3 IQR, respectively.

The interquartile range is often used to find outliers in data. Outliers here are defined as observations that fall below Q1 − 1.5 IQR or above Q3 + 1.5 IQR. In a boxplot, the highest and lowest occurring value within this limit are indicated by *whiskers* of the box (frequently with an additional bar at the end of the whisker) and any outliers as individual points.

Average Absolute Deviation

The average absolute deviation (or mean absolute deviation) of a data set is the average of the absolute deviations from a central point. It is a summary statistic of statistical dispersion or variability. In this general form, the central point can be the mean, median, mode, or the result of another measure of central tendency. Furthermore, as described in the article about averages, the deviation averaging operation may refer to the mean or the median. Thus the total number of combinations amounts to at least four types of average absolute deviation.

Measures of Dispersion

Several measures of statistical dispersion are defined in terms of the absolute deviation. The term "average absolute deviation" does not uniquely identify a measure of statistical dispersion, as there are several measures that can be used to measure absolute deviations, and there are several measures of central tendency that can be used as well. Thus, to uniquely identify the absolute deviation it is necessary to specify both the measure of deviation and the measure of central tendency. Unfortunately, the statistical literature has not yet adopted a standard notation, as both the #Mean absolute deviation around the mean and the #Median absolute deviation around the median have been denoted by their initials "MAD" in the literature, which may lead to confusion, since in general, they may have values considerably different from each other.

Mean Absolute Deviation Around a Central Point

The mean absolute deviation of a set $\{x_1, x_2, ..., x_n\}$ is

$$\frac{1}{n}\sum_{i=1}^{n}|x_i - m(X)|.$$

The choice of measure of central tendency, $m(X)$, has a marked effect on the value of the mean deviation. For example, for the data set {2, 2, 3, 4, 14}:

Measure of central tendency *m (X)*	**Mean absolute deviation**
Mean = 5	$\frac{\|2-5\|+\|2-5\|+\|3-5\|+\|4-5\|+\|14-5\|}{5} = 3.6$
Median = 3	$\frac{\|2-3\|+\|2-3\|+\|3-3\|+\|4-3\|+\|14-3\|}{5} = 2.8$
Mode = 2	$\frac{\|2-2\|+\|2-2\|+\|3-2\|+\|4-2\|+\|14-2\|}{5} = 3.0$

The mean absolute deviation from the median is less than or equal to the mean absolute deviation from the mean. In fact, the mean absolute deviation from the median is always less than or equal to the mean absolute deviation from any other fixed number.

The mean absolute deviation from the mean is less than or equal to the standard deviation; one way of proving this relies on Jensen's inequality.

Proof

Jensen's inequality is $\varphi(\mathbb{E}[X]) \leq \mathbb{E}[\varphi(X)]$,where φ is a convex function, this implies that:

$$\mathbb{E}(|x-\mu|)^2 \leq \mathbb{E}\left(|x-\mu|^2\right)$$

$$(|x- \quad |) \leq \mathrm{Var}(x)$$

Since both sides are positive, and the square root is a monotonically increasing function in the positive domain:

$$\mathbb{E}(|x-\mu|) \leq \sqrt{\mathrm{Var}(x)}$$

For a general case of this statement.

For the normal distribution, the ratio of mean absolute deviation to standard deviation is $\sqrt{2/\pi} = 0.79788456$..Thus if X is a normally distributed random variable with expected value 0 then:

$$w = \frac{E|X|}{\sqrt{E(X^2)}} = \sqrt{\frac{2}{\pi}}.$$

In other words, for a normal distribution, mean absolute deviation is about 0.8 times the standard deviation. However in-sample measurements deliver values of the ratio of mean average deviation / standard deviation for a given Gaussian sample n with the following bounds: $w_n \in [0,1]$, with a bias for small n.

Mean Absolute Deviation Around the Mean

The mean absolute deviation (MAD), also referred to as the "mean deviation" or sometimes "average absolute deviation", is the mean of the data's absolute deviations around the data's mean: the average (absolute) distance from the mean. "Average absolute deviation" can refer to either this usage, or to the general form with respect to a specified central point.

MAD has been proposed to be used in place of standard deviation since it corresponds better to real life. Because the MAD is a simpler measure of variability than the standard deviation, it can be useful in school teaching.

This method's forecast accuracy is very closely related to the mean squared error (MSE) method which is just the average squared error of the forecasts. Although these methods are very closely related, MAD is more commonly used because it is both easier to compute (avoiding the need for squaring) and easier to understand.

Mean Absolute Deviation Around the Median

Mean absolute deviation around the median (MAD median) offers a direct measure of the scale of a random variable around its median

$$D_{med} = E|X - \text{median}|$$

This is the maximum likelihood estimator of the scale parameter b of the Laplace distribution. For the normal distribution we have $D_{med} = \sigma\sqrt{2/\pi}$. Since the median minimizes the average absolute distance, we have $D_{med} \le D_{mean}$. By using the general dispersion function, Habib (2011) defined MAD about median as

$$D_{med} = E|X - \text{median}| = 2\,\text{Cov}(X, I_O)$$

where the indicator function is

$$\mathbf{I}_O := \begin{cases} 1 & \text{if } x > \text{median}, \\ 0 & \text{otherwise.} \end{cases}$$

This representation allows for obtaining MAD median correlation coefficients;

Median Absolute Deviation Around the Mean

In principle the mean could be taken as the central point for the median absolute deviation, but more often the median value is taken instead.

Median Absolute Deviation Around the Median

The median absolute deviation (also MAD) is the *median* of the absolute deviation from the *median*. It is a robust estimator of dispersion.

For the example {2, 2, 3, 4, 14}: 3 is the median, so the absolute deviations from the median are {1, 1, 0, 1, 11} (reordered as {0, 1, 1, 1, 11}) with a median of 1, in this case unaffected by the value of the outlier 14, so the median absolute deviation (also called MAD) is 1.

Maximum Absolute Deviation

The maximum absolute deviation around an arbitrary point is the maximum of the absolute deviations of a sample from that point. While not strictly a measure of central tendency, the maximum absolute deviation can be found using the formula for the average absolute deviation as above with $m(X) = \max(X)$, where $\max(X)$ is the sample maximum.

Minimization

The measures of statistical dispersion derived from absolute deviation characterize various measures of central tendency as *minimizing* dispersion: The median is the measure of central tendency most associated with the absolute deviation. Some location parameters can be compared as follows:

- L^2 norm statistics: the mean minimizes the mean squared error

- L^1 norm statistics: the median minimizes *average* absolute deviation,
- L^∞ norm statistics: the mid-range minimizes the *maximum* absolute deviation
- trimmed L^∞ norm statistics: for example, the midhinge (average of first and third quartiles) which minimizes the *median* absolute deviation of the whole distribution, also minimizes the *maximum* absolute deviation of the distribution after the top and bottom 25% have been trimmed off..

Estimation

The mean absolute deviation of a sample is a biased estimator of the mean absolute deviation of the population. In order for the absolute deviation to be an unbiased estimator, the expected value (average) of all the sample absolute deviations must equal the population absolute deviation. However, it does not. For the population 1,2,3 both the population absolute deviation about the median and the population absolute deviation about the mean are 2/3. The average of all the sample absolute deviations about the mean of size 3 that can be drawn from the population is 44/81, while the average of all the sample absolute deviations about the median is 4/9. Therefore the absolute deviation is a biased estimator. However, this argument is based on the notion of mean-unbiasedness. Each measure of location has its own form of unbiasedness. The relevant form of unbiasedness here is median unbiasedness.

Standard Deviation

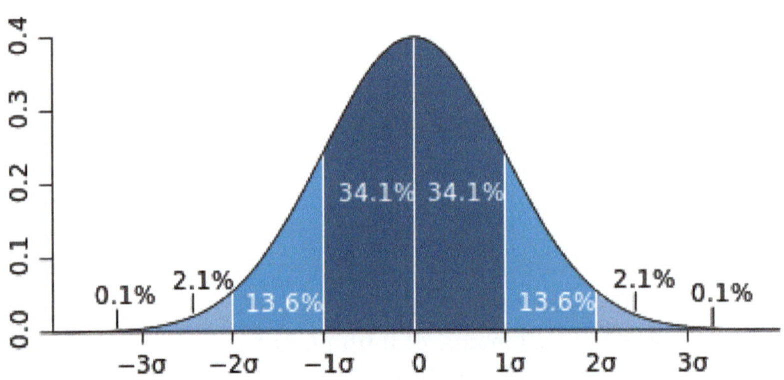

A plot of normal distribution (or bell-shaped curve) where each band has a width of 1 standard deviation

In statistics, the standard deviation (SD, also represented by the Greek letter sigma σ or the Latin letter s) is a measure that is used to quantify the amount of variation or dispersion of a set of data values. A low standard deviation indicates that the data points tend to be close to the mean (also called the expected value) of the set, while a high standard deviation indicates that the data points are spread out over a wider range of values.

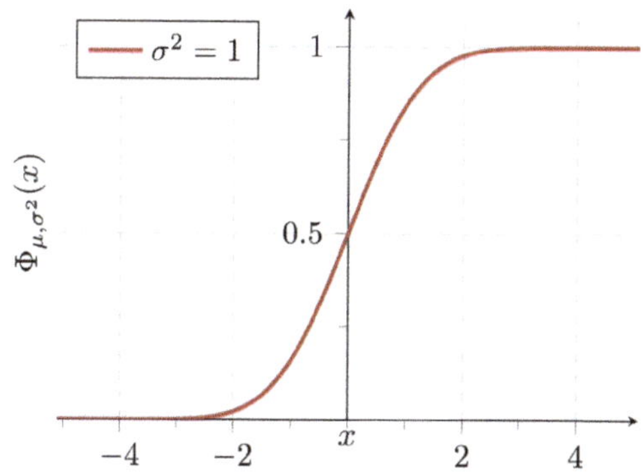

Cumulative probability of a normal distribution with expected value 0 and standard deviation 1.

The standard deviation of a random variable, statistical population, data set, or probability distribution is the square root of its variance. It is algebraically simpler, though in practice less robust, than the average absolute deviation. A useful property of the standard deviation is that, unlike the variance, it is expressed in the same units as the data. There are also other measures of deviation from the norm, including mean absolute deviation, which provide different mathematical properties from standard deviation.

In addition to expressing the variability of a population, the standard deviation is commonly used to measure confidence in statistical conclusions. For example, the margin of error in polling data is determined by calculating the expected standard deviation in the results if the same poll were to be conducted multiple times. This derivation of a standard deviation is often called the "standard error" of the estimate or "standard error of the mean" when referring to a mean. It is computed as the standard deviation of all the means that would be computed from that population if an infinite number of samples were drawn and a mean for each sample were computed. It is very important to note that the standard deviation of a population and the standard error of a statistic derived from that population (such as the mean) are quite different but related (related by the inverse of the square root of the number of observations). The reported margin of error of a poll is computed from the standard error of the mean (or alternatively from the product of the standard deviation of the population and the inverse of the square root of the sample size, which is the same thing) and is typically about twice the standard deviation—the half-width of a 95 percent confidence interval. In science, researchers commonly report the standard deviation of experimental data, and only effects that fall much farther than two standard deviations away from what would have been expected are considered statistically significant—normal random error or variation in the measurements is in this way distinguished from likely genuine effects or associations. The standard deviation is also important in finance, where the standard deviation on the rate of return on an investment is a measure of the volatility of the investment.

When only a sample of data from a population is available, the term standard deviation of the sample or sample standard deviation can refer to either the above-mentioned quantity as applied to those data or to a modified quantity that is an unbiased estimate of the population standard deviation (the standard deviation of the entire population).

Basic Examples

For a finite set of numbers, the standard deviation is found by taking the square root of the average of the squared deviations of the values from their average value. For example, the marks of a class of eight students (that is, a statistical population) are the following eight values:

$$2, 4, 4, 4, 5, 5, 7, 9.$$

These eight data points have the mean (average) of 5:

$$\frac{2+4+4+4+5+5+7+9}{8}=5.$$

First, calculate the deviations of each data point from the mean, and square the result of each:

$$\begin{array}{ll} (2-5)^2=(-3)^2=9 & (5-5)^2=0^2=0 \\ (4-5)^2=(-1)^2=1 & (5-5)^2=0^2=0 \\ (4-5)^2=(-1)^2=1 & (7-5)^2=2^2=4 \\ (4-5)^2=(-1)^2=1 & (9-5)^2=4^2=16. \end{array}$$

The variance is the mean of these values:

$$\frac{9+1+1+1+0+0+4+16}{8}=4.$$

and the *population* standard deviation is equal to the square root of the variance:

$$\sqrt{4}=2.$$

This formula is valid only if the eight values with which we began form the complete population. If the values instead were a random sample drawn from some large parent population (for example, they were 8 marks randomly and independently chosen from a class of 2 million), then one often divides by 7 (which is $n - 1$) instead of 8 (which is n) in the denominator of the last formula. In that case the result would be called the *sample* standard deviation. Dividing by $n - 1$ rather than by n gives an unbiased estimate of the variance of the larger parent population. This is known as *Bessel's correction*.

As a slightly more complicated real-life example, the average height for adult men in the United States is about 70 inches (177.8 cm), with a standard deviation of around 3 inches (7.62 cm). This means that most men (about 68%, assuming a normal distribution) have a height within 3 inches (7.62 cm) of the mean (67–73 inches (170.18–185.42 cm)) – one standard deviation – and almost all men (about 95%) have a height within 6 inches (15.24 cm) of the mean (64–76 inches (162.56–193.04 cm)) – two standard deviations. If the standard deviation were zero, then all men would be exactly 70 inches (177.8 cm) tall. If the standard deviation were 20 inches (50.8 cm), then men would have much more variable heights, with a typical range of about 50–90 inches (127–228.6 cm). Three standard deviations account for 99.7% of the sample population being studied, assuming the distribution is normal (bell-shaped).

Definition of Population Values

Let X be a random variable with mean value μ:

$$\mathrm{E[X]} = \mu.$$

Here the operator E denotes the average or expected value of X. Then the standard deviation of X is the quantity

$$\begin{aligned}\sigma &= \sqrt{\mathrm{E}[(\mathrm{X}-\mu)^2]}\\ &= \sqrt{\mathrm{E}[\mathrm{X}^2]+\mathrm{E}[-2\mu \mathrm{X}]+\mathrm{E}[\mu^2]} = \sqrt{\mathrm{E}[\mathrm{X}^2]-2\mu\,\mathrm{E}[\mathrm{X}]+\mu^2}\\ &= \sqrt{\mathrm{E}[\mathrm{X}^2]-2\mu^2+\mu^2} = \sqrt{\mathrm{E}[\mathrm{X}^2]-\mu^2}\\ &= \sqrt{\mathrm{E}[\mathrm{X}^2]-(\mathrm{E}[\mathrm{X}])^2}\end{aligned}$$

(derived using the properties of expected value).

In other words, the standard deviation σ (sigma) is the square root of the variance of X; i.e., it is the square root of the average value of $(X - \mu)^2$.

The standard deviation of a (univariate) probability distribution is the same as that of a random variable having that distribution. Not all random variables have a standard deviation, since these expected values need not exist. For example, the standard deviation of a random variable that follows a Cauchy distribution is undefined because its expected value μ is undefined.

Discrete Random Variable

In the case where X takes random values from a finite data set $x_1, x_2, \ldots, x_N$, with each value having the same probability, the standard deviation is

$$\sigma = \sqrt{\frac{1}{\mathrm{N}}\left[(\mathrm{x}_1-\mu)^2+(\mathrm{x}_2-\mu)^2+\cdots+(\mathrm{x}_\mathrm{N}-\mu)^2\right]}, \text{ where } \mu = \frac{1}{\mathrm{N}}(\mathrm{x}_1+\cdots+\mathrm{x}_\mathrm{N}),$$

or, using summation notation,

$$\sigma = \sqrt{\frac{1}{N}\sum_{i=1}^{N}(x_i - \mu)^2}, \text{ where } \mu = \frac{1}{N}\sum_{i=1}^{N} x_i.$$

If, instead of having equal probabilities, the values have different probabilities, let x_1 have probability p_1, x_2 have probability p_2, ..., x_N have probability p_N. In this case, the standard deviation will be

$$\sigma = \sqrt{\sum_{i=1}^{N} p_i (x_i - \mu)^2}, \text{ where } \mu = \sum_{i=1}^{N} p_i x_i.$$

Continuous Random Variable

The standard deviation of a continuous real-valued random variable *X* with probability density function *p*(*x*) is

$$\sigma = \sqrt{\int_X (x - \mu)^2 p(x) dx}, \text{ where } \mu = \int_X x p(x) dx,$$

and where the integrals are definite integrals taken for *x* ranging over the set of possible values of the random variable *X*.

In the case of a parametric family of distributions, the standard deviation can be expressed in terms of the parameters. For example, in the case of the log-normal distribution with parameters μ and σ^2, the standard deviation is $[(\exp(\sigma^2) - 1)\exp(2\mu + \sigma^2)]^{1/2}$.

Estimation

One can find the standard deviation of an entire population in cases (such as standardized testing) where every member of a population is sampled. In cases where that cannot be done, the standard deviation σ is estimated by examining a random sample taken from the population and computing a statistic of the sample, which is used as an estimate of the population standard deviation. Such a statistic is called an estimator, and the estimator (or the value of the estimator, namely the estimate) is called a sample standard deviation, and is denoted by *s* (possibly with modifiers). However, unlike in the case of estimating the population mean, for which the sample mean is a simple estimator with many desirable properties (unbiased, efficient, maximum likelihood), there is no single estimator for the standard deviation with all these properties, and unbiased estimation of standard deviation is a very technically involved problem. Most often, the standard deviation is estimated using the *corrected sample standard deviation* (using $N - 1$), defined below, and this is often referred to as the "sample standard deviation", without qualifiers. However, other estimators are better in other respects: the uncorrected estimator (using *N*) yields lower mean squared error, while using $N - 1.5$ (for the normal distribution) almost completely eliminates bias.

Uncorrected Sample Standard Deviation

The formula for the *population* standard deviation (of a finite population) can be applied to the sample, using the size of the sample as the size of the population (though the actual population size from which the sample is drawn may be much larger). This estimator, denoted by s_N, is known as the uncorrected sample standard deviation, or sometimes the standard deviation of the sample (considered as the entire population), and is defined as follows:

$$s_N = \sqrt{\frac{1}{N}\sum_{i=1}^{N}(x_i - \overline{x})^2},$$

where $\{x_1, x_2, \ldots, x_N\}$ are the observed values of the sample items and $\overline{x}$ is the mean value of these observations, while the denominator *N* stands for the size of the sample: this is the square root of the sample variance, which is the average of the squared deviations about the sample mean.

This is a consistent estimator (it converges in probability to the population value as the number of samples goes to infinity), and is the maximum-likelihood estimate when the population is normally distributed. However, this is a biased estimator, as the estimates are generally too low. The bias decreases as sample size grows, dropping off as $1/N$, and thus is most significant for small or moderate sample sizes; for $N > 75$ the bias is below 1%. Thus for very large sample sizes, the uncorrected sample standard deviation is generally acceptable. This estimator also has a uniformly smaller mean squared error than the corrected sample standard deviation.

Corrected Sample Standard Deviation

If the *biased sample variance* (the second central moment of the sample, which is a downward-biased estimate of the population variance) is used to compute an estimate of the population's standard deviation, the result is

$$s_N = \sqrt{\frac{1}{N}\sum_{i=1}^{N}(x_i - \overline{x})^2}.$$

Here taking the square root introduces further downward bias, by Jensen's inequality, due to the square root being a concave function. The bias in the variance is easily corrected, but the bias from the square root is more difficult to correct, and depends on the distribution in question.

An unbiased estimator for the *variance* is given by applying Bessel's correction, using $N-1$ instead of N to yield the *unbiased sample variance,* denoted s^2:

$$s^2 = \frac{1}{N-1}\sum_{i=1}^{N}(x_i - \bar{x})^2.$$

This estimator is unbiased if the variance exists and the sample values are drawn independently with replacement. $N-1$ corresponds to the number of degrees of freedom in the vector of deviations from the mean, $(x_1 - \bar{x}, \ldots, x_n - \bar{x})$.

Taking square roots reintroduces bias (because the square root is a nonlinear function, which does not commute with the expectation), yielding the corrected sample standard deviation, denoted by *s:*

$$s = \sqrt{\frac{1}{N-1}\sum_{i=1}^{N}(x_i - \bar{x})^2}.$$

As explained above, while s^2 is an unbiased estimator for the population variance, *s* is still a biased estimator for the population standard deviation, though markedly less biased than the uncorrected sample standard deviation. The bias is still significant for small samples (N less than 10), and also drops off as $1/N$ as sample size increases. This estimator is commonly used and generally known simply as the "sample standard deviation".

Unbiased Sample Standard Deviation

For unbiased estimation of standard deviation, there is no formula that works across all distributions, unlike for mean and variance. Instead, *s* is used as a basis, and is scaled by a correction factor to produce an unbiased estimate. For the normal distribution, an unbiased estimator is given by s/c_4, where the correction factor (which depends on N) is given in terms of the Gamma function, and equals:

$$c_4(N) = \sqrt{\frac{2}{N-1}}\frac{\Gamma\left(\frac{N}{2}\right)}{\Gamma\left(\frac{N-1}{2}\right)}.$$

This arises because the sampling distribution of the sample standard deviation follows a (scaled) chi distribution, and the correction factor is the mean of the chi distribution.

An approximation can be given by replacing $N-1$ with $N-1.5$, yielding:

$$\hat{\sigma} = \sqrt{\frac{1}{N-1.5}\sum_{i=1}^{N}(x_i - \bar{x})^2},$$

The error in this approximation decays quadratically (as $1/N^2$), and it is suited for all but the smallest samples or highest precision: for n = 3 the bias is equal to 1.3%, and for n = 9 the bias is already less than 0.1%.

For other distributions, the correct formula depends on the distribution, but a rule of thumb is to use the further refinement of the approximation:

$$\hat{\sigma} = \sqrt{\frac{1}{N - 1.5 - \frac{1}{4}\gamma_2} \sum_{i=1}^{N} (x_i - \overline{x})^2},$$

where γ_2 denotes the population excess kurtosis. The excess kurtosis may be either known beforehand for certain distributions, or estimated from the data.

Confidence Interval of a Sampled Standard Deviation

The standard deviation we obtain by sampling a distribution is itself not absolutely accurate, both for mathematical reasons (explained here by the confidence interval) and for practical reasons of measurement (measurement error). The mathematical effect can be described by the confidence interval or CI. To show how a larger sample will make the confidence interval narrower, consider the following examples: A small population of $N = 2$ has only 1 degree of freedom for estimating the standard deviation. The result is that a 95% CI of the SD runs from 0.45 × SD to 31.9 × SD; the factors here are as follows:

$$\Pr\left(q_{\alpha/2} < k\frac{s^2}{\sigma^2} < q_{1-\alpha/2} \right) = 1 - \alpha,$$

where q_p is the *p*-th quantile of the chi-square distribution with *k* degrees of freedom, and $1 - \acute{a}$ is the confidence level. This is equivalent to the following:

$$\Pr\left(k\frac{s^2}{q_{1-\alpha/2}} < \sigma^2 < k\frac{s^2}{q_{\alpha/2}} \right) = 1 - \alpha.$$

With $k = 1$, $q_{0.025} = 0.000982$ and $q_{0.975} = 5.024$. The reciprocals of the square roots of these two numbers give us the factors 0.45 and 31.9 given above.

A larger population of $N = 10$ has 9 degrees of freedom for estimating the standard deviation. The same computations as above give us in this case a 95% CI running from 0.69*SD to 1.83*SD. So even with a sample population of 10, the actual SD can still be almost a factor 2 higher than the sampled SD. For a sample population N=100, this is down to 0.88*SD to 1.16*SD. To be more certain that the sampled SD is close to the actual SD we need to sample a large number of points.

These same formulae can be used to obtain confidence intervals on the variance of residuals from a least squares fit under standard normal theory, where *k* is now the number of degrees of freedom for error.

Identities and Mathematical Properties

The standard deviation is invariant under changes in location, and scales directly with the scale of the random variable. Thus, for a constant *c* and random variables *X* and *Y*:

$$\sigma(c) = 0$$

$$\sigma(X + c) = \sigma(X),$$

$$\sigma(cX) = |c|\,\sigma(X).$$

The standard deviation of the sum of two random variables can be related to their individual standard deviations and the covariance between them:

$$\sigma(X + Y) = \sqrt{\operatorname{var}(X) + \operatorname{var}(Y) + 2\operatorname{cov}(X, Y)}.$$

where $\text{var}=\sigma^2$ and cov stand for variance and covariance, respectively.

The calculation of the sum of squared deviations can be related to moments calculated directly from the data. In the following formula, the letter E is interpreted to mean expected value, i.e., mean.

$$\sigma(X) = \sqrt{E[(X - E(X))^2]} = \sqrt{E[X^2] - (E[X])^2}.$$

The sample standard deviation can be computed as:

$$\sigma(X) = \sqrt{\frac{N}{N-1}}\sqrt{E[(X - E(X))^2]}.$$

For a finite population with equal probabilities at all points, we have

$$\sqrt{\frac{1}{N}\sum_{i=1}^{N}(x_i - \overline{x})^2} = \sqrt{\frac{1}{N}\left(\sum_{i=1}^{N}x_i^2\right) - \overline{x}^2} = \sqrt{\left(\frac{1}{N}\sum_{i=1}^{N}x_i^2\right) - \left(\frac{1}{N}\sum_{i=1}^{N}x_i\right)^2}.$$

This means that the standard deviation is equal to the square root of the difference between the average of the squares of the values and the square of the average value.

Interpretation and Application

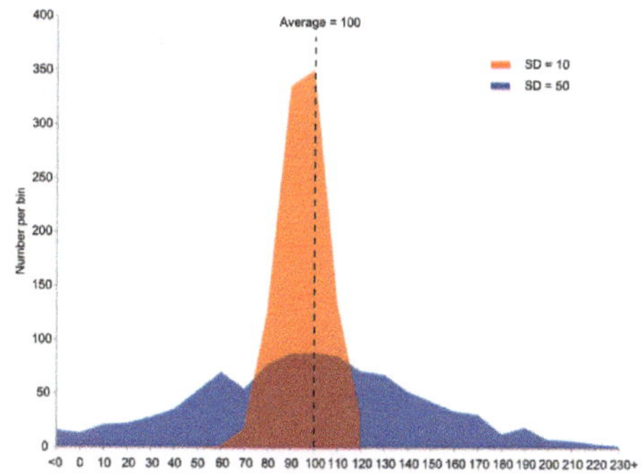

Example of samples from two populations with the same mean but different standard deviations. Red population has mean 100 and SD 10; blue population has mean 100 and SD 50.

A large standard deviation indicates that the data points can spread far from the mean and a small standard deviation indicates that they are clustered closely around the mean.

For example, each of the three populations {0, 0, 14, 14}, {0, 6, 8, 14} and {6, 6, 8, 8} has a mean of 7. Their standard deviations are 7, 5, and 1, respectively. The third population has a much smaller standard deviation than the other two because its values are all close to 7. It will have the same units as the data points themselves. If, for instance, the data set {0, 6, 8, 14} represents the ages of a population of four siblings in years, the standard deviation is 5 years. As another example, the population {1000, 1006, 1008, 1014} may represent the distances traveled by four athletes, measured in meters. It has a mean of 1007 meters, and a standard deviation of 5 meters.

Standard deviation may serve as a measure of uncertainty. In physical science, for example, the reported standard deviation of a group of repeated measurements gives the precision of those measurements. When deciding whether measurements agree with a theoretical prediction, the standard deviation of those measurements is of crucial importance: if the mean of the measurements is too far away from the prediction (with the distance measured in standard deviations), then the theory being tested probably needs to be revised. This makes sense since they fall outside the range of values that could reasonably be expected to occur, if the prediction were correct and the standard deviation appropriately quantified.

While the standard deviation does measure how far typical values tend to be from the mean, other measures are available. An example is the mean absolute deviation, which might be considered a more direct measure of average distance, compared to the root mean square distance inherent in the standard deviation.

Application Examples

The practical value of understanding the standard deviation of a set of values is in appreciating how much variation there is from the average (mean).

Experiment, Industrial and Hypothesis Testing

Standard deviation is often used to compare real-world data against a model to test the model. For example, in industrial applications the weight of products coming off a production line may need to comply with a legally required value. By weighing some fraction of the products an average weight can be found, which will always be slightly different to the long-term average. By using standard deviations, a minimum and maximum value can be calculated that the averaged weight will be within some very high percentage of the time (99.9% or more). If it falls outside the range then the production process may need to be corrected. Statistical tests such as these are particularly important when the testing is relatively expensive. For example, if the product needs to be opened and drained and weighed, or if the product was otherwise used up by the test.

In experimental science, a theoretical model of reality is used. Particle physics conventionally uses a standard of "5 sigma" for the declaration of a discovery. A five-sigma level translates to one chance in 3.5 million that a random fluctuation would yield the result. This level of certainty was required in order to assert that a particle consistent with the Higgs boson had been discovered in two independent experiments at CERN, and this was also the significance level leading to the declaration of the first detection of gravitational waves.

Weather

As a simple example, consider the average daily maximum temperatures for two cities, one inland and one on the coast. It is helpful to understand that the range of daily maximum temperatures for cities near the coast is smaller than for cities inland. Thus, while these two cities may each have the same average maximum temperature, the standard deviation of the daily maximum temperature for the coastal city will be less than that of the inland city as, on any particular day, the actual maximum temperature is more likely to be farther from the average maximum temperature for the inland city than for the coastal one.

Finance

In finance, standard deviation is often used as a measure of the risk associated with price-fluctuations of a given asset (stocks, bonds, property, etc.), or the risk of a portfolio of assets (actively managed mutual funds, index mutual funds, or ETFs). Risk is an important factor in determining how to efficiently manage a portfolio of investments because it determines the variation in returns on the asset and/or portfolio and gives investors a mathematical basis for investment decisions (known as mean-variance optimization). The fundamental concept of risk is that as it increases, the expected return on an investment should increase as well, an increase known as the risk premium. In other words, investors should expect a higher return on an investment when that investment carries a higher level of risk or uncertainty. When evaluating investments, investors should estimate both the expected return and the uncertainty of future returns. Standard deviation provides a quantified estimate of the uncertainty of future returns.

For example, assume an investor had to choose between two stocks. Stock A over the past 20 years had an average return of 10 percent, with a standard deviation of 20 percentage points (pp) and Stock B, over the same period, had average returns of 12 percent but a higher standard deviation of 30 pp. On the basis of risk and return, an investor may decide that Stock A is the safer choice, because Stock B's additional two percentage points of return is not worth the additional 10 pp standard deviation (greater risk or uncertainty of the expected return). Stock B is likely to fall short of the initial investment (but also to exceed the initial investment) more often than Stock A under the same circumstances, and is estimated to return only two percent more on average. In this example, Stock A is expected to earn about 10 percent, plus or minus 20 pp (a range of 30 percent to −10 percent), about two-thirds of the future year returns. When considering more extreme possible returns or outcomes in future, an investor should expect results of as much as 10 percent plus or minus 60 pp, or a range from 70 percent to −50 percent, which includes outcomes for three standard deviations from the average return (about 99.7 percent of probable returns).

Calculating the average (or arithmetic mean) of the return of a security over a given period will generate the expected return of the asset. For each period, subtracting the expected return from the actual return results in the difference from the mean. Squaring the difference in each period and taking the average gives the overall variance of the return of the asset. The larger the variance, the greater risk the security carries. Finding the square root of this variance will give the standard deviation of the investment tool in question.

Population standard deviation is used to set the width of Bollinger Bands, a widely adopted technical analysis tool. For example, the upper Bollinger Band is given as $x + n\sigma_x$. The most commonly used value for n is 2; there is about a five percent chance of going outside, assuming a normal distribution of returns.

Financial time series are known to be non-stationary series, whereas the statistical calculations above, such as standard deviation, apply only to stationary series. To apply the above statistical tools to non-stationary series, the series first must be transformed to a stationary series, enabling use of statistical tools that now have a valid basis from which to work.

Geometric Interpretation

To gain some geometric insights and clarification, we will start with a population of three values, x_1, x_2, x_3. This defines a point $P = (x_1, x_2, x_3)$ in $\mathbb{R}^3$. Consider the line $L = \{(r, r, r) : r \in \mathbb{R}\}$. This is the "main diagonal" going through the origin. If our three given values were all equal, then the standard deviation would be zero and P would lie on L. So it is not unreasonable to assume that the standard deviation is related to the *distance* of P to L. That is indeed the case. To move orthogonally from L to the point P, one begins at the point:

$$M = (\overline{x}, \overline{x}, \overline{x})$$

whose coordinates are the mean of the values we started out with.

Derivation of $M = (\overline{x}, \overline{x}, \overline{x})$

M is on L therefore $M = (l, l, l)$ with $l \in R$

The line L is to be orthogonal to the vector from M to P. Therefore:

$$\begin{aligned}
&L \cdot (P - M) = 0 \\
&(r, r, r) \cdot (x_1 - l, x_2 - l, x_3 - l) = 0 \\
&r * (x_1 - l + x_2 - l + x_3 - l) = 0 \\
&r * (\sum_i x_i - 3l) = 0 \\
&\sum_i x_i - 3l = 0 \\
&\frac{1}{3} \sum_i x_i = l \\
&\overline{x} = l
\end{aligned}$$

A little algebra shows that the distance between *P* and *M* (which is the same as the orthogonal distance between *P* and the line *L*) $\sqrt{\sum_i (x_i - \overline{x})^2}$ is equal to the standard deviation of the vector x_1, x_2, x_3, multiplied by the square root of the number of dimensions of the vector (3 in this case.)

Chebyshev's Inequality

An observation is rarely more than a few standard deviations away from the mean. Chebyshev's inequality ensures that, for all distributions for which the standard deviation is defined, the amount of data within a number of standard deviations of the mean is at least as much as given in the following table.

Distance from mean	**Minimum population**
$\sqrt{2}\sigma$	50%
2σ	75%
3σ	89%
4σ	94%
5σ	96%
6σ	97%

$k\sigma$	$1-\frac{1}{k^2}$
$\frac{1}{\sqrt{1-\ell}}\sigma$	ℓ

Rules for Normally Distributed Data

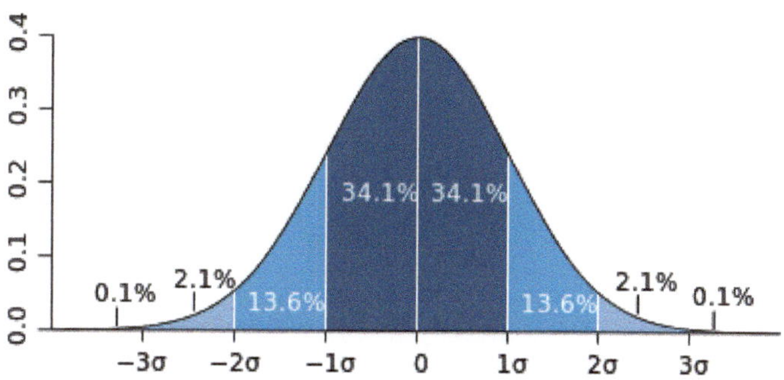

Dark blue is one standard deviation on either side of the mean. For the normal distribution, this accounts for 68.27 percent of the set; while two standard deviations from the mean (medium and dark blue) account for 95.45 percent; three standard deviations (light, medium, and dark blue) account for 99.73 percent; and four standard deviations account for 99.994 percent. The two points of the curve that are one standard deviation from the mean are also the inflection points.

The central limit theorem says that the distribution of an average of many independent, identically distributed random variables tends toward the famous bell-shaped normal distribution with a probability density function of

$$f(x;\mu,\sigma^2)=\frac{1}{\sigma\sqrt{2\pi}}e^{-\frac{1}{2}\left(\frac{x-\mu}{\sigma}\right)^2}$$

where μ is the expected value of the random variables, σ equals their distribution's standard deviation divided by $n^{1/2}$, and n is the number of random variables. The standard deviation therefore is simply a scaling variable that adjusts how broad the curve will be, though it also appears in the normalizing constant.

If a data distribution is approximately normal, then the proportion of data values within z standard deviations of the mean is defined by:

$$\text{Proportion}=\text{erf}\left(\frac{z}{\sqrt{2}}\right)$$

where erf is the error function. The proportion that is less than or equal to a number, x, is given by the cumulative distribution function:

$$\text{Proportion} \leq x = \frac{1}{2}\left[1+\operatorname{erf}\left(\frac{x-\mu}{\sigma\sqrt{2}}\right)\right] = \frac{1}{2}\left[1+\operatorname{erf}\left(\frac{z}{\sqrt{2}}\right)\right].$$

If a data distribution is approximately normal then about 68 percent of the data values are within one standard deviation of the mean (mathematically, μ ± σ, where μ is the arithmetic mean), about 95 percent are within two standard deviations (μ ± 2σ), and about 99.7 percent lie within three standard deviations (μ ± 3σ). This is known as the *68-95-99.7 rule*, or *the empirical rule.*

For various values of z, the percentage of values expected to lie in and outside the symmetric interval, CI = $(-z\sigma, z\sigma)$, are as follows:

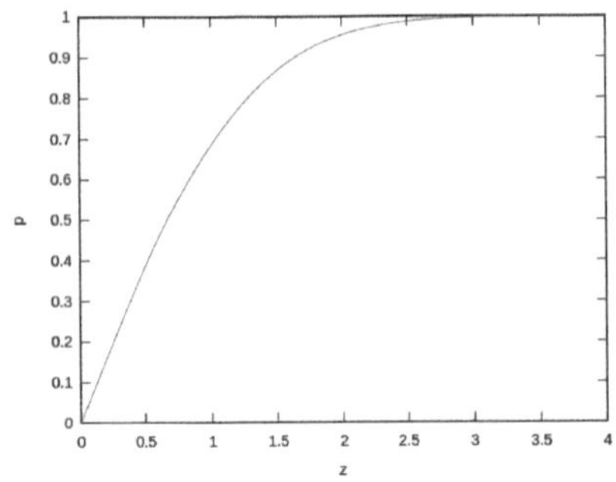

Percentage within(z)

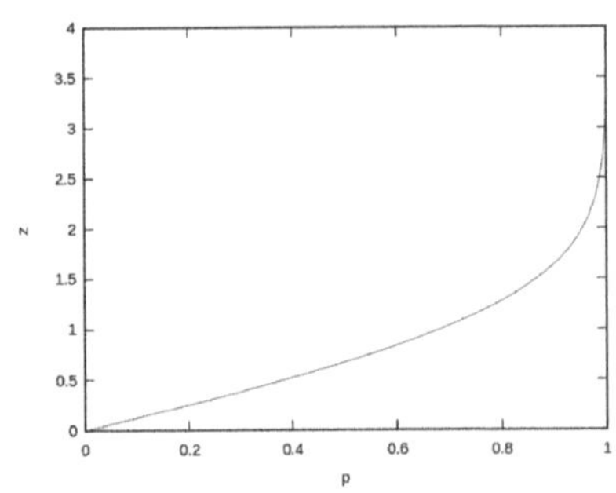

z(Percentage within)

Confidence interval	Proportion within	Proportion without	
	Percentage	Percentage	Fraction
0.674490σ	50%	50%	1 / 2
0.994458σ	68%	32%	1 / 3.125
1σ	68.2689492%	31.7310508%	1 / 3.1514872
1.281552σ	80%	20%	1 / 5
1.644854σ	90%	10%	1 / 10
1.959964σ	95%	5%	1 / 20
2σ	95.4499736%	4.5500264%	1 / 21.977895

2.575829σ	99%	1%	1 / 100
3σ	99.7300204%	0.2699796%	1 / 370.398
3.290527σ	99.9%	0.1%	1 / 1000
3.890592σ	99.99%	0.01%	1 / 10000
4σ	99.993666%	0.006334%	1 / 15787
4.417173σ	99.999%	0.001%	1 / 100000
4.5σ	*99.9993204653751%*	*0.0006795346249%*	*3.4 / 1000000 (on each side of mean)*
4.891638σ	99.9999%	0.0001%	1 / 1000000
5σ	99.9999426697%	0.0000573303%	1 / 1744278
5.326724σ	99.99999%	0.00001%	1 / 10000000
5.730729σ	99.999999%	0.000001%	1 / 100000000
6σ	99.9999998027%	0.0000001973%	1 / 506797346
6.109410σ	99.9999999%	0.0000001%	1 / 1000000000
6.466951σ	99.99999999%	0.00000001%	1 / 10000000000
6.806502σ	99.999999999%	0.000000001%	1 / 100000000000
7σ	99.9999999997440%	0.000000000256%	1 / 390682215445

Relationship Between Standard Deviation and Mean

The mean and the standard deviation of a set of data are descriptive statistics usually reported together. In a certain sense, the standard deviation is a "natural" measure of statistical dispersion if the center of the data is measured about the mean. This is because the standard deviation from the mean is smaller than from any other point. The precise statement is the following: suppose $x_1, \ldots, x_n$ are real numbers and define the function:

$$\sigma(r) = \sqrt{\frac{1}{N-1}\sum_{i=1}^{N}(x_i - r)^2}.$$

Using calculus or by completing the square, it is possible to show that σ(*r*) has a unique minimum at the mean:

$$r = \overline{x}.$$

Variability can also be measured by the coefficient of variation, which is the ratio of the standard deviation to the mean. It is a dimensionless number.

Standard Deviation of the Mean

Often, we want some information about the precision of the mean we obtained. We can obtain this by determining the standard deviation of the sampled mean. Assuming statistical independence of the values in the sample, the standard deviation of the mean is related to the standard deviation of the distribution by:

$$\sigma_{\text{mean}} = \frac{1}{\sqrt{N}}\sigma$$

where N is the number of observations in the sample used to estimate the mean. This can easily be proven with:

$$\text{var}(X) \equiv \sigma_X^2$$
$$\text{var}(X_1 + X_2) \equiv \text{var}(X_1) + \text{var}(X_2)$$

(Statistical Independence is assumed.)

$$\text{var}(cX_1) \equiv c^2\,\text{var}(X_1)$$

hence

$$\text{var(mean)} = \text{var}\left(\frac{1}{N}\sum_{i=1}^{N} X_i\right) = \frac{1}{N^2}\text{var}\left(\sum_{i=1}^{N} X_i\right)$$
$$= \frac{1}{N^2}\sum_{i=1}^{N}\text{var}(X_i) = \frac{N}{N^2}\text{var}(X) = \frac{1}{N}\text{var}(X).$$

Resulting in:

$$\sigma_{\text{mean}} = \frac{\sigma}{\sqrt{N}}.$$

It should be emphasized that in order to estimate the standard deviation of the mean σ_{mean} it is necessary to know the standard deviation of the entire population σ beforehand. However, in most applications this parameter is unknown. For example, if a series of 10 measurements of a previously unknown quantity is performed in a laboratory, it is possible to calculate the resulting sample mean and sample standard deviation, but it is impossible to calculate the standard deviation of the mean.

Rapid Calculation Methods

The following two formulas can represent a running (repeatedly updated) standard deviation. A set of two power sums s_1 and s_2 are computed over a set of N values of x, denoted as $x_1, \ldots, x_N$:

$$s_j = \sum_{k=1}^{N} x_k^j.$$

Given the results of these running summations, the values N, s_1, s_2 can be used at any time to compute the *current* value of the running standard deviation:

$$\sigma = \frac{\sqrt{Ns_2 - s_1^2}}{N}$$

Where N, as mentioned above, is the size of the set of values (or can also be regarded as s_0).

Similarly for sample standard deviation,

$$s = \sqrt{\frac{Ns_2 - s_1^2}{N(N-1)}}.$$

In a computer implementation, as the three s_j sums become large, we need to consider round-off error, arithmetic overflow, and arithmetic underflow. The method below calculates the running sums method with reduced rounding errors. This is a "one pass" algorithm for calculating variance of n samples without the need to store prior data during the calculation. Applying this method to a time series will result in successive values of standard deviation corresponding to n data points as n grows larger with each new sample, rather than a constant-width sliding window calculation.

For $k = 1, \ldots, n$:

$$A_0 = 0$$

$$A_k = A_{k-1} + \frac{x_k - A_{k-1}}{k}$$

where A is the mean value.

$$Q_0 = 0$$

$$Q_k = Q_{k-1} + \frac{k-1}{k}(x_k - A_{k-1})^2 = Q_{k-1} + (x_k - A_{k-1})(x_k - A_k)$$

Note: $Q_1 = 0$ since $k - 1 = 0$ or $x_1 = A_1$

Sample variance:

$$s_n^2 = \frac{Q_n}{n-1}$$

Population variance:

$$\sigma_n^2 = \frac{Q_n}{n}$$

Weighted Calculation

When the values x_i are weighted with unequal weights w_i, the power sums s_0, s_1, s_2 are each computed as:

$$s_j = \sum_{k=1}^{N} w_k x_k^j.$$

And the standard deviation equations remain unchanged. Note that s_0 is now the sum of the weights and not the number of samples N.

The incremental method with reduced rounding errors can also be applied, with some additional complexity.

A running sum of weights must be computed for each k from 1 to n:

$$W_0 = 0$$

$$W_k = W_{k-1} + w_k$$

and places where $1/n$ is used above must be replaced by w_i/W_n:

$$A_0 = 0$$

$$A_k = A_{k-1} + \frac{w_k}{W_k}(x_k - A_{k-1})$$

$$Q_0 = 0$$

$$Q_k = Q_{k-1} + \frac{w_k W_{k-1}}{W_k}(x_k - A_{k-1})^2 = Q_{k-1} + w_k(x_k - A_{k-1})(x_k - A_k)$$

In the final division,

$$\sigma_n^2 = \frac{Q_n}{W_n}$$

and

$$s_n^2 = \frac{Q_n}{W_n - 1},$$

or

$$s_n^2 = \frac{n'}{n' - 1}\sigma_n^2,$$

where n is the total number of elements, and n' is the number of elements with non-zero weights. The above formulas become equal to the simpler formulas given above if weights are taken as equal to one.

History

The term *standard deviation* was first used in writing by Karl Pearson in 1894, following his use of it in lectures. This was as a replacement for earlier alternative names for the same idea: for example, Gauss used *mean error*.

Variance

In probability theory and statistics, variance is the expectation of the squared deviation of a random variable from its mean, and it informally measures how far a set of (random) numbers are spread out from their mean. The variance has a central role in statistics. It is used in descriptive statistics, statistical inference, hypothesis testing, goodness of fit, and Monte Carlo sampling, amongst many others. This makes it a central quantity in numerous fields such as physics, biology, chemistry, cryptography, economics, and finance. The variance is the square of the standard deviation, the second central moment of a distribution, and the covariance of the random variable with itself, and it is often represented by σ^2, s^2, or $\mathrm{Var}(X)$.

Definition

The variance of a random variable X is the expected value of the squared deviation from the mean of X, $\mu = E[X]$

$$\mathrm{Var}(X) = E\left[(X-\mu)^2\right].$$

This definition encompasses random variables that are generated by processes that are discrete, continuous, neither, or mixed. The variance can also be thought of as the covariance of a random variable with itself:

$$\mathrm{Var}(X) = \mathrm{Cov}(X, X).$$

The variance is also equivalent to the second cumulant of a probability distribution that generates X. The variance is typically designated as $\mathrm{Var}(X)$, σ_X^2, or simply σ^2 (pronounced "sigma squared"). The expression for the variance can be expanded:

$$\begin{aligned}\mathrm{Var}(X) &= E\left[(X-E[X])^2\right]\\ &= E\left[X^2 - 2X\,E[X] + E[X]^2\right]\\ &= E\left[X^2\right] - 2\,E[X]E[X] + E[X]^2\\ &= E\left[X^2\right] - E[X]^2\end{aligned}$$

A mnemonic for the above expression is "mean of square minus square of mean". On computational floating point arithmetic, this equation should not be used, because it suffers from catastrophic cancellation if the two components of the equation are similar in magnitude. There exist numerically stable alternatives.

Continuous Random Variable

If the random variable X represents samples generated by a continuous distribution with probability density function $f(x)$, then the population variance is given by:

$$\mathrm{Var}(X) = \sigma^2 = \int (x-\mu)^2 f(x)dx = \int x^2 f(x)dx - 2\mu\int xf(x)dx + \int \mu^2 f(x)dx = \int x^2 f(x)dx - \mu^2$$

where μ is the expected value

$$\mu = \int x f(x)dx$$

and where the integrals are definite integrals taken for x ranging over the range of X.

If a continuous distribution does not have an expected value, as is the case for the Cauchy distribution, it does not have a variance either. Many other distributions for which the expected value does exist also do not have a finite variance because the integral in the variance definition diverges. An example is a Pareto distribution whose index k satisfies $1 < k \leq 2$.

Discrete Random Variable

If the generator of random variable X is discrete with probability mass function $x_1 \mapsto p_1, x_2 \mapsto p_2, \ldots, x_n \mapsto p_n$ then:

$$\mathrm{Var}(X) = \sum_{i=1}^{n} p_i \cdot (x_i - \mu)^2,$$

or equivalently

$$\mathrm{Var}(X) = \sum_{i=1}^{n} p_i x_i^2 - \mu^2,$$

where μ is the average value, i.e.

$$\mu = \sum_{i=1}^{n} p_i \cdot x_i.$$

(When such a discrete weighted variance is specified by weights whose sum is not 1, then one divides by the sum of the weights.)

The variance of a set of n equally likely values can be written as:

$$\mathrm{Var}(X)=\frac{1}{n}\sum_{i=1}^{n}(x_i-\mu)^2,$$

where μ is the expected value, i.e.,

$$\mu=\frac{1}{n}\sum_{i=1}^{n}x_i.$$

The variance of a set of n equally likely values can be equivalently expressed, without directly referring to the mean, in terms of squared deviations of all points from each other:

$$\mathrm{Var}(X)=\frac{1}{n^2}\sum_{i=1}^{n}\sum_{j=1}^{n}\frac{1}{2}(x_i-x_j)^2=\frac{1}{n^2}\sum_{i}\sum_{j>i}(x_i-x_j)^2.$$

Examples

Normal Distribution

The normal distribution with parameters μ and σ is a continuous distribution whose probability density function is given by

$$f(x)=\frac{1}{\sqrt{2\pi\sigma^2}}e^{-\frac{(x-\mu)^2}{2\sigma^2}}.$$

In this distribution, $E[X]=\mu$ and the variance $\mathrm{Var}(X)$ is related with σ via

$$\mathrm{Var}(X)=\int_{-\infty}^{\infty}\frac{x^2}{\sqrt{2\pi\sigma^2}}e^{-\frac{(x-\mu)^2}{2\sigma^2}}dx-\mu^2=\sigma^2.$$

The role of the normal distribution in the central limit theorem is in part responsible for the prevalence of the variance in probability and statistics.

Exponential Distribution

The exponential distribution with parameter λ is a continuous distribution whose support is the semi-infinite interval $[0,\infty)$. Its probability density function is given by

$$f(x)=\lambda e^{-\lambda x}$$

and it has expected value $\mu=\lambda^{-1}$. The variance is equal to

$$\mathrm{Var}(X)=\int_{0}^{\infty}x^2\lambda e^{-\lambda x}dx-\mu^2=\lambda^{-2}.$$

So for an exponentially distributed random variable, $\sigma^2 = \mu^2$.

Poisson Distribution

The Poisson distribution with parameter λ is a discrete distribution for $k = 0, 1, 2, \ldots$. Its probability mass function is given by

$$p(k) = \frac{\lambda^k}{k!} e^{-\lambda},$$

and it has expected value $\mu = \lambda$. The variance is equal to

$$\operatorname{Var}(X) = \left(\sum_{k=0}^{\infty} k^2 \frac{\lambda^k}{k!} e^{-\lambda} \right) - \mu^2 = \lambda,$$

So for a Poisson-distributed random variable, $\sigma^2 = \mu$.

Binomial Distribution

The binomial distribution with parameters n and p is a discrete distribution for $k = 0, 1, 2, \ldots, n$. Its probability mass function is given by

$$p(k) = \binom{n}{k} p^k (1-p)^{n-k},$$

and it has expected value $\mu = np$. The variance is equal to

$$\operatorname{Var}(X) = \left(\sum_{k=0}^{n} k^2 \binom{n}{k} p^k (1-p)^{n-k} \right) - \mu^2 = np(1-p).$$

As a simple example, the binomial distribution with $p = 1/2$ describes the probability of getting k heads in n tosses. Thus the expected value of the number of heads is $\frac{n}{2}$, and the variance is $\frac{n}{4}$.

Fair Die

A six-sided fair die can be modelled with a discrete random variable with outcomes 1 through 6, each with equal probability $\frac{1}{6}$. The expected value is $\frac{1+2+3+4+5+6}{6} = 3.5$. Therefore, the variance can be computed to be

$$\sum_{i=1}^{6}\tfrac{1}{6}(i-3.5)^2=\tfrac{1}{6}\sum_{i=1}^{6}(i-3.5)^2=\tfrac{1}{6}\left((-2.5)^2+(-1.5)^2+(-0.5)^2+0.5^2+1.5^2+2.5^2\right)$$
$$=\tfrac{1}{6}\cdot 17.50=\tfrac{35}{12}\approx 2.92.$$

The general formula for the variance of the outcome X of a die of n sides is

$$\sigma^2=E(X^2)-(E(X))^2=\frac{1}{n}\sum_{i=1}^{n}i^2-\left(\frac{1}{n}\sum_{i=1}^{n}i\right)^2$$
$$=\tfrac{1}{6}(n+1)(2n+1)-\tfrac{1}{4}(n+1)^2$$
$$=\frac{n^2-1}{12}.$$

Properties

Basic Properties

Variance is non-negative because the squares are positive or zero:

$$\mathrm{Var}(X)\geq 0.$$

The variance of a constant random variable is zero, and if the variance of a variable in a data set is 0, then all the entries have the same value:

$$P(X=a)=1\Leftrightarrow \mathrm{Var}(X)=0.$$

Variance is invariant with respect to changes in a location parameter. That is, if a constant is added to all values of the variable, the variance is unchanged:

$$\mathrm{Var}(X+a)=\mathrm{Var}(X).$$

If all values are scaled by a constant, the variance is scaled by the square of that constant:

$$\mathrm{Var}(aX)=a^2\,\mathrm{Var}(X).$$

The variance of a sum of two random variables is given by

$$\mathrm{Var}(aX+bY)=a^2\,\mathrm{Var}(X)+b^2\,\mathrm{Var}(Y)+2ab\mathrm{Cov}(X,Y),$$

$$\mathrm{Var}(aX-bY)=a^2\,\mathrm{Var}(X)+b^2\,\mathrm{Var}(Y)-2ab\mathrm{Cov}(X,Y),$$

where Cov(·, ·) is the covariance. In general we have for the sum of N random variables $\{X_1,\ldots,X_N\}$:

$$\operatorname{Var}\left(\sum_{i=1}^{N} X_i\right)=\sum_{i,j=1}^{N}\operatorname{cov}(X_i,X_j)=\sum_{i=1}^{N}\operatorname{Var}(X_i)+\sum_{i\neq j}\operatorname{cov}(X_i,X_j).$$

These results lead to the variance of a linear combination as:

$$\begin{aligned}\operatorname{Var}\left(\sum_{i=1}^{N} a_i X_i\right)&=\sum_{i,j=1}^{N} a_i a_j \operatorname{Cov}(X_i,X_j)\\ &=\sum_{i=1}^{N} a_i^2 \operatorname{Var}(X_i)+\sum_{i\neq j} a_i a_j \operatorname{Cov}(X_i,X_j)\\ &=\sum_{i=1}^{N} a_i^2 \operatorname{Var}(X_i)+2\sum_{1\le i<j\le N} a_i a_j \operatorname{Cov}(X_i,X_j).\end{aligned}$$

If the random variables $X_1,\ldots,X_N$ are such that

$$\operatorname{Cov}(X_i,X_j)=0,\ \forall\,(i\neq j),$$

they are said to be uncorrelated. It follows immediately from the expression given earlier that if the random variables $X_1,\ldots,X_N$ are uncorrelated, then the variance of their sum is equal to the sum of their variances, or, expressed symbolically:

$$\operatorname{Var}\left(\sum_{i=1}^{N} X_i\right)=\sum_{i=1}^{N}\operatorname{Var}(X_i).$$

Since independent random variables are always uncorrelated, the equation above holds in particular when the random variables $X_1,\ldots,X_n$ are independent. Thus independence is sufficient but not necessary for the variance of the sum to equal the sum of the variances.

Sum of Uncorrelated Variables (Bienaymé Formula)

One reason for the use of the variance in preference to other measures of dispersion is that the variance of the sum (or the difference) of uncorrelated random variables is the sum of their variances:

$$\operatorname{Var}\left(\sum_{i=1}^{n} X_i\right)=\sum_{i=1}^{n}\operatorname{Var}(X_i).$$

This statement is called the Bienaymé formula and was discovered in 1853. It is often made with the stronger condition that the variables are independent, but being uncorrelated suffices. So if all the variables have the same variance σ^2, then, since division by n is a linear transformation, this formula immediately implies that the variance of their mean is

$$\mathrm{Var}(\bar{X}) = \mathrm{Var}\left(\frac{1}{n}\sum_{i=1}^{n} X_i\right) = \frac{1}{n^2}\sum_{i=1}^{n}\mathrm{Var}(X_i) = \frac{\sigma^2}{n}.$$

That is, the variance of the mean decreases when n increases. This formula for the variance of the mean is used in the definition of the standard error of the sample mean, which is used in the central limit theorem.

To prove the initial statement, it suffices to show that

$$\mathrm{Var}(X+Y) = \mathrm{Var}(X) + \mathrm{Var}(Y).$$

The general result then follows by induction. Starting with the definition,

$$\begin{aligned}\mathrm{Var}(X+Y) &= E[(X+Y)^2] - (E[X+Y])^2 \\ &= E[X^2 + 2XY + Y^2] - (E[X]+E[Y])^2.\end{aligned}$$

Using the linearity of the expectation operator and the assumption of independence (or uncorrelatedness) of X and Y, this further simplifies as follows:

$$\begin{aligned}\mathrm{Var}(X+Y) &= E[X^2] + 2E[XY] + E[Y^2] - (E[X]^2 + 2E[X]E[Y] + E[Y]^2) \\ &= E[X^2] + E[Y^2] - E[X]^2 - E[Y]^2 \\ &= \mathrm{Var}(X) + \mathrm{Var}(Y).\end{aligned}$$

Sum of Correlated Variables

In general, if the variables are correlated, then the variance of their sum is the sum of their covariances:

$$\mathrm{Var}\left(\sum_{i=1}^{n} X_i\right) = \sum_{i=1}^{n}\sum_{j=1}^{n}\mathrm{Cov}(X_i, X_j) = \sum_{i=1}^{n}\mathrm{Var}(X_i) + 2\sum_{1\le i<j\le n}\mathrm{Cov}(X_i, X_j).$$

(Note: The second equality comes from the fact that $\mathrm{Cov}(X_i, X_i) = \mathrm{Var}(X_i)$.)

Here Cov(·, ·) is the covariance, which is zero for independent random variables (if it exists). The formula states that the variance of a sum is equal to the sum of all elements in the covariance matrix of the components. The next expression states equivalently that the variance of the sum is the sum of the diagonal of covariance matrix plus two times the sum of its upper triangular elements (or its lower triangular elements); this emphasizes that the covariance matrix is symmetric. This formula is used in the theory of Cronbach's alpha in classical test theory.

So if the variables have equal variance σ^2 and the average correlation of distinct variables is ρ, then the variance of their mean is

$$\operatorname{Var}(\overline{X}) = \frac{\sigma^2}{n} + \frac{n-1}{n}\rho\sigma^2.$$

This implies that the variance of the mean increases with the average of the correlations. In other words, additional correlated observations are not as effective as additional independent observations at reducing the uncertainty of the mean. Moreover, if the variables have unit variance, for example if they are standardized, then this simplifies to

$$\operatorname{Var}(\overline{X}) = \frac{1}{n} + \frac{n-1}{n}\rho.$$

This formula is used in the Spearman–Brown prediction formula of classical test theory. This converges to ρ if n goes to infinity, provided that the average correlation remains constant or converges too. So for the variance of the mean of standardized variables with equal correlations or converging average correlation we have

$$\lim_{n\to\infty} \operatorname{Var}(\overline{X}) = \rho.$$

Therefore, the variance of the mean of a large number of standardized variables is approximately equal to their average correlation. This makes clear that the sample mean of correlated variables does not generally converge to the population mean, even though the Law of large numbers states that the sample mean will converge for independent variables.

Matrix Notation for the Variance of A Linear Combination

Define X as a column vector of n random variables $X_1,\ldots,X_n$, and c as a column vector of n scalars $c_1,\ldots,c_n$. Therefore, $c^T X$ is a linear combination of these random variables, where c^T denotes the transpose of c. Also let Σ be the covariance matrix of X. The variance of $c^T X$ is then given by:

$$\operatorname{Var}(c^T X) = c^T \Sigma c.$$

Weighted Sum of Variables

The scaling property and the Bienaymé formula, along with the property of the covariance $\operatorname{Cov}(aX, bY) = ab \operatorname{Cov}(X, Y)$ jointly imply that

$$\operatorname{Var}(aX \pm bY) = a^2 \operatorname{Var}(X) + b^2 \operatorname{Var}(Y) \pm 2ab\operatorname{Cov}(X, Y).$$

This implies that in a weighted sum of variables, the variable with the largest weight will have a disproportionally large weight in the variance of the total. For example, if *X* and *Y* are uncorrelated and the weight of *X* is two times the weight of *Y*, then the weight of the variance of *X* will be four times the weight of the variance of *Y*.

The expression above can be extended to a weighted sum of multiple variables:

$$\mathrm{Var}\left(\sum_{i}^{n} a_i X_i\right) = \sum_{i=1}^{n} a_i^2 \,\mathrm{Var}(X_i) + 2\sum_{1\le i}\sum_{<j\le n} a_i a_j \,\mathrm{Cov}(X_i, X_j)$$

Product of Independent Variables

If two variables X and Y are independent, the variance of their product is given by

$$\mathrm{Var}(XY) = [E(X)]^2\,\mathrm{Var}(Y) + [E(Y)]^2\,\mathrm{Var}(X) + \mathrm{Var}(X)\,\mathrm{Var}(Y).$$

Equivalently, using the basic properties of expectation, it is given by

$$\mathrm{Var}(XY) = E(X^2)E(Y^2) - [E(X)]^2[E(Y)]^2.$$

Product of Statistically Dependent Variables

In general, if two variables are statistically dependent, the variance of their product is given by:

$$\begin{aligned}
&\mathrm{Var}(XY) = E[X^2Y^2] - [E(XY)]^2\\
&= \mathrm{Cov}(X^2, Y^2) + E(X^2)E(Y^2) - [E(XY)]^2\\
&= \mathrm{Cov}(X^2, Y^2) + (\mathrm{Var}(X) + [E(X)]^2)(\mathrm{Var}(Y) + [E(Y)]^2) - [\mathrm{Cov}(X, Y) + E(X)E(Y)]^2
\end{aligned}$$

Decomposition

The general formula for variance decomposition or the law of total variance is: If X and Y are two random variables, and the variance of X exists, then

$$\mathrm{Var}[X] = E_Y(\mathrm{Var}[X \mid Y]) + \mathrm{Var}_Y(E[X \mid Y]).$$

where $E(X \mid Y)$ is the conditional expectation of X given Y, and $\mathrm{Var}(X \mid Y)$ is the conditional variance of X given Y. (A more intuitive explanation is that given a particular value of Y, then X follows a distribution with mean $E(X \mid Y)$ and variance $\mathrm{Var}(X \mid Y)$). As $E(X \mid Y)$ is a function of the variable Y, the outer expectation or variance is taken with respect to Y. The above formula tells how to find $\mathrm{Var}(X)$ based on the distributions of these two quantities when Y is allowed to vary.

In particular, if Y is a discrete random variable assuming $y_1, y_2, \ldots, y_n$ with corresponding probability masses $p_1, p_2, \ldots, p_n$, then in the formula for total variance, the first term on the right-hand side becomes

$$E_Y(\mathrm{Var}[X \mid Y]) = \sum_{i=1}^{n} p_i \sigma_i^2,$$

where $\sigma_i^2 = \mathrm{Var}[X \mid y_i]$. Similarly, the second term on the right-hand side becomes

$$\mathrm{Var}_Y(E[X \mid Y]) = \sum_{i=1}^{n} p_i \mu_i^2 - \left(\sum_{i=1}^{n} p_i \mu_i \right)^2 = \sum_{i=1}^{n} p_i \mu_i^2 - \mu^2,$$

where $\mu_i = E[X \mid y_i]$ and $\mu = \sum_{i=1}^{n} p_i \mu_i$. Thus the total variance is given by

$$\mathrm{Var}[X] = \sum_{i=1}^{n} p_i \sigma_i^2 + \left(\sum_{i=1}^{n} p_i \mu_i^2 - \mu^2 \right).$$

A similar formula is applied in analysis of variance, where the corresponding formula is

$$MS_{\text{total}} = MS_{\text{between}} + MS_{\text{within}};$$

here MS refers to the Mean of the Squares. In linear regression analysis the corresponding formula is

$$MS_{\text{total}} = MS_{\text{regression}} + MS_{\text{residual}}.$$

This can also be derived from the additivity of variances, since the total (observed) score is the sum of the predicted score and the error score, where the latter two are uncorrelated.

Similar decompositions are possible for the sum of squared deviations (sum of squares, SS):

$$SS_{\text{total}} = SS_{\text{between}} + SS_{\text{within}},$$

$$SS_{\text{total}} = SS_{\text{regression}} + SS_{\text{residual}}.$$

Formulae for the Variance

A formula often used for deriving the variance of a theoretical distribution is as follows:

$$\mathrm{Var}(X) = E(X^2) - (E(X))^2.$$

This will be useful when it is possible to derive formulae for the expected value and for the expected value of the square.

This formula is also sometimes used in connection with the sample variance. While useful for hand calculations, it is not advised for computer calculations as it suffers from catastrophic cancellation if the two components of the equation are similar in magnitude and floating point arithmetic is used.

Calculation from the CDF

The population variance for a non-negative random variable can be expressed in terms of the cumulative distribution function F using

$$2\int_0^\infty u(1-F(u))du - \left(\int_0^\infty 1-F(u)du\right)^2.$$

This expression can be used to calculate the variance in situations where the CDF, but not the density, can be conveniently expressed.

Characteristic Property

The second moment of a random variable attains the minimum value when taken around the first moment (i.e., mean) of the random variable, i.e. $argmin_m E((X-m)^2) = E(X)$. Conversely, if a continuous function φ satisfies $argmin_m E(\varphi(X-m)) = E(X)$ for all random variables X, then it is necessarily of the form $\varphi(x) = ax^2 + b$, where $a > 0$. This also holds in the multidimensional case.

Units of Measurement

Unlike expected absolute deviation, the variance of a variable has units that are the square of the units of the variable itself. For example, a variable measured in meters will have a variance measured in meters squared. For this reason, describing data sets via their standard deviation or root mean square deviation is often preferred over using the variance. In the dice example the standard deviation is $\sqrt{2.9} \approx 1.7$, slightly larger than the expected absolute deviation of 1.5.

The standard deviation and the expected absolute deviation can both be used as an indicator of the "spread" of a distribution. The standard deviation is more amenable to algebraic manipulation than the expected absolute deviation, and, together with variance and its generalization covariance, is used frequently in theoretical statistics; however the expected absolute deviation tends to be more robust as it is less sensitive to outliers arising from measurement anomalies or an unduly heavy-tailed distribution.

Approximating the Variance of a Function

The delta method uses second-order Taylor expansions to approximate the variance of a function of one or more random variables. For example, the approximate variance of a function of one variable is given by

$$\operatorname{Var}[f(X)] \approx (f'(E[X]))^2 \operatorname{Var}[X]$$

provided that *f* is twice differentiable and that the mean and variance of *X* are finite.

Population Variance and Sample Variance

Real-world observations such as the measurements of yesterday's rain throughout the day typically cannot be complete sets of all possible observations that could be made. As such, the variance calculated from the finite set will in general not match the variance that would have been calculated from the full population of possible observations. This means that one estimates the mean and variance that would have been calculated from an omniscient set of observations by using an estimator equation. The estimator is a function of the sample of n observations drawn without observational bias from the whole population of potential observations. In this example that sample would be the set of actual measurements of yesterday's rainfall from available rain gauges within the geography of interest.

The simplest estimators for population mean and population variance are simply the mean and variance of the sample, the sample mean and (uncorrected) sample variance – these are consistent estimators (they converge to the correct value as the number of samples increases), but can be improved. Estimating the population variance by taking the sample's variance is close to optimal in general, but can be improved in two ways. Most simply, the sample variance is computed as an average of squared deviations about the (sample) mean, by dividing by n. However, using values other than n improves the estimator in various ways. Four common values for the denominator are n, $n - 1$, $n + 1$, and $n - 1.5$: n is the simplest (population variance of the sample), $n - 1$ eliminates bias, $n + 1$ minimizes mean squared error for the normal distribution, and $n - 1.5$ mostly eliminates bias in unbiased estimation of standard deviation for the normal distribution.

Firstly, if the omniscient mean is unknown (and is computed as the sample mean), then the sample variance is a biased estimator: it underestimates the variance by a factor of $(n - 1) / n$; correcting by this factor (dividing by $n - 1$ instead of n) is called Bessel's correction. The resulting estimator is unbiased, and is called the (corrected) sample variance or unbiased sample variance. For example, when $n = 1$ the variance of a single observation about the sample mean (itself) is obviously zero regardless of the population variance. If the mean is determined in some other way than from the same samples used to estimate the variance then this bias does not arise and the variance can safely be estimated as that of the samples about the (independently known) mean.

Secondly, the sample variance does not generally minimize mean squared error between sample variance and population variance. Correcting for bias often makes this worse: one can always choose a scale factor that performs better than the corrected sample variance, though the optimal scale factor depends on the excess kurtosis of the population, and introduces bias. This always consists of scaling down the unbiased estimator (dividing by a number larger than $n - 1$), and is a simple example of a shrinkage estimator: one "shrinks" the unbiased estimator towards zero. For the normal distribution, dividing by $n + 1$ (instead of $n - 1$ or n) minimizes mean squared error. The resulting estimator is biased, however, and is known as the biased sample variation.

Population Variance

In general, the *population variance* of a *finite* population of size N with values x_i is given by

$$\sigma^2 = \frac{1}{N}\sum_{i=1}^{N}(x_i - \mu)^2 = \frac{1}{N}\sum_{i=1}^{N}(x_i^2 - 2\mu x_i + \mu^2) = \left(\frac{1}{N}\sum_{i=1}^{N}x_i^2\right) - 2\mu\left(\frac{1}{N}\sum_{i=1}^{N}x_i\right) + \mu^2 = \left(\frac{1}{N}\sum_{i=1}^{N}x_i^2\right) - \mu^2$$

where the population mean is

$$\mu = \frac{1}{N}\sum_{i=1}^{N}x_i\,.$$

The population variance can also be computed using

$$\sigma^2 = \frac{1}{N^2}\sum_{i<j}(x_i - x_j)^2 = \frac{1}{2N^2}\sum_{i,j=1}^{N}(x_i - x_j)^2$$

This is true because

$$\frac{1}{2N^2}\sum_{i,j=1}^{N}(x_i - x_j)^2 = \frac{1}{2N^2}\sum_{i,j=1}^{N}(x_i^2 - 2x_i x_j + x_j^2)$$
$$= \frac{1}{2N}\sum_{j=1}^{N}\left(\frac{1}{N}\sum_{i=1}^{N}x_i^2\right) - \left(\frac{1}{N}\sum_{i=1}^{N}x_i\right)\left(\frac{1}{N}\sum_{j=1}^{N}x_j\right) + \frac{1}{2N}\sum_{i=1}^{N}\left(\frac{1}{N}\sum_{j=1}^{N}x_j^2\right)$$
$$= \frac{1}{2}(\sigma^2 + \mu^2) - \mu^2 + \frac{1}{2}(\sigma^2 + \mu^2) = \sigma^2$$

The population variance matches the variance of the generating probability distribution. In this sense, the concept of population can be extended to continuous random variables with infinite populations.

Sample Variance

In many practical situations, the true variance of a population is not known *a priori* and must be computed somehow. When dealing with extremely large populations, it is not possible to count every object in the population, so the computation must be performed on a sample of the population. Sample variance can also be applied to the estimation of the variance of a continuous distribution from a sample of that distribution.

We take a sample with replacement of n values $y_1, \ldots, y_n$ from the population, where $n < N$, and estimate the variance on the basis of this sample. Directly taking the variance of the sample data gives the average of the squared deviations:

$$\sigma_y^2 = \frac{1}{n}\sum_{i=1}^{n}(y_i - \bar{y})^2 = \left(\frac{1}{n}\sum_{i=1}^{n} y_i^2\right) - \bar{y}^2 = \frac{1}{n^2}\sum_{i<j}(y_i - y_j)^2.$$

Here, $\bar{y}$ denotes the sample mean:

$$\bar{y} = \frac{1}{n}\sum_{i=1}^{n} y_i.$$

Since the y_i are selected randomly, both $\bar{y}$ and σ_y^2 are random variables. Their expected values can be evaluated by averaging over the ensemble of all possible samples $\{y_i\}$ of size n from the population. For σ_y^2 this gives:

$$E[\sigma_y^2] = E\left[\frac{1}{n}\sum_{i=1}^{n}\left(y_i - \frac{1}{n}\sum_{j=1}^{n} y_j\right)^2\right]$$

$$= \frac{1}{n}\sum_{i=1}^{n} E\left[y_i^2 - \frac{2}{n} y_i \sum_{j=1}^{n} y_j + \frac{1}{n^2}\sum_{j=1}^{n} y_j \sum_{k=1}^{n} y_k\right]$$

$$= \frac{1}{n}\sum_{i=1}^{n}\left[\frac{n-2}{n} E[y_i^2] - \frac{2}{n}\sum_{j\neq i} E[y_i y_j] + \frac{1}{n^2}\sum_{j=1}^{n}\sum_{k\neq j}^{n} E[y_j y_k] + \frac{1}{n^2}\sum_{j=1}^{n} E[y_j^2]\right]$$

$$= \frac{1}{n}\sum_{i=1}^{n}\left[\frac{n-2}{n}(\sigma^2 + \mu^2) - \frac{2}{n}(n-1)\mu^2 + \frac{1}{n^2} n(n-1)\mu^2 + \frac{1}{n}(\sigma^2 + \mu^2)\right]$$

$$= \frac{n-1}{n}\sigma^2.$$

Hence σ_y^2 gives an estimate of the population variance that is biased by a factor of $\frac{n-1}{n}$.

For this reason, σ_y^2 is referred to as the *biased sample variance*. Correcting for this bias yields the *unbiased sample variance*:

$$s^2 = \frac{n}{n-1}\sigma_y^2 = \frac{n}{n-1}\left(\frac{1}{n}\sum_{i=1}^{n}(y_i - \bar{y})^2\right) = \frac{1}{n-1}\sum_{i=1}^{n}(y_i - \bar{y})^2$$

Either estimator may be simply referred to as the *sample variance* when the version can be determined by context. The same proof is also applicable for samples taken from a continuous probability distribution.

The use of the term $n - 1$ is called Bessel's correction, and it is also used in sample covariance and the sample standard deviation (the square root of variance). The square root is a concave function and thus introduces negative bias (by Jensen's inequality), which depends on the distribution, and thus the corrected sample standard deviation (using Bessel's correction) is biased. The unbiased estimation of standard deviation is a technically involved problem, though for the normal distribution using the term $n - 1.5$ yields an almost unbiased estimator.

The unbiased sample variance is a U-statistic for the function $f(y_1, y_2) = (y_1 - y_2)^2/2$, meaning that it is obtained by averaging a 2-sample statistic over 2-element subsets of the population.

Distribution of the Sample Variance

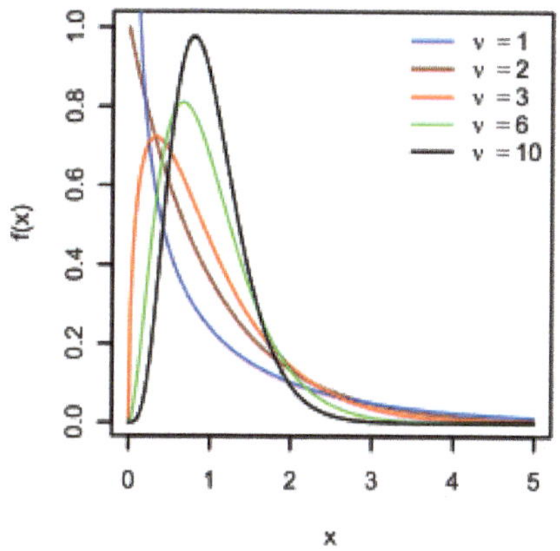

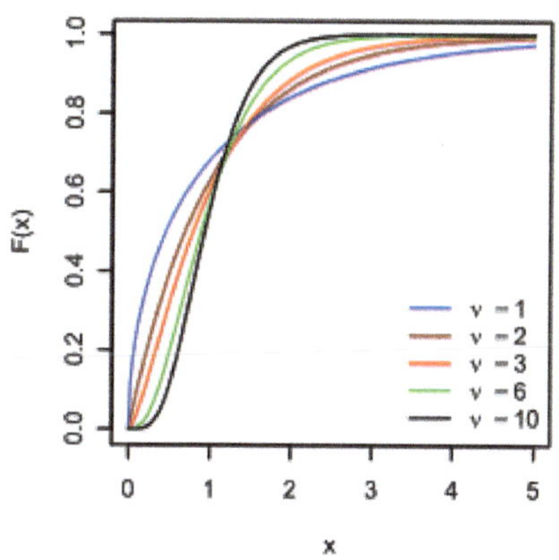

Distribution and cumulative distribution of s^2/σ^2, for various values of $\nu = n - 1$, when the y_i are independent normally distributed.

Being a function of random variables, the sample variance is itself a random variable, and it is natural to study its distribution. In the case that y_i are independent observations from a normal distribution, Cochran's theorem shows that s^2 follows a scaled chi-squared distribution:

$$(n-1)\frac{s^2}{\sigma^2} \sim \chi^2_{n-1}.$$

As a direct consequence, it follows that

$$E(s^2) = E\left(\frac{\sigma^2}{n-1}\chi^2_{n-1}\right) = \sigma^2,$$

and

$$\mathrm{Var}[s^2] = \mathrm{Var}\left(\frac{\sigma^2}{n-1}\chi^2_{n-1}\right) = \frac{\sigma^4}{(n-1)^2}\mathrm{Var}\left(\chi^2_{n-1}\right) = \frac{2\sigma^4}{n-1}.$$

If the y_i are independent and identically distributed, but not necessarily normally distributed, then

$$E[s^2] = \sigma^2, \quad \mathrm{Var}[s^2] = \frac{\sigma^4}{n}\left((\kappa-1) + \frac{2}{n-1}\right) = \frac{1}{n}\left(\mu_4 - \frac{n-3}{n-1}\sigma^4\right),$$

where κ is the kurtosis of the distribution and μ_4 is the fourth central moment.

If the conditions of the law of large numbers hold for the squared observations, s^2 is a consistent estimator of σ^2. One can see indeed that the variance of the estimator tends asymptotically to zero. An asymptotically equivalent formula was given in Kenney and Keeping (1951:164), Rose and Smith (2002:264), and Weisstein (n.d.).

Samuelson's Inequality

Samuelson's inequality is a result that states bounds on the values that individual observations in a sample can take, given that the sample mean and (biased) variance have been calculated. Values must lie within the limits $\bar{y} \pm \sigma_y(n-1)^{1/2}$.

Relations with the Harmonic and Arithmetic Means

It has been shown that for a sample $\{y_i\}$ of real numbers,

$$\sigma_y^2 \le 2y_{max}(A-H),$$

where y_{max} is the maximum of the sample, A is the arithmetic mean, H is the harmonic mean of the sample and σ_y^2 is the (biased) variance of the sample.

This bound has been improved, and it is known that variance is bounded by

$$\sigma_y^2 \le \frac{y_{max}(A-H)(y_{max}-A)}{y_{max}-H},$$

$$\sigma_y^2 \ge \frac{y_{min}(A-H)(A-y_{min})}{H-y_{min}},$$

where y_{min} is the minimum of the sample.

Tests of Equality of Variances

Testing for the equality of two or more variances is difficult. The F test and chi square tests are both adversely affected by non-normality and are not recommended for this purpose.

Several non parametric tests have been proposed: these include the Barton–David–Ansari–Freund–Siegel–Tukey test, the Capon test, Mood test, the Klotz test and the Sukhatme test. The Sukhatme test applies to two variances and requires that both medians be known and equal to zero. The Mood, Klotz, Capon and Barton–David–Ansari–Freund–Siegel–Tukey tests also apply to two variances. They allow the median to be unknown but do require that the two medians are equal.

The Lehmann test is a parametric test of two variances. Of this test there are several variants known. Other tests of the equality of variances include the Box test, the Box–Anderson test and the Moses test.

Resampling methods, which include the bootstrap and the jackknife, may be used to test the equality of variances.

History

The term *variance* was first introduced by Ronald Fisher in his 1918 paper *The Correlation Between Relatives on the Supposition of Mendelian Inheritance*:

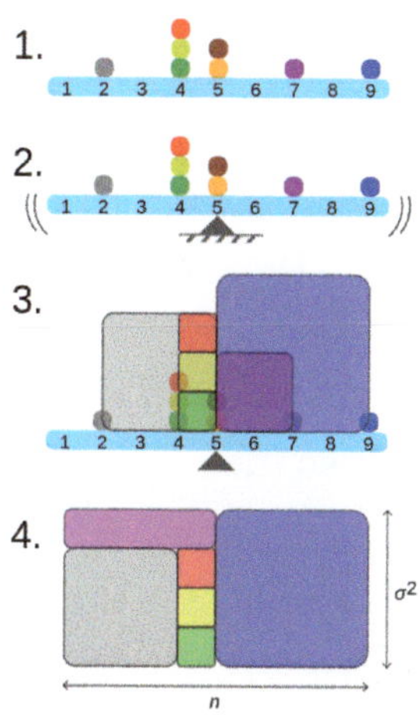

Geometric visualisation of the variance of an arbitrary distribution (2, 4, 4, 4, 5, 5, 7, 9):

1. A frequency distribution is constructed.
2. The centroid of the distribution gives its mean.
3. A square with sides equal to the difference of each value from the mean is formed for each value.
4. Arranging the squares into a rectangle with one side equal to the number of values, n, results in the other side being the distribution's variance, σ^2.

The great body of available statistics show us that the deviations of a human measurement from its mean follow very closely the Normal Law of Errors, and, therefore, that the variability may be uniformly measured by the standard deviation corresponding to the square root of the mean square error. When there are two independent causes of variability capable of producing in an otherwise uniform population distributions with standard deviations σ_1 and σ_2, it is found that the distribution, when both causes act together, has a standard deviation $\sqrt{\sigma_1^2+\sigma_2^2}$. It is therefore desirable in analysing the causes of variability to deal with the square of the standard deviation as the measure of variability. We shall term this quantity the Variance...

Moment of Inertia

The variance of a probability distribution is analogous to the moment of inertia in classical mechanics of a corresponding mass distribution along a line, with respect to rotation about its center of mass. It is because of this analogy that such things as the variance are called *moments* of probability distributions. The covariance matrix is related to the moment of inertia tensor for multivariate distributions. The moment of inertia of a cloud of n points with a covariance matrix of Σ is given by

$$I = n(1_{3\times 3}\,\mathrm{tr}(\Sigma) - \Sigma).$$

This difference between moment of inertia in physics and in statistics is clear for points that are gathered along a line. Suppose many points are close to the x axis and distributed along it. The covariance matrix might look like

$$\Sigma = \begin{bmatrix} 10 & 0 & 0 \\ 0 & 0.1 & 0 \\ 0 & 0 & 0.1 \end{bmatrix}.$$

That is, there is the most variance in the x direction. Physicists would consider this to have a low moment *about* the x axis so the moment-of-inertia tensor is

$$I = n\begin{bmatrix} 0.2 & 0 & 0 \\ 0 & 10.1 & 0 \\ 0 & 0 & 10.1 \end{bmatrix}.$$

Semivariance

The *semivariance* is calculated in the same manner as the variance but only those observations that fall below the mean are included in the calculation. It is sometimes described as a measure of downside risk in an investments context. For skewed distributions, the semivariance can provide additional information that a variance does not.

Generalizations

If x is a scalar complex-valued random variable, with values in $\mathbb{C}$, then its variance is $E\left[(x-\mu)(x-\mu)^*\right]$, where x^* is the complex conjugate of x This variance is a real scalar.

If X is a vector-valued random variable, with values in $\mathbb{R}^n$, and thought of as a column vector, then a natural generalization of variance is $E\left[(X-\mu)(X-\mu)^T\right]$, where $\mu = E(X)$ and X^T is the transpose of X and so is a row vector. The result is a positive semi-definite square matrix, commonly referred to as the variance-covariance matrix (or simply as the *covariance matrix*).

Another natural generalization of variance for such vector-valued random variables X which results in a scalar value rather than in a matrix, is obtained by interpreting the deviation between the random variable and its mean as the Euclidean distance. This results in $E\left[(X-\mu)^T(X-\mu)\right] = \text{tr}(C)$, which is the trace of the covariance matrix.

If X is a vector- and complex-valued random variable, with values in $\mathbb{C}^n$, then the covariance matrix is $E\left[(X-\mu)(X-\mu)^\dagger\right]$, where $X^\dagger$ is the conjugate transpose of X This matrix is also positive semi-definite and square.

Univariate Analysis

Univariate analysis is perhaps the simplest form of statistical analysis. Like other forms of statistics, it can be inferential or descriptive. The key fact is that only one variable is involved.

Descriptive Methods

Descriptive statistics describe a sample or population. They can be part of exploratory data analysis.

The appropriate statistic depends on the level of measurement. For nominal variables, a frequency table and a listing of the mode(s) is sufficient. For ordinal variables the median can be calculated as a measure of central tendency and the range (and variations of it) as a measure of dispersion. For interval level variables, the arithmetic mean (average) and standard deviation are added to the toolbox and, for ratio level variables, we add the geometric mean and harmonic mean as measures of central tendency and the coefficient of variation as a measure of dispersion.

For interval and ratio level data, further descriptors include the variable's skewness and kurtosis.

Inferential Methods

Inferential methods allow us to infer from a sample to a population. For a nominal variable a one-way chi-square (goodness of fit) test can help determine if our sample matches that of some population. For interval and ratio level data, a one-sample t-test can let us infer whether the mean in our sample matches some proposed number (typically 0). Other available tests of location include the one-sample sign test and Wilcoxon signed rank test.

Bivariate Analysis

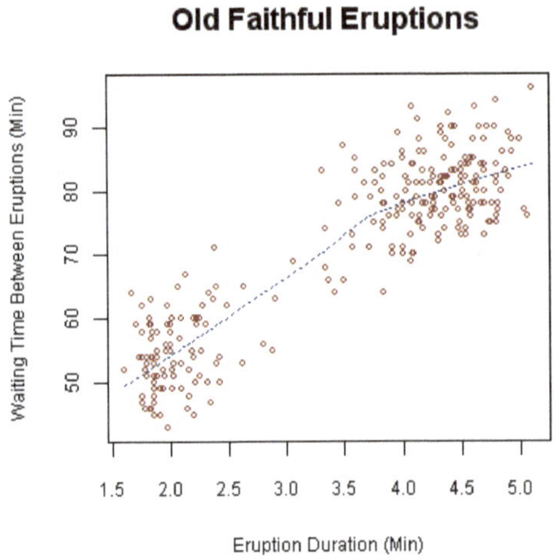

Waiting time between eruptions and the duration of the eruption for the Old Faithful Geyser in Yellowstone National Park, Wyoming, USA. This scatterplot suggests there are generally two "types" of eruptions: short-wait-short-duration, and long-wait-long-duration.

Bivariate analysis is one of the simplest forms of quantitative (statistical) analysis. It involves the analysis of two variables (often denoted as *X*, *Y*), for the purpose of determining the empirical relationship between them.

Bivariate analysis can be helpful in testing simple hypotheses of association. Bivariate analysis can help determine to what extent it becomes easier to know and predict a value for one variable (possibly a dependent variable) if we know the value of the other variable (possibly the independent variable).

Bivariate analysis can be contrasted with univariate analysis in which only one variable is analysed. Like univariate analysis, bivariate analysis can be descriptive or inferential. It is the analysis of the relationship between the two variables. Bivariate analysis is a simple (two variable) special case of multivariate analysis (where multiple relations between multiple variables are examined simultaneously).

There are 2 types, one is inferential and the other is descriptive.

When there is a Dependent Variable

If the dependent variable—the one whose value is determined to some extent by the other, independent variable— is a categorical variable, such as the preferred brand of cereal, then probit or logit regression (or multinomial probit or multinomial logit) can be used. If both variables are ordinal, meaning they are ranked in a sequence as first, second, etc., then a rank correlation coefficient can be computed. If just the dependent variable is ordinal, ordered probit or ordered logit can be used. If the dependent variable is continuous—either interval level or ratio level, such as a temperature scale or an income scale—then simple regression can be used.

If both variables are time series, a particular type of causality known as Granger causality can be tested for, and vector autoregression can be performed to examine the intertemporal linkages between the variables.

When there is not a Dependent Variable

When neither variable can be regarded as dependent on the other, regression is not appropriate but some form of correlation analysis may be.

Graphical Methods

Graphs that are appropriate for bivariate analysis depend on the type of variable. For two continuous variables, a scatterplot is a common graph. When one variable is categorical and the other continuous, a box plot is common and when both are categorical a mosaic plot is common. These graphs are part of descriptive statistics.

Structure Of Bivariate Econometric Modeling

The model starts with the condition that there are two variables in the system (say Y and X), where Y is dependent variable and X is independent variable. The sampling structures of Y and X are as follows:

$$Y = [Y_1, Y_2, Y_3, \ldots Y_n] \text{ and } X = [X_1, X_2, X_3, \ldots X_n]$$

The relation between the two can be presented as follows:

$$Y_i = \beta_1 + \beta_2 X_i + u_i$$

Where, β_1 is intercept and β_2 is slope. The u $[u_1, u_2, \ldots u_n]$ is error term, which is unexplained in nature, and i represent sample observation.

Reasons for Introducing Error Term in Econometric Modelling

- Exclusion of relevant variables
- Inclusion of unnecessary variables
- Human errors
- Wrong observations
- Misspecification of mathematical form of the model
- Poor proxy variables
- Variables cannot be measured but identified and so on.

The Graphic Representation of the Econometric Relationship Between Dependent and Independent Variable

The relationship can be established in non-linear format. The graphic representations between

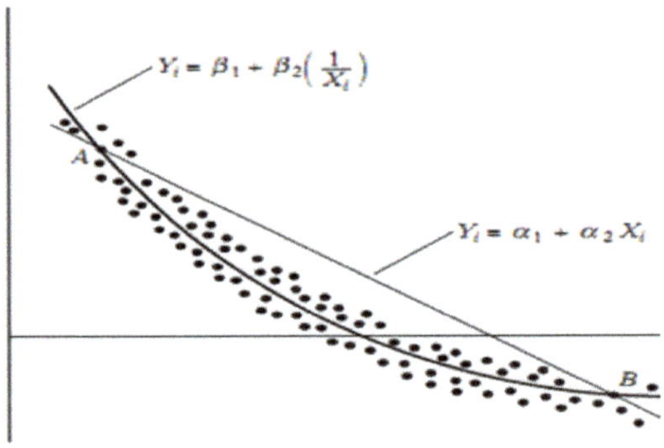

The Estimation Process

The objective of the above mentioned model is to have the estimated model for prediction and forecasting. The estimated model requires the estimation of two unknown parameters (β_1 and β_2). The process of the estimation is as follows:

$$\begin{aligned} Y_i &= \hat{\beta}_1 + \hat{\beta}_2 X_i + \hat{u}_i \\ &= \hat{Y}_i + \hat{u}_i \end{aligned}$$

where $\hat{Y}$ is read as "Y – hat" or "Y – cap"

$$\hat{Y}_i = \text{estimator of } E(Y|X_i)$$

$$\hat{\beta}_1 = \text{estimator of } \beta_1$$

$$\hat{\beta}_2 = \text{estimator of } \beta_2$$

The above is the sample regression function where the corresponding Betas are the estimated values and the u term is the error term of the residuals that is the difference between the actual and the estimated values. Y cap is the conditional mean of the Y variable in the population regression function.

$$\hat{u}_i = Y_i - \ddot{Y}_i$$
$$= Y_i - \hat{\beta}_1 - \hat{\beta}_2 X_i$$

$$\text{PRF, it can be exp ressed as}$$
$$Y_i = E(Y|X_i) + u_i$$

Now we have to choose the sample regression function in such a way that the sum of residuals that is $\sum \hat{u}_i = \sum (Y_i - \hat{Y}_i)$ is as small as possible. For convenience we take squared values of the residual term that is given below:

$$\sum \hat{u}_i^2 = \sum (Y_i - \hat{Y}_i)^2$$
$$= \sum (Y_i - \hat{\beta}_1 - \hat{\beta}_2 X_i)^2$$

The Estimated Model

As discussed the estimation process to have the estimated model. For Y and X, the estimated model is

$$Y_i = \hat{\beta}_1 + \hat{\beta}_2 X_i + \hat{u}_i$$
$$= \hat{Y}_i + \hat{u}_i$$

$$\text{Where, } \hat{\beta}_2 = \frac{\sum x_i y_i}{\sum x_i^2} \text{ and}$$

$$\hat{\beta}_2 = \frac{\sum X_i^2 \sum Y_i - \sum X_i \sum X_i Y_i}{n \sum x_i^2 - (X_i)^2}$$
$$= \overline{Y} - \hat{\beta}_2 \overline{X}$$

After specifying a model and estimating its parameters, it is good practice to check the reliability of the fitted model. If the estimated is reliable, you can go for prediction and forecasting. Or else, we have to redesign and re-estimate to have the best fitted model.

It is, in fact, a continuous process till you get a better fitted model. Here our primary concern is to check the followings:

- Violations of model assumptions, potentially resulting in bias and inaccurate standard errors
- Poor predictive performance
- Missing explanatory variables

The procedure to check the reliability of estimated econometric model depends upon:

- Specification Test
- Goodness Fit Test

The detail discussions of these two tests are as follows

Specification Test

The aim of this test is to know the validity of estimated parameters (i.e. β_1 and β_2). This follows the statistical process of hypothesis testing. We start with the hypothesis that both β_1 and β_2 are significantly different from zero. The t-statistics is deployed for the same. The process of t-test requires fixing the level of significance, t-calculated of β_1 and β_2 and t-tabulated of β_1 and β_2. The process starts with setting the null hypothesis and alternative hypothesis. This is as follows:

For β_1, H_0: $\beta_1 = 0$ against HA: $\beta_1 \neq 0$ and for β_2, H_0: $\beta_2 = 0$ against H_A: $\beta_2 \neq 0$. To validate this hypothesis, we have to first calculate t-β_1 and t-β_2. To have that, we must have variance (and standard errors) of $\beta_1$and β_2. This is as follows:

$$\operatorname{var}\left(\hat{\beta}_2\right)=\frac{\sigma^2}{\sum x_i^2}$$

$$\operatorname{se}\left(\hat{\beta}_2\right)=\frac{\sigma}{\sqrt{\sum x_i^2}}$$

$$\operatorname{var}\left(\hat{\beta}_1\right)=\frac{\sum X_i^2}{n\sum x_i^2}\sigma^2$$

$$\operatorname{se}\left(\hat{\beta}_1\right)=\sqrt{\frac{\sum X_i^2}{n\sum x_i^2}}\sigma$$

Now, the t- of corresponding parameters is calculated by this following formula:

$$t = \frac{\hat{\beta}_2 - \beta_2}{se\left(\hat{\beta}_2\right)} = \frac{\text{estimator} - \text{parameter}}{\text{estimated s tan dard error of estimator}}$$

In the similar fashion, we can calculate the β_1.

To test this hypothesis, we have to compute the acceptance region (confidence interval) or rejection region based upon the sampling distribution. This can be seen in the following diagram:

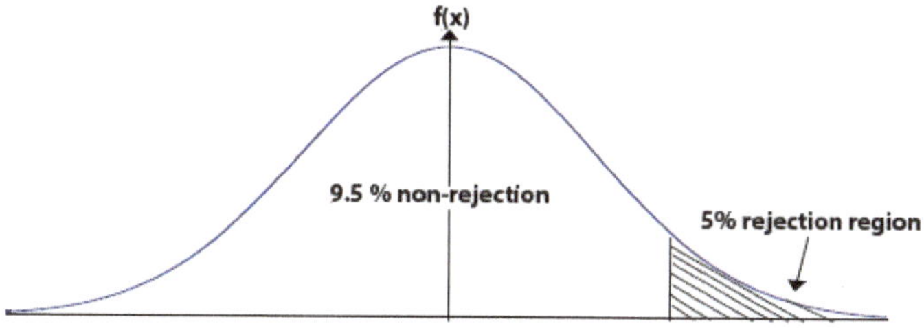

The above diagram represents a one tail test. Similarly we can have a two tailed test as well. We use the t-tables to obtain a critical value or values with which to compare the test statistic. We need some tabulated distribution with which to compare the estimated test statistics. Test statistics derived in this way can be shown to follow a t-distribution with n-2 degrees of freedom.

Goodness Fit Test

This test projects the overall fitness of the estimated model. It depends upon two statistical tools: coefficient of determination (R^2) and corresponding F- statistics. The entire process of overall fitness test is presented in the form of analysis of variance (ANOVA). The ANOVA brings two components: explained sum of squares (ESS) and residual sum of squares (RSS). The sum of these two (ESS and RSS) is called total sum of squares (TSS). The model is technically best fitted, if ESS is greater than to RSS and vice versa. On the basis of ESS, RSS and TSS, we calculate R^2 and F. R^2 is the ratio between ESS to TSS, which explains percentage variation of Y that is explained by X. And F is the ration between ESS and RSS with integration of degree of freedom. The F-test validity is very similar to t-test. The details structures of ANOVA are as follows:

Anova table

Source	SS	DF	MS	F
Treatments	SST	k-1	SST / (k-1)	MST/MSE
Error	SSE	N-k	SSE / (N-k)	
Total (corrected)	SS	N-1		

It can be noted that the value of R^2 lies between 0- 1. If R^2 is zero, the model is treated as unfit or misfit. If R^2 is one, the model is treated as best fitted. So, if it closer to zero, it is less fit and closer to one means high fit. If R^2 is one, then RSS will be zero and ESS will 100%; and if R^2 is zero, RSS will be 100 and ESS is zero. The details can be explained with a suitable example.

The Modelling Building Process

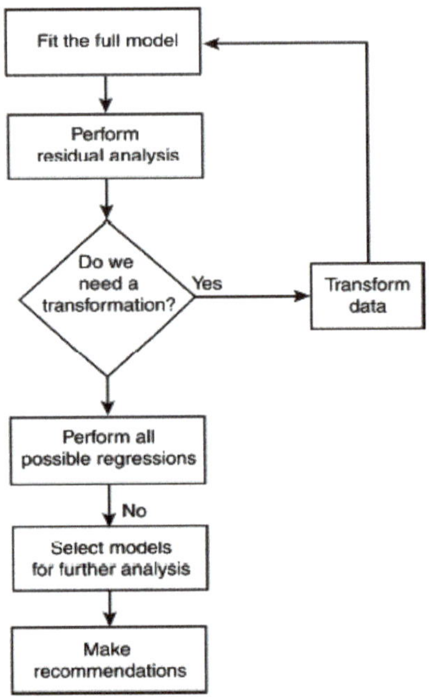

Flowchart of the model-building process

The Sample Problem

Units	Price	County	Size	Elevation	Sewer	Date	Flood	Distance
1	4.5	1	138.4	10	3000	-103	0	0.3
2	10.6	1	52	4	0	-103	0	2.5
3	1.7	0	16.1	0	2640	-98	1	10.3
4	5	0	1695.2	1	3500	-93	0	14
5	5	0	845	1	1000	-92	1	14
6	3.3	1	6.9	2	10000	-86	0	0
7	5.7	1	105.9	4	0	-68	0	0
8	6.2	1	56.6	4	0	-64	0	0
9	19.4	1	51.4	20	1300	-63	0	1.2
10	3.2	1	22.1	0	6000	-62	0	0
11	4.7	1	22.1	0	6000	-61	0	0
12	6.9	1	27.7	3	4500	-60	0	0

13	8.1	1	18.6	5	5000	-59	0	0.5
14	11.6	1	69.9	8	0	-59	0	4.4
15	19.3	1	145.7	10	0	-59	0	4.2
16	11.7	1	77.2	9	0	-59	0	4.5
17	13.3	1	26.2	8	0	-59	0	4.7
18	15.1	1	102.3	6	0	-59	0	4.9
19	12.4	1	49.5	11	0	-59	0	4.6
20	15.3	1	12.2	8	0	-59	0	5
21	12.2	0	320.6	0	4000	-54	0	16.5
22	18.1	1	9.9	5	0	-54	0	5.2
23	16.8	1	15.3	2	0	-53	0	5.5
24	5.9	0	55.2	0	1320	-49	1	11.9
25	4	0	116.2	2	900	-45	1	5.5
26	37.2	0	15	5	0	-39	0	7.2
27	18.2	0	23.4	5	4420	-39	0	5.5
28	15.1	0	132.8	2	2640	-35	0	10.2
29	22.9	0	12	5	3400	-16	0	5.5
30	15.2	0	67	2	900	-5	1	5.5
31	21.9	0	30.8	2	900	-4	0	5.5

$$\text{Price} = \beta_1 + \beta_2 * \text{Elevation} + u$$

Solutions:

Two parts:

Dependent Variable: Price

Independent variables: Elevation

Objectives:

With respect to Parameters:

If β_2 is found to be statistically significant then, we can say that elevation affects price;

So, we look for the significance of β_2

With respect to overall fit:

R^2

Tests:

Specification test: Coefficients

Goodness fit test: Model summary and ANOVA

Coefficients[a]

Model		Unstandardized Coefficients B	Unstandardized Coefficients Std. Error	Standardized Coefficients Beta	t	Sig.
1	(Constant)	9.057	1.946		4.655	.000
	Elevation	.623	.308	.352	2.024	.052

a. Dependent Variable: Price

Model Summary

Model	R	R Square	Adjusted R Square	Std. Error of the Estimate
1	.352a	.124	.094	7.34487

a. Predictors: (Constant), Elevation

ANOVAb

Model		Sum of Squares	df	Mean Square	F	Sig.
1	Regression	221.033	1	221.033	4.097	.052a
	Residual	1564.464	29	53.947		
	Total	1785.497	30			

a. Predictors: (Constant), Elevation

b. Dependent Variable: Price

Structure of Trivariate Econometric Modelling

The model starts with the condition that there are three variables in the system (say Y and X_2, X_3), where Y is dependent variable and X_2 and X_3 are independent variables. The sampling structures of Y and X are as follows:

$Y = [Y_{11}, Y_{12}, Y_{13}, \ldots Y_{1n}]$, $X_2 = [x_{21}, X_{22}, X_{23}, \ldots X_{2n}]$ and $X_3 = [x_{31}, X_{32}, X_{33}, \ldots X_{3n}]$ and The structure of trivariate econometric modelling can be presented as follows:

$$Y_i = \beta_1 + \beta_2 X_{2i} + \beta_3 X_{3i} + u_i$$

Where, β_1 is intercept, β_2 is slope to X_2 and β_3 is slope to X_3. The u $[u_1, u_2, \ldots u_n]$ is error term, which is unexplained in nature, and i represent sample observation. The relationship can be established in non-linear format also.

The Estimation Process

The objective of the above process is to have the estimated model for prediction and forecasting. The estimated model requires the estimation of three unknown parameters (β_1, β_2 and β_3). The process requires minimizing error sum squares by the OLS technique. This is as follows:

$$\bar{Y} = \hat{\beta}_1 + \hat{\beta}_2 \bar{X}_3$$

$$Y_i = \hat{\beta}_1 + \hat{\beta}_2 \bar{X}_{2i} + \hat{\beta}_3 \bar{X}_{3i} + \hat{u}_i$$

$$\min \sum \hat{u}_i^2 = \sum \left(Y_i - \hat{\beta}_1 + \hat{\beta}_2 \bar{X}_{2i} + \hat{\beta}_3 \bar{X}_{3i} \right)^2$$

We need the normal equations in order to find out the estimated values of the betas. The normal equations are as follows:

$$\bar{Y} = \hat{\beta}_1 + \hat{\beta}_2 \bar{X}_2 + \hat{\beta}_3 \bar{X}_3$$

$$\sum Y_i X_{2i} = \hat{\beta}_1 \sum X_{2i} + \hat{\beta}_2 \sum X_{2i}^2 + \hat{\beta}_3 \sum X_{2i} X_{3i}$$

$$\sum Y_i X_{3i} = \hat{\beta}_1 \sum X_{3i} + \hat{\beta}_2 \sum X_{2i} X_{3i} + \hat{\beta}_3 \sum X_{3i}^2$$

ANOVA[b]

The estimated values for the betas are as follows:

$$\hat{\beta}_1 = \bar{Y} - \hat{\beta}_2 \bar{X}_2 - \hat{\beta}_3 \bar{X}_3$$

$$\hat{\beta}_2 = \frac{\left(\sum y_i x_{2i}\right)\left(\sum x_{3i}^2\right) - \left(\sum y_i x_{3i}\right)\left(\sum x_{2i} x_{3i}\right)}{\left(\sum x_{2i}^2\right)\left(\sum x_{3i}^2\right) - \left(\sum x_{2i} x_{3i}\right)^2}$$

$$\hat{\beta}_3 = \frac{\left(\sum y_i x_{3i}\right)\left(\sum x_{2i}^2\right) - \left(\sum y_i x_{2i}\right)\left(\sum x_{2i} x_{3i}\right)}{\left(\sum x_{2i}^2\right)\left(\sum x_{3i}^2\right) - \left(\sum x_{2i} x_{3i}\right)^2}$$

The Reliability Of Estimated Model

The procedure to check the reliability of estimated econometric model depends upon:

- Specification test
- Goodness fit test

The detail discussions of these two tests are as follows

Specification Test

The aim of this test is to know the validity of estimated parameters (i.e. β_1, β_2 and β_3). This follows the statistical process of hypothesis testing. We start with the hypothesis that β_1, β_2 and β_3 are significantly different from zero. The t-statistics is deployed for the same. The process of t test requires fixing the level of significance, t-calculated of β_1, β_2 and β_3 and t-tabulated of β_1, β_2 and β_3. The process starts with setting the null hypothesis and alternative hypothesis. This is as follows:

For β_1, H_0: $\beta_1 = 0$ against H_A: $\beta_1 \neq 0$; and for β_2, H_0: $\beta_2 = 0$ against H_A: $\beta_2 \neq 0$; and for β_3, H_0: $\beta_3 = 0$ against H_A: $\beta_3 \neq 0$

To validate this hypothesis, we have to first calculate t-β_1, t-β_2 and t-β_3. To have that, we must have variance (and standard errors) of β_1, β_2 and β_3. This is as follows:

$$\operatorname{var}\left(\hat{\beta}_1\right)=\left[\frac{1}{n}+\frac{\bar{X}_2^2\sum x_{3i}^2+\bar{X}_3^2\sum x_{2i}^2-2\bar{X}_2\bar{X}_3\sum x_{2i}x_{3i}}{\sum x_{2i}^2\sum x_{3i}^2-\left(\sum x_{2i}x_{3i}\right)^2}\right].\sigma^2$$

$$\operatorname{se}\left(\hat{\beta}_1\right)=+\sqrt{\operatorname{var}\left(\hat{\beta}_1\right)}$$

$$\operatorname{var}\left(\hat{\beta}_2\right)=\frac{\sum x_{3i}^2}{\left(\sum x_{2i}^2\right)\left(\sum x_{3i}^2\right)-\left(\sum x_{2i}x_{3i}\right)^2}\sigma^2$$

$$\operatorname{se}\left(\hat{\beta}_2\right)=+\sqrt{\operatorname{var}\left(\hat{\beta}_2\right)}$$

$$\operatorname{var}\left(\hat{\beta}_3\right)=\frac{\sum x_{2i}^2}{\left(\sum x_{2i}^2\right)\left(\sum x_{3i}^2\right)-\left(\sum x_{2i}x_{3i}\right)^2}\sigma^2$$

$$\operatorname{var}\left(\hat{\beta}_3\right)=\frac{\sigma^2}{\sum x_{3i}^2\left(1-r_{23}^2\right)}$$

$$\operatorname{se}\left(\hat{\beta}_3\right)=+\sqrt{\operatorname{var}\left(\hat{\beta}_3\right)}$$

Now, the t- of corresponding parameters is calculated by this following formula:

$$t=\frac{\hat{\beta}_2-\beta_2}{\operatorname{se}\left(\hat{\beta}_2\right)}=\frac{\text{estimator}-\text{parameter}}{\text{estimated s tan dard error of estimator}}$$

In the similar fashion, we can calculate the β_1 and β_3.

To test this hypothesis, we have to compute the acceptance region (confidence interval) or rejection region based upon the sampling distribution. This can be seen in the following diagram:

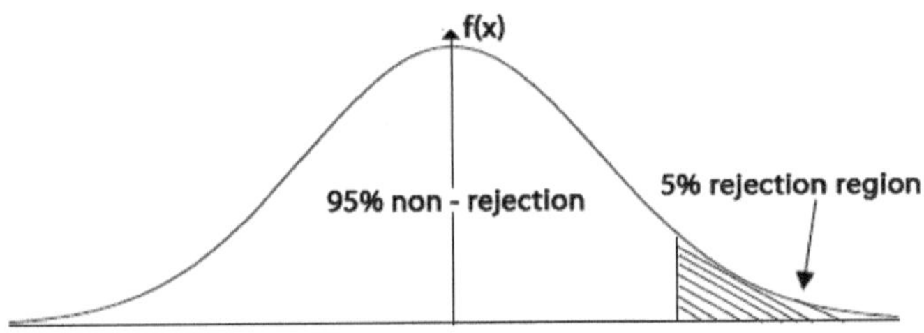

The above diagram represents a one tail test. Similarly we can have a two tailed test as well. We use the t-tables to obtain a critical value or values with which to compare the test statistic. We need some tabulated distribution with which to compare the estimated test statistics. Test statistics derived in this way can be shown to follow a t-distribution with n-2 degrees of freedom.

Goodness Fit Test

This test projects the overall fitness of the estimated model. It depends upon two statistical tools: coefficient of determination (R^2) and corresponding F- statistics. The entire process of overall fitness test is presented in the form of analysis of variance (ANOVA). The ANOVA brings two components: explained sum of squares (ESS) and residual sum of squares (RSS). The sum of these two (ESS and RSS) is called total sum of squares (TSS). The model is technically best fitted, if ESS is greater than to RSS and vice versa. On the basis of ESS, RSS and TSS, we calculate R^2 and F. R^2 is the ratio between ESS to TSS, which explains percentage variation of Y that is explained by X. This is as follows:

$$R^2 = \frac{ESS}{TSS}$$

$$= \frac{\hat{\beta}_2 \sum y_i x_{2i} + \hat{\beta}_3 \sum y_i x_{3i}}{\sum y_i^2}$$

Similarly, we can calculate F-stat. which is the ration between ESS and RSS with integration of degree of freedom. The F-test validity is very similar to t-test that explained above in the previous section. The details structures of ANOVA are as follows:

ANOVA table

Source	SS	DF	MS	F
Treatments	SST	k-1	SST / (k-1)	MST/MSE
Error	SSE	N-k	SSE / (N-k)	
Total (corrected)	SS	N-1		

It can be noted that the value of R^2 lies between 0- 1. If R^2 is zero, the model is treated as unfit or misfit. If R^2 is one, the model is treated as best fitted. So, if it closer to zero, it is less fit and closer to one means high fit. If R^2 is one, then RSS will be zero and ESS will 100%; and if R^2 is zero, RSS will be 100 and ESS is zero. The details can be explained with a suitable example. It is simply the standard deviation of the Y values about the estimated regression line and is often used as a summary measure of the "goodness of fit" of the estimated regression line.

Multivariate Analysis

Multivariate analysis (MVA) is based on the statistical principle of multivariate statistics, which involves observation and analysis of more than one statistical outcome variable at a time. In design and analysis, the technique is used to perform trade studies across multiple dimensions while taking into account the effects of all variables on the responses of interest.

Uses for multivariate analysis include:

- design for capability (also known as capability-based design)
- inverse design, where any variable can be treated as an independent variable
- Analysis of Alternatives (AoA), the selection of concepts to fulfil a customer need
- analysis of concepts with respect to changing scenarios
- identification of critical design-drivers and correlations across hierarchical levels.

Multivariate analysis can be complicated by the desire to include physics-based analysis to calculate the effects of variables for a hierarchical "system-of-systems". Often, studies that wish to use multivariate analysis are stalled by the dimensionality of the problem. These concerns are often eased through the use of surrogate models, highly accurate approximations of the physics-based code. Since surrogate models take the form of an equation, they can be evaluated very quickly. This becomes an enabler for large-scale MVA studies: while a Monte Carlo simulation across the design space is difficult with physics-based codes, it becomes trivial when evaluating surrogate models, which often take the form of response-surface equations.

Factor Analysis

Overview: Factor analysis is used to uncover the latent structure (dimensions) of a set of variables. It reduces attribute space from a larger number of variables to a smaller number of factors. Factor analysis originated a century ago with Charles Spearman's attempts to show that a wide variety of mental tests could be explained by a single underlying intelligence factor.

Applications

- To reduce a large number of variables to a smaller number of factors for data modeling
- To validate a scale or index by demonstrating that its constituent items load on the same factor, and to drop proposed scale items which cross-load on more than one factor.
- To select a subset of variables from a larger set, based on which original variables have the highest correlations with some other factors.
- To create a set of factors to be treated as uncorrelated variables as one approach to handling multi-collinearity in such procedures as multiple regression

- To integrate different data in earth sciences and geo-modeling. For example, integration of drilling and seismic data

Factor analysis is part of the general linear model (GLM) family of procedures and makes many of the same assumptions as multiple regression, but it uses multiple outcomes.

History

Anderson's 1958 textbook, *An Introduction to Multivariate Analysis*, educated a generation of theorists and applied statisticians; Anderson's book emphasizes hypothesis testing via likelihood ratio tests and the properties of power functions: Admissibility, unbiasedness and monotonicity.

Commercial

- NCSS (statistical software) includes multivariate analysis.
- The Unscrambler® X is a multivariate analysis tool.

Structure of Multivariate Econometric Modeling

The model starts with the condition that there are more variables in the system (say Y, X_2, X_3,....X_k), where Y is dependent variable and X_2, X_3, ...X_k are independent variables. The sampling structures of Y and Xs are as follows:

$Y = [Y_{11}, Y_{12}, Y_{13},....Y_{1n}]$, $X_2 = [x_{21}, X_{22}, X_{23},....X_{2n}]$, $X_3 = [x_{31}, X_{32}, X_{33},....X_{3n}]$ and $X_k = [X_{k1}, X_{k2}, X_{k3},....X_{kn}]$

The structure of multivariate econometric modelling can be presented as follows:

$$Y_i = \beta_1 + \beta_2 X_{2i} + \beta_3 X_{3i} + \ldots + \beta_k X_{ki} + u_i$$

$$\hat{\beta}_1 = \bar{Y} - \beta_2 \bar{X}_2 - \beta_3 \bar{X}_3 - \ldots - \beta_k \bar{X}_k$$

Where, β_1 is intercept, β_2 is slope to X_2, β_3, is slope to X_3 and β_k is slope to X_k. The u [u_1, u_2,...u_n] is error term, which is unexplained in nature, and i represents sample observation.

The Estimation Process

The objective of the above process is to have the estimated model for prediction and forecasting. The estimated model requires the estimation of k unknown parameters (β_1, β_2, β_3,...β_k). The process requires minimizing error sum squares by the OLS technique. This is as follows:

$$Y_i = \beta_1 + \beta_2 X_{2i} + \beta_3 X_{3i} + \ldots + \beta_k X_{ki} + u_i$$
$$\hat{\beta}_1 = \bar{Y} - \beta_2 \bar{X}_2 - \beta_3 \bar{X}_3 - \ldots - \beta_k \bar{X}_k$$
$$\sum \hat{u}_i^2 = \sum \left(Y_i - \hat{\beta}_1 - \hat{\beta}_2 X_{2i} - \ldots - \beta_k \bar{X}_{ki} \right)^2$$

We need the normal equations in order to find out the estimated values of the betas. The normal equations are as follows:

$$\sum Y_i = n\hat{\beta}_1 + \hat{\beta}_2 \sum X_{2i} + \hat{\beta}_3 \sum X_{3i} + \ldots + \hat{\beta}_k \sum X_{ki}$$
$$\sum Y_i X_{2i} = \hat{\beta}_1 \sum X_{2i} + \hat{\beta}_2 \sum X_{2i}^2 + \hat{\beta}_3 \sum X_{2i} X_{3i} + \ldots + \hat{\beta}_k \sum X_{2i} X_{ki}$$
$$\sum Y_i X_{3i} = \hat{\beta}_1 \sum X_{3i} + \hat{\beta}_2 \sum X_{2i} X_{3i} + \hat{\beta}_3 \sum X_{3i}^2 + \ldots + \hat{\beta}_k \sum X_{3i} X_{ki}$$

....

$$\sum Y_i X_{ki} = \hat{\beta}_1 \sum X_{ki} + \hat{\beta}_2 \sum X_{2i} X_{ki} + \hat{\beta}_3 \sum X_{3i} X_{ki} + \ldots + \hat{\beta}_k \sum X_{ki}^2$$

The Reliability of Estimated Model

The procedure to check the reliability of estimated econometric model depends upon:

- Specification Test
- Goodness Fit Test

The detail discussions of these two tests are as follows

Specification Test

The aim of this test is to know the validity of estimated parameters (i.e. β_1, β_2, β_3,...β_k). This follows the statistical process of hypothesis testing. We start with the hypothesis that β_1, β_2, β_3,...β_k are significantly different from zero. The t-statistics is deployed for the same. The process of t-test requires fixing the level of significance, t-calculated of β_1, β_2, β_3,...β_k and t-tabulated of β_1, β_2, β_3,...β_k. The process starts with setting the null hypothesis and alternative hypothesis. This is as follows:

For β_1, H_0: $\beta_1 = 0$ against H_A: $\beta_1 \neq 0$; and for β_2, H_0: $\beta_2 = 0$ against H_A: $\beta_2 \neq 0$; for β_3, H_0: $\beta_3 = 0$ against H_A: $\beta_3 \neq 0$; and forβ_k, H_0: $\beta_k = 0$ against H_A: $\beta_k \neq 0$

To validate this hypothesis, we have to first calculate t- β_1, t-β_2, t- β_3,... t-β_k To have that, we must have variance (and standard errors) of β_1, β_2, β_3,...β_k.

Now, the t- of corresponding parameters is calculated by this following formula:

$$t = \frac{\hat{\beta}_2 - \beta_2}{se\left(\hat{\beta}_2\right)} = \frac{\text{estimator} - \text{parameter}}{\text{estimated standard error of estimator}}$$

In the similar fashion, we can calculate for other parameters.

To test this hypothesis, we have to compute the acceptance region (confidence interval) or rejection region based upon the sampling distribution. This can be seen in the following diagram:

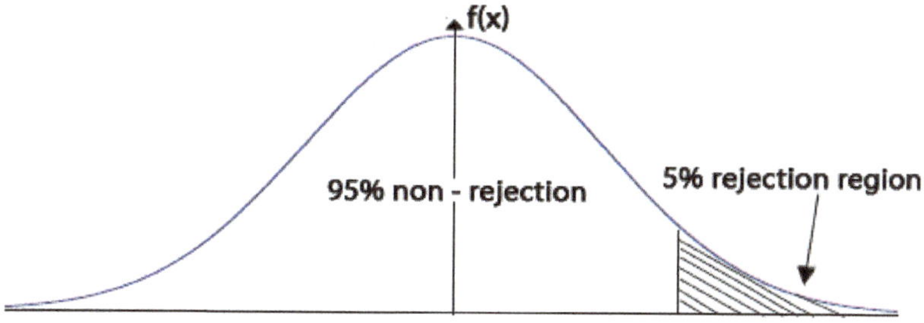

The above diagram represents a one tail test. Similarly we can have a two tailed test as well. We use the t-tables to obtain a critical value or values with which to compare the test statistic. We need some tabulated distribution with which to compare the estimated test statistics. Test statistics derived in this way can be shown to follow a t-distribution with n-2 degrees of freedom.

Goodness Fit Test

This test projects the overall fitness of the estimated model. It depends upon two statistical tools: coefficient of determination (R^2) and corresponding F- statistics. The entire process of overall fitness test is presented in the form of analysis of variance (ANOVA). The ANOVA brings two components: explained sum of squares (ESS) and residual sum of squares (RSS). The sum of these two (ESS and RSS) is called total sum of squares (TSS). The model is technically best fitted, if ESS is greater than to RSS and vice versa. On the basis of ESS, RSS and TSS, we calculate R^2 and F. R^2 is the ratio between ESS to TSS, which explains percentage variation of Y that is explained by X. Similarly, we can calculate F-stat. which is the ration between ESS and RSS with integration of degree of freedom. The F-test validity is very similar to t-test. The details structures of ANOVA are as follows:

ANOVA TABLE IN TERMS OF R^2		
Source of variation	SS	df
Due to regression	$R^2\left(\sum y_i^2\right)$	2
Due to residuals	$\left(1-R^2\right)\left(\sum y_i^2\right)$	$n-3$
Total	$\sum y_i^2$	$n-1$

Decision Rule. Given the k – variable regression model

$$Y_i = \beta_1 + \beta_2 X_{2i} + \beta_3 X_{3i} + \ldots + \beta_k X_{ki} + u_i$$

To test the hypothesis

$$H_0 : \beta_2 = \beta_3 = \ldots = \beta_k = 0$$

(i.e., all slope coefficients are simultaneously zero) versus

H_1 : Not all slope coefficients are simultaneously zero

compute

$$F = \frac{ESS/df}{RSS/df} = \frac{ESS/(k-1)}{RSS/(n-k)}$$

It can be noted that the value of R^2 lies between 0- 1. If R^2 is zero, the model is treated as unfit or misfit. If R^2 is one, the model is treated as best fitted. So, if it closer to zero, it is less fit and closer to one means high fit. If R^2 is one, then RSS will be zero and ESS will 100%; and if R^2 is zero, RSS will be 100 and ESS is zero. The details can be explained with a suitable example. It is simply the standard deviation of the Y values about the estimated regression line and is often used as a summary measure of the "goodness of fit" of the estimated regression line.

The Sample Problem

Units	Price	County	Size	Elevation	Sewer	Date	Flood	Distance
1	4.5	1	138.4	10	3000	-103	0	0.3
2	10.6	1	52	4	0	-103	0	2.5
3	1.7	0	16.1	0	2640	-98	1	10.3
4	5	0	1695.2	1	3500	-93	0	14
5	5	0	845	1	1000	-92	1	14
6	3.3	1	6.9	2	10000	-86	0	0
7	5.7	1	105.9	4	0	-68	0	0
8	6.2	1	56.6	4	0	-64	0	0
9	19.4	1	51.4	20	1300	-63	0	1.2
10	3.2	1	22.1	0	6000	-62	0	0
11	4.7	1	22.1	0	6000	-61	0	0
12	6.9	1	27.7	3	4500	-60	0	0
13	8.1	1	18.6	5	5000	-59	0	0.5
14	11.6	1	69.9	8	0	-59	0	4.4
15	19.3	1	145.7	10	0	-59	0	4.2
16	11.7	1	77.2	9	0	-59	0	4.5
17	13.3	1	26.2	8	0	-59	0	4.7
18	15.1	1	102.3	6	0	-59	0	4.9

19	12.4	1	49.5	11	0	-59	0	4.6
20	15.3	1	12.2	8	0	-59	0	5
21	12.2	0	320.6	0	4000	-54	0	16.5
22	18.1	1	9.9	5	0	-54	0	5.2
23	16.8	1	15.3	2	0	-53	0	5.5
24	5.9	0	55.2	0	1320	-49	1	11.9
25	4	0	116.2	2	900	-45	1	5.5
26	37.2	0	15	5	0	-39	0	7.2
27	18.2	0	23.4	5	4420	-39	0	5.5
28	15.1	0	132.8	2	2640	-35	0	10.2
29	22.9	0	12	5	3400	-16	0	5.5
30	15.2	0	67	2	900	-5	1	5.5
31	21.9	0	30.8	2	900	-4	0	5.5

$$\text{Price} = \beta_1 + \beta_2 * \text{size} + \beta_3 * \text{Elevation} + u$$

Solutions:

Two parts:

Dependent Variable: Price

Independent variables: size and Elevation

Objectives:

With respect to Parameters:

If β_2 is found to be statistically significant then, we can say that country affects price;

If β_3 is found to be statistically significant then, we can say that size affects price;

So, we look for the significance of β_2 and β_3

With respect to overall fit:

R^2 and Adjusted R^2

Tests:

Specification test: Coefficients

Goodness fit test: Model summary and ANOVA

Coefficientsa						
Model		Unstandardized Coefficients		Standardized Coefficients	t	Sig.
		B	Std. Error	Beta		
1	(Constant)	9.929	2.143		4.634	.000
	Size	-.004	.004	-.174	-.976	.337
	Elevation	.559	.315	.315	1.773	.087
a. Dependent Variable: Price						

ANOVA[b]						
Model		Sum of Squares	df	Mean Square	F	Sig.
1	Regression	272.515	2	136.258	2.522	.098a
	Residual	1512.982	28	54.035		
	Total	1785.497	30			
a. Predictors: (Constant), Elevation, Size						
b. Dependent Variable: Price						

Model Summary				
Model	R	R Square	Adjusted R Square	Std. Error of the Estimate
1	.391a	.153	.092	7.35086
a. Predictors: (Constant), Elevation, Size				

References

- Trochim, William M. K. (2006). "Descriptive statistics". Research Methods Knowledge Base. Retrieved 14 March 2011
- E. J. Gumbel (1947). "The Distribution of the Range". The Annals of Mathematical Statistics. 18 (3): 384–412. JSTOR 2235736. doi:10.1214/aoms/1177730387
- Weisberg H.F (1992) Central Tendency and Variability, Sage University Paper Series on Quantitative Applications in the Social Sciences, ISBN 0-8039-4007-6 p.2
- Rothschild, Michael; Stiglitz, Joseph (1970). "Increasing risk I: A definition". Journal of Economic Theory. 2 (3): 225–243. doi:10.1016/0022-0531(70)90038-4
- H. O. Hartley; H. A. David (1954). "Universal Bounds for Mean Range and Extreme Observation". The Annals of Mathematical Statistics. 25 (1): 85–99. JSTOR 2236514. doi:10.1214/aoms/1177728848
- Tsimashenka, I.; Knottenbelt, W.; Harrison, P. (2012). "Controlling Variability in Split-Merge Systems". Analytical and Stochastic Modeling Techniques and Applications (PDF). Lecture Notes in Computer Science. 7314. p. 165. ISBN 978-3-642-30781-2. doi:10.1007/978-3-642-30782-9_12
- Evans, D. L.; Leemis, L. M.; Drew, J. H. (2006). "The Distribution of Order Statistics for Discrete Random Variables with Applications to Bootstrapping". INFORMS Journal on Computing. 18: 19. doi:10.1287/ijoc.1040.0105
- L. H. C. Tippett (1925). "On the Extreme Individuals and the Range of Samples Taken from a Normal Population". Biometrika. 17 (3/4): 364–387. JSTOR 2332087. doi:10.1093/biomet/17.3-4.364
- Kader, Gary (March 1999). "Means and MADS". Mathematics Teaching in the Middle School. 4 (6): 398–403. Retrieved 20 February 2013
- Bertil., Westergren, (1988). Beta [beta] mathematics handbook : concepts, theorems, methods, algorithms, formulas, graphs, tables. Studentlitteratur. p. 348. ISBN 9144250517. OCLC 18454776

- Paul R. Rider (1951). "The Distribution of the Range in Samples from a Discrete Rectangular Population". Journal of the American Statistical Association. 46 (255): 375–378. JSTOR 2280515. doi:10.1080/01621459.1951.10500796
- Irving W. Burr (1955). "Calculation of Exact Sampling Distribution of Ranges from a Discrete Population". The Annals of Mathematical Statistics. 26 (3): 530–532. JSTOR 2236482. doi:10.1214/aoms/1177728500
- Nahmias, Steven; Olsen, Tava Lennon (2015), Production and Operations Analysis (7th ed.), Waveland Press, p. 62, ISBN 9781478628248, MAD is often the preferred method of measuring the forecast error because it does not require squaring
- Habib, Elsayed A.E. (2011). "Correlation coefficients based on mean absolute deviation about median". International Journal of Statistics and Systems. 6 (4): 413–428
- Abdel-Aty, S. H. (1954). "Ordered variables in discontinuous distributions". Statistica Neerlandica. 8 (2): 61–82. doi:10.1111/j.1467-9574.1954.tb00442.x
- "CERN experiments observe particle consistent with long-sought Higgs boson | CERN press office". Press.web.cern.ch. 2012-07-04. Retrieved 2015-05-30
- Everitt, Brian (1998). The Cambridge Dictionary of Statistics. Cambridge, UK New York: Cambridge University Press. ISBN 0521593468
- Siotani, M. (1956). "Order statistics for discrete case with a numerical application to the binomial distribution". Annals of the Institute of Statistical Mathematics. 8: 95–96. doi:10.1007/BF02863574

4

Regression Analysis: An Econometric Model

The process used for assessing the relationship between variables is known as regression analysis. It is mostly used for prediction and forecasting. The chapter strategically encompasses and incorporates the major components and key concepts of econometrics, providing a complete understanding.

Regression Analysis

In statistical modeling, regression analysis is a statistical process for estimating the relationships among variables. It includes many techniques for modeling and analyzing several variables, when the focus is on the relationship between a dependent variable and one or more independent variables (or 'predictors'). More specifically, regression analysis helps one understand how the typical value of the dependent variable (or 'criterion variable') changes when any one of the independent variables is varied, while the other independent variables are held fixed. Most commonly, regression analysis estimates the conditional expectation of the dependent variable given the independent variables – that is, the average value of the dependent variable when the independent variables are fixed. Less commonly, the focus is on a quantile, or other location parameter of the conditional distribution of the dependent variable given the independent variables. In all cases, the estimation target is a function of the independent variables called the regression function. In regression analysis, it is also of interest to characterize the variation of the dependent variable around the regression function which can be described by a probability distribution. A related but distinct approach is necessary condition analysis (NCA), which estimates the maximum (rather than average) value of the dependent variable for a given value of the independent variable (ceiling line rather than central line) in order to identify what value of the independent variable is necessary but not sufficient for a given value of the dependent variable.

Regression analysis is widely used for prediction and forecasting, where its use has substantial overlap with the field of machine learning. Regression analysis is also used to understand which among the independent variables are related to the dependent variable, and to explore the forms of these relationships. In restricted circumstances, regression analysis can be used to infer causal relationships between the independent and dependent variables. However this can lead to illusions or false relationships, so caution is advisable; for example, correlation does not imply causation.

Many techniques for carrying out regression analysis have been developed. Familiar methods such as linear regression and ordinary least squares regression are parametric, in that the regression function is defined in terms of a finite number of unknown parameters that are estimated from the data. Nonparametric regression refers to techniques that allow the regression function to lie in a specified set of functions, which may be infinite-dimensional.

The performance of regression analysis methods in practice depends on the form of the data generating process, and how it relates to the regression approach being used. Since the true form of the data-generating process is generally not known, regression analysis often depends to some extent on making assumptions about this process. These assumptions are sometimes testable if a sufficient quantity of data is available. Regression models for prediction are often useful even when the assumptions are moderately violated, although they may not perform optimally. However, in many applications, especially with small effects or questions of causality based on observational data, regression methods can give misleading results.

In a narrower sense, regression may refer specifically to the estimation of continuous response variables, as opposed to the discrete response variables used in classification. The case of a continuous output variable may be more specifically referred to as metric regression to distinguish it from related problems.

History

The earliest form of regression was the method of least squares, which was published by Legendre in 1805, and by Gauss in 1809. Legendre and Gauss both applied the method to the problem of determining, from astronomical observations, the orbits of bodies about the Sun (mostly comets, but also later the then newly discovered minor planets). Gauss published a further development of the theory of least squares in 1821, including a version of the Gauss–Markov theorem.

The term "regression" was coined by Francis Galton in the nineteenth century to describe a biological phenomenon. The phenomenon was that the heights of descendants of tall ancestors tend to regress down towards a normal average (a phenomenon also known as regression toward the mean). For Galton, regression had only this biological meaning, but his work was later extended by Udny Yule and Karl Pearson to a more general statistical context. In the work of Yule and Pearson, the joint distribution of the response and explanatory variables is assumed to be Gaussian. This assumption was weakened by R.A. Fisher in his works of 1922 and 1925. Fisher assumed that the conditional distribution of the response variable is Gaussian, but the joint distribution need not be. In this respect, Fisher's assumption is closer to Gauss's formulation of 1821.

In the 1950s and 1960s, economists used electromechanical desk calculators to calculate regressions. Before 1970, it sometimes took up to 24 hours to receive the result from one regression.

Regression methods continue to be an area of active research. In recent decades, new methods have been developed for robust regression, regression involving correlated responses such as time series and growth curves, regression in which the predictor (independent variable) or response variables are curves, images, graphs, or other complex data objects, regression methods accommodating various types of missing data, nonparametric regression, Bayesian methods for regression, regression in which the predictor variables are measured with error, regression with more predictor variables than observations, and causal inference with regression.

Regression Models

Regression models involve the following variables:

- The unknown parameters, denoted as β, which may represent a scalar or a vector.
- The independent variables, X.
- The dependent variable, Y.

In various fields of application, different terminologies are used in place of dependent and independent variables.

A regression model relates Y to a function of X and β.

$$Y \approx f(X, \beta)$$

The approximation is usually formalized as $E(Y \mid X) = f(X, \beta)$. To carry out regression analysis, the form of the function f must be specified. Sometimes the form of this function is based on knowledge about the relationship between Y and X that does not rely on the data. If no such knowledge is available, a flexible or convenient form for f is chosen.

Assume now that the vector of unknown parameters β is of length k. In order to perform a regression analysis the user must provide information about the dependent variable Y:

- If N data points of the form (Y, X) are observed, where $N < k$, most classical approaches to regression analysis cannot be performed: since the system of equations defining the regression model is underdetermined, there are not enough data to recover β.
- If exactly $N = k$ data points are observed, and the function f is linear, the equations $Y = f(X, \beta)$ can be solved exactly rather than approximately. This reduces to solving a set of N equations with N unknowns (the elements of β), which has a unique solution as long as the X are linearly independent. If f is nonlinear, a solution may not exist, or many solutions may exist.

- The most common situation is where $N > k$ data points are observed. In this case, there is enough information in the data to estimate a unique value for β that best fits the data in some sense, and the regression model when applied to the data can be viewed as an overdetermined system in β.

In the last case, the regression analysis provides the tools for:

1. Finding a solution for unknown parameters β that will, for example, minimize the distance between the measured and predicted values of the dependent variable Y (also known as method of least squares).

2. Under certain statistical assumptions, the regression analysis uses the surplus of information to provide statistical information about the unknown parameters β and predicted values of the dependent variable Y.

Necessary Number of Independent Measurements

Consider a regression model which has three unknown parameters, β_0, β_1, and β_2. Suppose an experimenter performs 10 measurements all at exactly the same value of independent variable vector X (which contains the independent variables X_1, X_2, and X_3). In this case, regression analysis fails to give a unique set of estimated values for the three unknown parameters; the experimenter did not provide enough information. The best one can do is to estimate the average value and the standard deviation of the dependent variable Y. Similarly, measuring at two different values of X would give enough data for a regression with two unknowns, but not for three or more unknowns.

If the experimenter had performed measurements at three different values of the independent variable vector X, then regression analysis would provide a unique set of estimates for the three unknown parameters in β.

In the case of general linear regression, the above statement is equivalent to the requirement that the matrix X^TX is invertible.

Statistical Assumptions

When the number of measurements, N, is larger than the number of unknown parameters, k, and the measurement errors ε_i are normally distributed then *the excess of information* contained in $(N - k)$ measurements is used to make statistical predictions about the unknown parameters. This excess of information is referred to as the degrees of freedom of the regression.

Underlying Assumptions

Classical assumptions for regression analysis include:

- The sample is representative of the population for the inference prediction.

- The error is a random variable with a mean of zero conditional on the explanatory variables.
- The independent variables are measured with no error. (Note: If this is not so, modeling may be done instead using errors-in-variables model techniques).
- The independent variables (predictors) are linearly independent, i.e. it is not possible to express any predictor as a linear combination of the others.
- The errors are uncorrelated, that is, the variance–covariance matrix of the errors is diagonal and each non-zero element is the variance of the error.
- The variance of the error is constant across observations (homoscedasticity). If not, weighted least squares or other methods might instead be used.

These are sufficient conditions for the least-squares estimator to possess desirable properties; in particular, these assumptions imply that the parameter estimates will be unbiased, consistent, and efficient in the class of linear unbiased estimators. It is important to note that actual data rarely satisfies the assumptions. That is, the method is used even though the assumptions are not true. Variation from the assumptions can sometimes be used as a measure of how far the model is from being useful. Many of these assumptions may be relaxed in more advanced treatments. Reports of statistical analyses usually include analyses of tests on the sample data and methodology for the fit and usefulness of the model.

Assumptions include the geometrical support of the variables. Independent and dependent variables often refer to values measured at point locations. There may be spatial trends and spatial autocorrelation in the variables that violate statistical assumptions of regression. Geographic weighted regression is one technique to deal with such data. Also, variables may include values aggregated by areas. With aggregated data the modifiable areal unit problem can cause extreme variation in regression parameters. When analyzing data aggregated by political boundaries, postal codes or census areas results may be very distinct with a different choice of units.

Linear Regression

In linear regression, the model specification is that the dependent variable, y_i is a linear combination of the *parameters* (but need not be linear in the *independent variables*). For example, in simple linear regression for modeling n data points there is one independent variable: x_i, and two parameters, β_0 and β_1:

straight line: $y_i = \beta_0 + \beta_1 x_i + \varepsilon_i, \quad i = 1, \ldots, n.$

In multiple linear regression, there are several independent variables or functions of independent variables.

Adding a term in x_i^2 to the preceding regression gives:

parabola: $y_i = \beta_0 + \beta_1 x_i + \beta_2 x_i^2 + \varepsilon_i, i = 1, \ldots, n.$

This is still linear regression; although the expression on the right hand side is quadratic in the independent variable x_i, it is linear in the parameters β_0, β_1 and β_2

In both cases, ε_i is an error term and the subscript i indexes a particular observation.

Returning our attention to the straight line case: Given a random sample from the population, we estimate the population parameters and obtain the sample linear regression model:

$$\widehat{y_i} = \hat{\beta}_0 + \hat{\beta}_1 x_i.$$

The residual, $e_i = y_i - \hat{y}_i$, is the difference between the value of the dependent variable predicted by the model, $\widehat{y_i}$, and the true value of the dependent variable, y_i. One method of estimation is ordinary least squares. This method obtains parameter estimates that minimize the sum of squared residuals, SSE, also sometimes denoted RSS:

$$SSE = \sum_{i=1}^{n} e_i^2.$$

Minimization of this function results in a set of normal equations, a set of simultaneous linear equations in the parameters, which are solved to yield the parameter estimators, $\hat{\beta}_0, \hat{\beta}_1$.

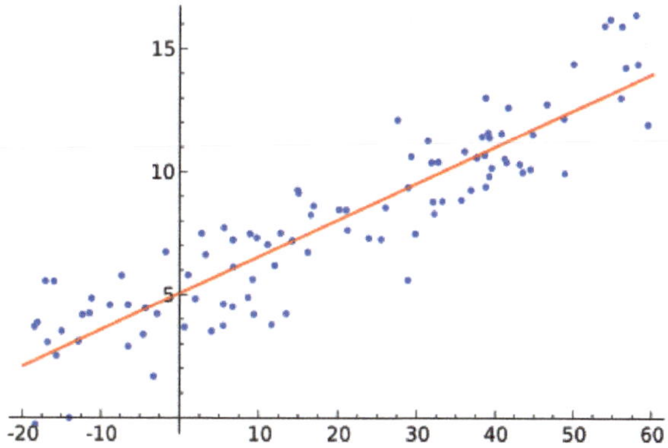

Illustration of linear regression on a data set.

In the case of simple regression, the formulas for the least squares estimates are

$$\widehat{\beta_1} = \frac{\sum (x_i - \overline{x})(y_i - \overline{y})}{\sum (x_i - \overline{x})^2} \text{ and } \widehat{\beta_0} = \overline{y} - \widehat{\beta_1}\overline{x}$$

where $\overline{x}$ is the mean (average) of the x values and $\overline{y}$ is the mean of the y values.

Under the assumption that the population error term has a constant variance, the estimate of that variance is given by:

$$\hat{\sigma}_{\varepsilon}^{2} = \frac{\text{SSE}}{n-2}.$$

This is called the mean square error (MSE) of the regression. The denominator is the sample size reduced by the number of model parameters estimated from the same data, (*n-p*) for *p* regressors or (*n-p-*1) if an intercept is used. In this case, *p*=1 so the denominator is *n*-2.

The standard errors of the parameter estimates are given by

$$\hat{\sigma}_{\beta_0} = \hat{\sigma}_{\varepsilon}\sqrt{\frac{1}{n} + \frac{\overline{x}^2}{\sum (x_i - \overline{x})^2}}$$

$$\hat{\sigma}_{\beta_1} = \hat{\sigma}_{\varepsilon}\sqrt{\frac{1}{\sum (x_i - \overline{x})^2}}.$$

Under the further assumption that the population error term is normally distributed, the researcher can use these estimated standard errors to create confidence intervals and conduct hypothesis tests about the population parameters.

General Linear Model

In the more general multiple regression model, there are *p* independent variables:

$$y_i = \beta_1 x_{i1} + \beta_2 x_{i2} + \cdots + \beta_p x_{ip} + \varepsilon_i,$$

where x_{ij} is the ith observation on the jth independent variable. If the first independent variable takes the value 1 for all *i*, x_{i1} = 1, then β_1 is called the regression intercept.

The least squares parameter estimates are obtained from *p* normal equations. The residual can be written as

$$\varepsilon_i = y_i - \hat{\beta}_1 x_{i1} - \cdots - \hat{\beta}_p x_{ip}.$$

The normal equations are

$$\sum_{i=1}^{n}\sum_{k=1}^{p} X_{ij}X_{ik}\hat{\beta}_k = \sum_{i=1}^{n} X_{ij}y_i,\ j = 1,\ldots,p.$$

In matrix notation, the normal equations are written as

$$(X^{\top}X)\widehat{\beta} = X^{\top}Y,$$

where the ij element of X is x_{ij}, the i element of the column vector Y is y_i, and the j element of $\hat{\beta}$ is $\hat{\beta}_j$. Thus X is $n \times p$, Y is $n \times 1$, and $\hat{\beta}$ is $p \times 1$. The solution is

$$\hat{\beta} = (X^{\top}X)^{-1}X^{\top}Y.$$

Diagnostics

Once a regression model has been constructed, it may be important to confirm the goodness of fit of the model and the statistical significance of the estimated parameters. Commonly used checks of goodness of fit include the R-squared, analyses of the pattern of residuals and hypothesis testing. Statistical significance can be checked by an F-test of the overall fit, followed by t-tests of individual parameters.

Interpretations of these diagnostic tests rest heavily on the model assumptions. Although examination of the residuals can be used to invalidate a model, the results of a t-test or F-test are sometimes more difficult to interpret if the model's assumptions are violated. For example, if the error term does not have a normal distribution, in small samples the estimated parameters will not follow normal distributions and complicate inference. With relatively large samples, however, a central limit theorem can be invoked such that hypothesis testing may proceed using asymptotic approximations.

"Limited Dependent" Variables

The phrase "limited dependent" is used in econometric statistics for categorical and constrained variables.

The response variable may be non-continuous ("limited" to lie on some subset of the real line). For binary (zero or one) variables, if analysis proceeds with least-squares linear regression, the model is called the linear probability model. Nonlinear models for binary dependent variables include the probit and logit model. The multivariate probit model is a standard method of estimating a joint relationship between several binary dependent variables and some independent variables. For categorical variables with more than two values there is the multinomial logit. For ordinal variables with more than two values, there are the ordered logit and ordered probit models. Censored regression models may be used when the dependent variable is only sometimes observed, and Heckman correction type models may be used when the sample is not randomly selected from the population of interest. An alternative to such procedures is linear regression based on polychoric correlation (or polyserial correlations) between the categorical variables. Such procedures differ in the assumptions made about the distribution of the variables in the population. If the variable is positive with low values and represents the repetition of the occurrence of an event, then count models like the Poisson regression or the negative binomial model may be used instead.

Interpolation and Extrapolation

Regression models predict a value of the Y variable given known values of the X variables. Prediction *within* the range of values in the dataset used for model-fitting is known informally as interpolation. Prediction *outside* this range of the data is known as extrapolation. Performing extrapolation relies strongly on the regression assumptions. The further the extrapolation goes outside the data, the more room there is for the model to fail due to differences between the assumptions and the sample data or the true values.

It is generally advised that when performing extrapolation, one should accompany the estimated value of the dependent variable with a prediction interval that represents the uncertainty. Such intervals tend to expand rapidly as the values of the independent variable(s) moved outside the range covered by the observed data.

For such reasons and others, some tend to say that it might be unwise to undertake extrapolation.

However, this does not cover the full set of modelling errors that may be being made: in particular, the assumption of a particular form for the relation between Y and X. A properly conducted regression analysis will include an assessment of how well the assumed form is matched by the observed data, but it can only do so within the range of values of the independent variables actually available. This means that any extrapolation is particularly reliant on the assumptions being made about the structural form of the regression relationship. Best-practice advice here is that a linear-in-variables and linear-in-parameters relationship should not be chosen simply for computational convenience, but that all available knowledge should be deployed in constructing a regression model. If this knowledge includes the fact that the dependent variable cannot go outside a certain range of values, this can be made use of in selecting the model – even if the observed dataset has no values particularly near such bounds. The implications of this step of choosing an appropriate functional form for the regression can be great when extrapolation is considered. At a minimum, it can ensure that any extrapolation arising from a fitted model is "realistic" (or in accord with what is known).

Nonlinear Regression

When the model function is not linear in the parameters, the sum of squares must be minimized by an iterative procedure. This introduces many complications which are summarized in Differences between linear and non-linear least squares

Power and Sample Size Calculations

There are no generally agreed methods for relating the number of observations versus the number of independent variables in the model. One rule of thumb suggested by Good and Hardin is $N = m^n$, where N is the sample size, n is the number of independent variables and m is the number of observations needed to reach the desired precision if the model had only one independent variable. For example, a researcher is building a linear regression model using a dataset that contains 1000 patients (N). If the researcher decides that five observations are needed to precisely define a straight line (m), then the maximum number of independent variables the model can support is 4, because

$$\frac{\log 1000}{\log 5} = 4.29.$$

Other Methods

Although the parameters of a regression model are usually estimated using the method of least squares, other methods which have been used include:

- Bayesian methods, e.g. Bayesian linear regression
- Percentage regression, for situations where reducing *percentage* errors is deemed more appropriate.
- Least absolute deviations, which is more robust in the presence of outliers, leading to quantile regression
- Nonparametric regression, requires a large number of observations and is computationally intensive
- Distance metric learning, which is learned by the search of a meaningful distance metric in a given input space.

Software

All major statistical software packages perform least squares regression analysis and inference. Simple linear regression and multiple regression using least squares can be done in some spreadsheet applications and on some calculators. While many statistical software packages can perform various types of nonparametric and robust regression, these methods are less standardized; different software packages implement different methods, and a method with a given name may be implemented differently in different packages. Specialized regression software has been developed for use in fields such as survey analysis and neuroimaging.

Basic Structure of Estimated Model by OLS Technique

The basic structure of simple econometric modelling for one dependent variable and two independent variables can be presented as follows:

$$Y_i = \beta_1 + \beta_2 X_{2i} + \beta_3 X_{3i} + u_i$$

Where, β_1 is intercept, β_2 is slope to X_2 and β_3 is slope to X_3. The u $[u_1, u_2, \ldots u_n]$ is error term, which is unexplained in nature, and i represent sample observation.

We use OLS technique to have the estimation of three unknown parameters (β_1, β_2 and β_3). The estimated model by OLS technique is as follows:

$$\bar{Y} = \hat{\beta}_1 + \hat{\beta}_2 \bar{X}_2 + \hat{\beta}_3 \bar{X}_3$$

Where,

$$\hat{\beta}_1 = \bar{Y} - \hat{\beta}_2 \bar{X}_2 - \hat{\beta}_3 \bar{X}_3$$

$$\hat{\beta}_2 = \frac{\left(\sum y_i x_{2i}\right)\left(\sum x_{3i}^2\right) - \left(\sum y_i x_{3i}\right)\left(\sum x_{2i} x_{3i}\right)}{\left(\sum x_{2i}^2\right)\left(\sum x_{3i}^2\right) - \left(\sum x_{2i} x_{3i}\right)^2}$$

$$\hat{\beta}_3 = \frac{\left(\sum y_i x_{3i}\right)\left(\sum x_{2i}^2\right) - \left(\sum y_i x_{2i}\right)\left(\sum x_{2i} x_{3i}\right)}{\left(\sum x_{2i}^2\right)\left(\sum x_{3i}^2\right) - \left(\sum x_{2i} x_{3i}\right)^2}$$

and

$$Y_i = \hat{\beta}_1 + \hat{\beta}_2 X_{2i} + \hat{\beta}_3 X_{3i} + \hat{u}_i$$

The reliability of this estimated model depends upon the specification test and good fitness test. This requires the followings:

$$\operatorname{var}\left(\hat{\beta}_1\right) = \left[\frac{1}{n} + \frac{\bar{X}_2^2 \sum x_{3i}^2 + \bar{X}_3^2 \sum x_{2i}^2 - 2\bar{X}_2 \bar{X}_3 \sum x_{2i} x_{3i}}{\sum x_{2i}^2 \sum x_{3i}^2 - \left(\sum x_{2i} x_{3i}\right)^2}\right] . \sigma^2$$

$$\operatorname{se}\left(\hat{\beta}_1\right) = +\sqrt{\operatorname{var}\left(\hat{\beta}_1\right)}$$

$$\operatorname{var}\left(\hat{\beta}_2\right) = \frac{\sum x_{3i}^2}{\left(\sum x_{2i}^2\right)\left(\sum x_{3i}^2\right) - \left(\sum x_{2i} x_{3i}\right)^2} \sigma^2$$

$$\operatorname{se}\left(\hat{\beta}_2\right) = +\sqrt{\operatorname{var}\left(\hat{\beta}_2\right)}$$

$$\operatorname{var}\left(\hat{\beta}_3\right) = \frac{\sum x_{2i}^2}{\left(\sum x_{2i}^2\right)\left(\sum x_{3i}^2\right) - \left(\sum x_{2i} x_{3i}\right)^2} \sigma^2$$

$$\operatorname{var}\left(\hat{\beta}_3\right) = \frac{\sigma^2}{\sum x_{3i}^2 \left(1 - r_{23}^2\right)}$$

$$\operatorname{se}\left(\hat{\beta}_3\right) = +\sqrt{\operatorname{var}\left(\hat{\beta}_3\right)}$$

$$t = \frac{\hat{\beta}_2 - \beta_2}{\operatorname{se}\left(\hat{\beta}_2\right)} = \frac{\text{estimator} - \text{parameter}}{\text{estimated standard error of estimator}}$$

$$R^2 = \frac{\text{ESS}}{\text{TSS}}$$

$$= \frac{\hat{\beta}_2 \sum y_i x_{2i} + \hat{\beta}_3 \sum y_i x_{3i}}{\sum y_i^2}$$

The OLS Assumptions

The discussion above exclusively depends on OLS assumption. These are as follows:

- The regression model is linear in parameters.
- The values of the regressors, the Xs are fixed or X values are independent of the error term. Here this means we require zero covariance between u and each X variable.
- For the given Xs the mean values of the disturbance u is zero.
- For the given Xs the variance of the u is constant.
- For the given Xs there is association between the disturbance terms.
- The number of observations n must be greater than the number of parameters to be estimated.
- There must be sufficient variation in the values of the X variables.
- There is no exact collinearity between the X variables.
- The model is correctly specified so there is no specification bias
- The stochastic term is normally distributed

Violations of OLS Assumptions

Assumption 1: The regression model is linear in parameters though it may or may not be linear in variables. The variables can be nonlinear. If the model is non-linear, it can be transformed to liner before you apply OLS technique.

Assumption 2: Values taken by the regressor X may be considered fixed in repeat samples or they might be sampled along with the dependent variable Y. If it violates, it affects the estimation process.

Assumption 3: Given the value X s the mean or the expected value of the random disturbance term is zero that is the expectation of the disturbance term given the fixed values of Xs is zero. If it violates, the estimated model cannot be best fitted.

Assumption 4: The variance of the error or disturbance term is the same regardless of the values of Xs. If so, we call it homoskedasticity issue and it is in favour of estimation process. If the assumption violates, it affects the reliability of the model. It is a situation, where error variance is unequal and we call it the problem of heteroskedasticity. The presence of heteroskedasticity leads to the estimated model is unreliable for prediction and forecasting.

Assumption 5: The correlation between the disturbance terms given any two X values is zero [i.e. correlation/ covariance (U_i, U_j) = 0 for i ≠ j]. If it violates, it is the question of serial correlation or autocorrelation. If the assumption violates, it affects the reliability of the model. It is a situation, where error covariance is equal to zero. The presence of autocorrelation leads to the estimated model is unreliable for prediction and forecasting.

Assumption 6: The number of observations must be greater than the number of parameters or no of variables in the system. For example, in the previously sited model equation where we come across three unknowns that is β_1, β_2 and β_3. In order to estimate those, we need at least four observations. But the need should not just sample size (n) > no of parameters (k). The estimation process is more practical and feasible, if n > k is sufficiently large.

Assumption 7: The X values in a given sample must not all is the same. Technically the variance must be a positive number. Furthermore there can be no outliers in the values of the X variable, which are the values that are very large in relation to the rest of the observations.

Assumption 8: There is no exact collinearity between the X variables. If so, it is the problem of multicollinearity. The OLS technique assumes that all Xs should completely independent. If it violates, the estimated model cannot be reliable.

The Testing Procedure OLS Estimation Process

We follow the below procedure to examine the violations of OLS assumptions:

- Looking first at the whole data set and then at individual observations.
- The first step is to calculate the residual for each observation.
- The residual is the numeric difference between the observed value that you entered into the data set and the predicted value derived from the model.
- Standardized residuals are calculated by dividing each residual by its standard error.
- These standardized residuals are plotted against the predicted values for the observations using a scatter plot.
- If the assumption of equal variance over the values of the independent variable is true (homoscedasticity), then the scatter of points across the predicted values will form a band with no obvious decreasing or increasing pattern of residuals with increase in the predicted values.
- If the sizes of the residuals change as the values of the predicted outcomes changes, then we know that the assumption of equal variance is not true. This

is a major violation of the linear regression. It will impact the calculation of the standard errors, which in turn will alter the size of the P value.

This therefore would be a serious flaw in the assumptions.

Multicollinearity

In statistics, multicollinearity (also collinearity) is a phenomenon in which two or more predictor variables in a multiple regression model are highly correlated, meaning that one can be linearly predicted from the others with a substantial degree of accuracy. In this situation the coefficient estimates of the multiple regression may change erratically in response to small changes in the model or the data. Multicollinearity does not reduce the predictive power or reliability of the model as a whole, at least within the sample data set; it only affects calculations regarding individual predictors. That is, a multiple regression model with correlated predictors can indicate how well the entire bundle of predictors predicts the outcome variable, but it may not give valid results about any individual predictor, or about which predictors are redundant with respect to others.

In case of perfect multicollinearity the design matrix X has less than full rank, and therefore the moment matrix $X^{T}X$ cannot be inverted. Under these circumstances, for a general linear model $y = X\beta + \epsilon$, the ordinary least-squares estimator $\hat{\beta}_{OLS} = (X^{T}X)^{-1}X^{T}y$ does not exist.

Note that in statements of the assumptions underlying regression analyses such as ordinary least squares, the phrase "no multicollinearity" is sometimes used to mean the absence of perfect multicollinearity, which is an exact (non-stochastic) linear relation among the regressors.

Definition

Collinearity is a linear association between *two* explanatory variables. Two variables are perfectly collinear if there is an exact linear relationship between them. For example, X_1 and X_2 are perfectly collinear if there exist parameters λ_0 and λ_1 such that, for all observations *i*, we have

$$X_{2i} = \lambda_0 + \lambda_1 X_{1i}.$$

Multicollinearity refers to a situation in which two or more explanatory variables in a multiple regression model are highly linearly related. We have perfect multicollinearity if, for example as in the equation above, the correlation between two independent variables is equal to 1 or −1. In practice, we rarely face perfect multicollinearity in a data set. More commonly, the issue of multicollinearity arises when there is an approximate linear relationship among two or more independent variables.

Mathematically, a set of variables is perfectly multicollinear if there exist one or more exact linear relationships among some of the variables. For example, we may have

$$\lambda_0 + \lambda_1 X_{1i} + \lambda_2 X_{2i} + \cdots + \lambda_k X_{ki} = 0$$

holding for all observations i, where λ_j are constants and X_{ji} is the ith observation on the jth explanatory variable. We can explore one issue caused by multicollinearity by examining the process of attempting to obtain estimates for the parameters of the multiple regression equation

$$Y_i = \beta_0 + \beta_1 X_{1i} + \cdots + \beta_k X_{ki} + \varepsilon_i.$$

The ordinary least squares estimates involve inverting the matrix

$$X^T X$$

where

$$X = \begin{bmatrix} 1 & X_{11} & \cdots & X_{k1} \\ \vdots & \vdots & & \vdots \\ 1 & X_{1N} & \cdots & X_{kN} \end{bmatrix}.$$

If there is an exact linear relationship (perfect multicollinearity) among the independent variables, the rank of X (and therefore of $X^T X$) is less than k+1, and the matrix $X^T X$ will not be invertible.

Perfect multicollinearity is fairly common when working with raw datasets, which frequently contain redundant information. Once redundancies are identified and removed, however, nearly multicollinear variables often remain due to correlations inherent in the system being studied. In such a case, instead of the above equation holding, we have that equation in modified form with an error term v_i:

$$\lambda_0 + \lambda_1 X_{1i} + \lambda_2 X_{2i} + \cdots + \lambda_k X_{ki} + v_i = 0.$$

In this case, there is no exact linear relationship among the variables, but the X_j variables are nearly perfectly multicollinear if the variance of v_i is small for some set of values for the λ's. In this case, the matrix $X^T X$ has an inverse, but is ill-conditioned so that a given computer algorithm may or may not be able to compute an approximate inverse, and if it does so the resulting computed inverse may be highly sensitive to slight variations in the data (due to magnified effects of rounding error) and so may be very inaccurate.

Detection of Multicollinearity

Indicators that multicollinearity may be present in a model include the following:

1. Large changes in the estimated regression coefficients when a predictor variable is added or deleted

2. Insignificant regression coefficients for the affected variables in the multiple regression, but a rejection of the joint hypothesis that those coefficients are all zero (using an *F*-test)

3. If a multivariable regression finds an insignificant coefficient of a particular explanator, yet a simple linear regression of the explained variable on this explanatory variable shows its coefficient to be significantly different from zero, this situation indicates multicollinearity in the multivariable regression.

4. Some authors have suggested a formal detection-tolerance or the variance inflation factor (VIF) for multicollinearity: $\text{tolerance} = 1 - R_j^2$, $\text{VIF} = \frac{1}{\text{tolerance}}$, where R_j^2 is the coefficient of determination of a regression of explanator *j* on all the other explanators. A tolerance of less than 0.20 or 0.10 and/or a VIF of 5 or 10 and above indicates a multicollinearity problem.

5. Condition number test: The standard measure of ill-conditioning in a matrix is the condition index. It will indicate that the inversion of the matrix is numerically unstable with finite-precision numbers (standard computer floats and doubles). This indicates the potential sensitivity of the computed inverse to small changes in the original matrix. The Condition Number is computed by finding the square root of (the maximum eigenvalue divided by the minimum eigenvalue). If the Condition Number is above 30, the regression may have significant multicollinearity; multicollinearity exists if, in addition, two or more of the variables related to the high condition number have high proportions of variance explained. One advantage of this method is that it also shows which variables are causing the problem.

6. Farrar–Glauber test: If the variables are found to be orthogonal, there is no multicollinearity; if the variables are not orthogonal, then at least some degree of multicollinearity is present. C. Robert Wichers has argued that Farrar–Glauber partial correlation test is ineffective in that a given partial correlation may be compatible with different multicollinearity patterns. The Farrar–Glauber test has also been criticized by other researchers.

7. Perturbing the data. Multicollinearity can be detected by adding random noise to the data and re-running the regression many times and seeing how much the coefficients change.

8. Construction of a correlation matrix among the explanatory variables will yield indications as to the likelihood that any given couplet of right-hand-side variables are creating multicollinearity problems. Correlation values (off-diagonal elements) of at least 0.4 are sometimes interpreted as indicating a multicollinearity problem. This procedure is, however, highly problematic and cannot be recommended. Intuitively, correlation describes a bivariate relationship, whereas collinearity is a multivariate phenomenon.

Consequences of Multicollinearity

One consequence of a high degree of multicollinearity is that, even if the matrix $X^\top X$ is invertible, a computer algorithm may be unsuccessful in obtaining an approximate inverse, and if it does obtain one it may be numerically inaccurate. But even in the presence of an accurate $X^\top X$ matrix, the following consequences arise.

In the presence of multicollinearity, the estimate of one variable's impact on the dependent variable Y while controlling for the others tends to be less precise than if predictors were uncorrelated with one another. The usual interpretation of a regression coefficient is that it provides an estimate of the effect of a one unit change in an independent variable, X_1, holding the other variables constant. If X_1 is highly correlated with another independent variable, X_2, in the given data set, then we have a set of observations for which X_1 and X_2 have a particular linear stochastic relationship. We don't have a set of observations for which all changes in X_1 are independent of changes in X_2, so we have an imprecise estimate of the effect of independent changes in X_1.

In some sense, the collinear variables contain the same information about the dependent variable. If nominally "different" measures actually quantify the same phenomenon then they are redundant. Alternatively, if the variables are accorded different names and perhaps employ different numeric measurement scales but are highly correlated with each other, then they suffer from redundancy.

One of the features of multicollinearity is that the standard errors of the affected coefficients tend to be large. In that case, the test of the hypothesis that the coefficient is equal to zero may lead to a failure to reject a false null hypothesis of no effect of the explanator, a type II error.

Another issue with multicollinearity is that small changes to the input data can lead to large changes in the model, even resulting in changes of sign of parameter estimates.

A principal danger of such data redundancy is that of overfitting in regression analysis models. The best regression models are those in which the predictor variables each correlate highly with the dependent (outcome) variable but correlate at most only minimally with each other. Such a model is often called "low noise" and will be statistically robust (that is, it will predict reliably across numerous samples of variable sets drawn from the same statistical population).

So long as the underlying specification is correct, multicollinearity does not actually bias results; it just produces large standard errors in the related independent variables. More importantly, the usual use of regression is to take coefficients from the model and then apply them to other data. Since multicollinearity causes imprecise estimates of coefficient values, the resulting out-of-sample predictions will also be imprecise. And if the pattern of multicollinearity in the new data differs from that in the data that was fitted, such extrapolation may introduce large errors in the predictions.

Remedies for Multicollinearity

1. Make sure you have not fallen into the dummy variable trap; including a dummy variable for every category (e.g., summer, autumn, winter, and spring) and including a constant term in the regression together guarantee perfect multicollinearity.

2. Try seeing what happens if you use independent subsets of your data for estimation and apply those estimates to the whole data set. Theoretically you should obtain somewhat higher variance from the smaller datasets used for estimation, but the expectation of the coefficient values should be the same. Naturally, the observed coefficient values will vary, but look at how much they vary.

3. Leave the model as is, despite multicollinearity. The presence of multicollinearity doesn't affect the efficiency of extrapolating the fitted model to new data provided that the predictor variables follow the same pattern of multicollinearity in the new data as in the data on which the regression model is based.

4. Drop one of the variables. An explanatory variable may be dropped to produce a model with significant coefficients. However, you lose information (because you've dropped a variable). Omission of a relevant variable results in biased coefficient estimates for the remaining explanatory variables that are correlated with the dropped variable.

5. Obtain more data, if possible. This is the preferred solution. More data can produce more precise parameter estimates (with lower standard errors), as seen from the formula in variance inflation factor for the variance of the estimate of a regression coefficient in terms of the sample size and the degree of multicollinearity.

6. Mean-center the predictor variables. Generating polynomial terms (i.e., for x_1, x_1^2, x_1^3, etc.) or interaction terms (i.e., $x_1 \times x_2$, etc.) can cause some multicollinearity if the variable in question has a limited range (e.g., [2,4]). Mean-centering will eliminate this special kind of multicollinearity. However, in general, this has no effect. It can be useful in overcoming problems arising from rounding and other computational steps if a carefully designed computer program is not used.

7. Standardize your independent variables. This may help reduce a false flagging of a condition index above 30.
8. It has also been suggested that using the Shapley value, a game theory tool, the model could account for the effects of multicollinearity. The Shapley value assigns a value for each predictor and assesses all possible combinations of importance.
9. Ridge regression or principal component regression or partial least squares regression can be used.
10. If the correlated explanators are different lagged values of the same underlying explanator, then a distributed lag technique can be used, imposing a general structure on the relative values of the coefficients to be estimated.

Note that one technique that does not work in offsetting the effects of multicollinearity is orthogonalizing the explanatory variables (linearly transforming them so that the transformed variables are uncorrelated with each other): By the Frisch–Waugh–Lovell theorem, using projection matrices to make the explanatory variables orthogonal to each other will lead to the same results as running the regression with all non-orthogonal explanators included.

Examples of Contexts in which Multicollinearity Arises

Survival Analysis

Multicollinearity may represent a serious issue in survival analysis. The problem is that time-varying covariates may change their value over the time line of the study. A special procedure is recommended to assess the impact of multicollinearity on the results.

Interest Rates for Different Terms to Maturity

In various situations it might be hypothesized that multiple interest rates of various terms to maturity all influence some economic decision, such as the amount of money or some other financial asset to hold, or the amount of fixed investment spending to engage in. In this case, including these various interest rates will in general create a substantial multicollinearity problem because interest rates tend to move together. If in fact each of the interest rates has its own separate effect on the dependent variable, it can be extremely difficult to separate out their effects.

Extension

The concept of *lateral collinearity* expands on the traditional view of multicollinearity, comprising also collinearity between explanatory and criteria (i.e., explained) variables, in the sense that they may be measuring almost the same thing as each other.

Autocorrelation

In general, autocorrelation means the correlation among the error terms. If it is present in the estimated model, it is the violation of OLS technique and hence, the estimated model cannot be used for prediction and forecasting. The structure of auto correlation is as follows:

$Y_t = \beta_0 + \beta_1 X_t + U_t$ and where $U_t = \rho U_{t-1} + v_t$

If $\rho = 0$, then there is no serial correlation; otherwise, there is presence of serial correlation. The range of ρ is between -1 and +1, indicating perfect negative and positive autocorrelation. So, if $\rho \neq 0$, it is autocorrelation and assumes that the error term follows the autoregressive scheme.

Consequences of Autocorrelation

The estimation process requires that OLS applications of estimated parameters should follow the BLUE theorem. If not, there is question on model reliability. In specific, the presence of autocorrelation makes the estimated parameters highly volatile and their standard errors are infinite. However, it will not affect the unbiasedness property; but affects minimum variance property.

Does it Really Cause a Problem?

On the first instance, any estimated parameters whose value does not follow BLUE theorem means it is really a problem. However, in the case of autocorrelation, it depends upon the objective specification. If the objective is for prediction (or forecasting), then the existence of autocorrelation (not in severe) is not a serious problem. But if the objective is model reliability, then it is serious issue, even if it is at the minor level. So we assume that the disturbance term is generated by a slightly different method and such error terms are also called the white noise error terms. If it is so, then there is no issue of serial correlation and estimated model can be used for forecasting.

Detection Criteria

The detection of autocorrelation can be done only after the estimation process. So, first we should have estimated model and then we can have the error term. Once we get the error term, the process of detecting autocorrelation is feasible. The residuals in case of autocorrelation can be calculated by plotting them in the time sequence plot or alternatively we can plot the standardized residuals against time. Apart from these there are several quantitative tests that one can apply in order to supplement the pure qualitative approach. These are as follows:

- Runs Test
- Durbin Watson 'D' Test

- Breusch- Godfrey Test
- Q-Test
- Von-Neuman Ratio Test

Among them, the most frequent used criteria to detect autocorrelation is

Here in case of detection of autocorrelation the most frequently used test is the Durbin Watson 'd' test. This can be analyzed as follows:

$d = cov(u_t, u_{t-1}) / var(ut)$

With some simplification, we can have $d = 2(1-\rho)$

If $\rho = 0$, $d = 2$ and the system has no autocorrelation;

If $\rho = -1$, $d = 4$ and the system has perfect negative autocorrelation;

If $\rho = 1$, $d = 0$ and the system has perfect positive autocorrelation.

So, d varies from 0 - 4. But the value of d = 2 is the best for the estimated model.

The Test, However, Depends upon the Following Assumptions

- The errors follow the autoregressive model
- There are no lagged dependent variables used as explanatory variables
- There is an intercept in the original model

Causes of Autocorrelation

- Sluggishness
- Interpolation or extrapolation
- Misspecification of the random term
- An over determined model
- An under-determined model
- Lag explanatory variables
- Wrong data transformation
- Manipulation of data
- Non-stationarity
- Presence of lagged variable in the system

Remedial Measures

- First we try to find out whether the autocorrelation present is pure autocorrelation or not and not the result of misspecification of the model
- We can then transform the original model just like in the case of heteroscedasticity we had to use the generalized least square method
- In case of large samples we can use the Newey –West method
- In some situations we might continue to use the OLS method

Heteroscedasticity-consistent Standard Error

The topic of heteroscedasticity-consistent (HC) standard errors arises in statistics and econometrics in the context of linear regression as well as time series analysis. These are also known as Eicker–Huber–White standard errors (also Huber–White standard errors or White standard errors), to recognize the contributions of Friedhelm Eicker, Peter J. Huber, and Halbert White.

In regression and time-series modelling, basic forms of models make use of the assumption that the errors or disturbances u_i have the same variance across all observation points. When this is not the case, the errors are said to be heteroscedastic, or to have heteroscedasticity, and this behaviour will be reflected in the residuals $\hat{u}_i$ estimated from a fitted model. Heteroscedasticity-consistent standard errors are used to allow the fitting of a model that does contain heteroscedastic residuals. The first such approach was proposed by Huber (1967), and further improved procedures have been produced since for cross-sectional data, time-series data and GARCH estimation.

Definition

Assume that we are studying the linear regression model

$$Y = X'\beta + U,$$

where X is the vector of explanatory variables and β is a $k \times 1$ column vector of parameters to be estimated.

The ordinary least squares (OLS) estimator is

$$\hat{\beta}_{\mathrm{OLS}} = (\mathbb{X}'\mathbb{X})^{-1}\mathbb{X}'\mathbb{Y}.$$

where $\mathbb{X}$ denotes the matrix of stacked X_i' values observed in the data.

If the sample errors have equal variance σ^2 and are uncorrelated, then the least-squares estimate of β is BLUE (best linear unbiased estimator), and its variance is easily estimated with

$$v_{OLS}[\hat{\beta}_{OLS}] = s^2(\mathbb{X}'\mathbb{X})^{-1}, s^2 = \frac{\sum_i \hat{u}_i^2}{n-k}$$

where $\hat{u}_i$ are regression residuals.

When the assumptions of $E[uu'] = \sigma^2 I_n$ are violated, the OLS estimator loses its desirable properties. Indeed,

$$V[\hat{\beta}_{OLS}] = V[(\mathbb{X}'\mathbb{X})^{-1}\mathbb{X}'\mathbb{Y}] = (\mathbb{X}'\mathbb{X})^{-1}\mathbb{X}'\Sigma\mathbb{X}(\mathbb{X}'\mathbb{X})^{-1}$$

where $\Sigma = V[u]$.

While the OLS point estimator remains unbiased, it is not "best" in the sense of having minimum mean square error, and the OLS variance estimator $v_{OLS}[\hat{\beta}_{OLS}]$ does not provide a consistent estimate of the variance of the OLS estimates.

For any non-linear model (for instance Logit and Probit models), however, heteroscedasticity has more severe consequences: the maximum likelihood estimates of the parameters will be biased (in an unknown direction), as well as inconsistent (unless the likelihood function is modified to correctly take into account the precise form of heteroscedasticity). As pointed out by Greene, "simply computing a robust covariance matrix for an otherwise inconsistent estimator does not give it redemption."

Eicker's Heteroscedasticity-consistent Estimator

If the regression errors u_i are independent, but have distinct variances σ_i^2, then $\Sigma = \text{diag}(\sigma_1^2, \ldots, \sigma_n^2)$ which can be estimated with $\hat{\sigma}_i^2 = \hat{u}_i^2$. This provides White's (1980) estimator, often referred to as *HCE* (heteroscedasticity-consistent estimator):

$$\begin{aligned} v_{HCE}[\hat{\beta}_{OLS}] &= \frac{1}{n}(\frac{1}{n}\sum_i X_i X_i')^{-1}(\frac{1}{n}\sum_i X_i X_i' \hat{u}_i^2)(\frac{1}{n}\sum_i X_i X_i')^{-1} \\ &= (\mathbb{X}'\mathbb{X})^{-1}(\mathbb{X}'\text{diag}(\hat{u}_1^2, \ldots, \hat{u}_n^2)\mathbb{X})(\mathbb{X}'\mathbb{X})^{-1}, \end{aligned}$$

where as above $\mathbb{X}$ denotes the matrix of stacked X_i' values from the data. The estimator can be derived in terms of the generalized method of moments (GMM).

Note that also often discussed in the literature (including in White's paper itself) is the covariance matrix $\hat{\Omega}_n$ of the $\sqrt{n}$-consistent limiting distribution:

$$\sqrt{n}(\hat{\beta}_n - \beta) \xrightarrow{d} N(0, \Omega),$$

where,

$$\Omega = E[XX']^{-1}\operatorname{Var}[Xu]E[XX']^{-1},$$

and

$$\begin{aligned}\hat{\Omega}_n &= \left(\frac{1}{n}\sum_i X_i X_i'\right)^{-1}\left(\frac{1}{n}\sum_i X_i X_i' \hat{u}_i^2\right)\left(\frac{1}{n}\sum_i X_i X_i'\right)^{-1} \\ &= n(\mathbb{X}'\mathbb{X})^{-1}(\mathbb{X}'\operatorname{diag}(\hat{u}_1^2,\ldots,\hat{u}_n^2)\mathbb{X})(\mathbb{X}'\mathbb{X})^{-1}.\end{aligned}$$

Thus,

$$\hat{\Omega}_n = n \cdot v_{HCE}[\hat{\beta}_{OLS}]$$

and

$$\widehat{Var}[Xu] = \frac{1}{n}\sum_i X_i X_i' \hat{u}_i^2 = \frac{1}{n}\mathbb{X}'\operatorname{diag}(\hat{u}_1^2,\ldots,\hat{u}_n^2)\mathbb{X}$$

Precisely which covariance matrix is of concern should be a matter of context.

Alternative estimators have been proposed in MacKinnon & White (1985) that correct for unequal variances of regression residuals due to different leverage. Unlike the asymptotic White's estimator, their estimators are unbiased when the data are homoscedastic.

Dummy Variable (Statistics)

In statistics and econometrics, particularly in regression analysis, a dummy variable (also known as an indicator variable, design variable, Boolean indicator, categorical variable, binary variable, or qualitative variable) is one that takes the value 0 or 1 to indicate the absence or presence of some categorical effect that may be expected to shift the outcome. Dummy variables are used as devices to sort data into mutually exclusive categories (such as smoker/non-smoker, etc.). For example, in econometric time series analysis, dummy variables may be used to indicate the occurrence of wars or major strikes. A dummy variable can thus be thought of as a truth value represented as a numerical value 0 or 1 (as is sometimes done in computer programming).

Dummy variables are "proxy" variables or numeric stand-ins for qualitative facts in a regression model. In regression analysis, the dependent variables may be influenced not only by quantitative variables (income, output, prices, etc.), but also by qualitative variables (gender, religion, geographic region, etc.). A dummy independent variable (also called a dummy explanatory variable) which for some observation has a value of 0 will cause that variable's coefficient to have no role in influencing the dependent variable, while when the dummy takes on a value 1 its coefficient acts to alter the intercept. For example, suppose membership in a group is one of the qualitative variables relevant to a regression. If group membership is arbitrarily assigned the value of 1, then all others would get the value 0. Then the intercept (the value of the dependent variable if all other explanatory variables hypothetically took on the value zero) would be the constant term for non-members but would be the constant term plus the coefficient of the membership dummy in the case of group members.

Dummy variables are used frequently in time series analysis with regime switching, seasonal analysis and qualitative data applications. Dummy variables are involved in studies for economic forecasting, bio-medical studies, credit scoring, response modelling, etc. Dummy variables may be incorporated in traditional regression methods or newly developed modeling paradigms.

Incorporating a Dummy Independent

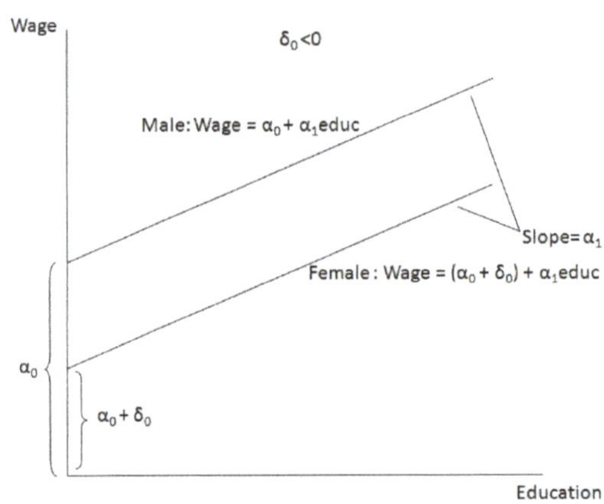

Graph showing wage = $\alpha_0 + \delta_0$female + $\alpha_1$education + U, $\delta_0 < 0$.

Dummy variables are incorporated in the same way as quantitative variables are included (as explanatory variables) in regression models. For example, if we consider a Mincer-type regression model of wage determination, wherein wages are dependent on gender (qualitative) and years of education (quantitative):

$$\ln \text{wage} = \alpha_0 + \delta_0 \text{female} + \alpha_1 \text{education} + u$$

where $u \sim N(0, \sigma^2)$ is the error term. In the model, *female* = 1 when the person is a female and *female* = 0 when the person is male. δ_0 can be interpreted as: the difference in wages between females and males, holding education constant. Thus, δ_0 helps to determine whether there is a discrimination in wages between males and females. For example, if $\delta_0 > 0$ (positive coefficient), then women earn a higher wage than men (keeping other factors constant). Note that the coefficients attached to the dummy variables are called differential intercept coefficients. The model can be depicted graphically as an intercept shift between females and males. In the figure, the case $\delta_0 < 0$ is shown (wherein, men earn a higher wage than women).

Dummy variables may be extended to more complex cases. For example, seasonal effects may be captured by creating dummy variables for each of the seasons: $D_1 = 1$ if the observation is for summer, and equals zero otherwise; $D_2 = 1$ if and only if autumn, otherwise equals zero; $D_3 = 1$ if and only if winter, otherwise equals zero; and $D_4 = 1$ if and only if spring, otherwise equals zero. In the panel data, fixed effects estimator dummies are created for each of the units in cross-sectional data (e.g. firms or countries) or periods in a pooled time-series. However in such regressions either the constant term has to be removed or one of the dummies has to be removed, with its associated category becoming the base category against which the others are assessed in order to avoid the dummy variable trap:

The constant term in all regression equations is a coefficient multiplied by a regressor equal to one. When the regression is expressed as a matrix equation, the matrix of regressors then consists of a column of ones (the constant term), vectors of zeros and ones (the dummies), and possibly other regressors. If one includes both male and female dummies, say, the sum of these vectors is a vector of ones, since every observation is categorized as either male or female. This sum is thus equal to the constant term's regressor, the first vector of ones. As result, the regression equation will be unsolvable, even by the typical pseudoinverse method. In other words: if both the vector-of-ones (constant term) regressor and an exhaustive set of dummies are present, perfect multicollinearity occurs, and the system of equations formed by the regression does not have a unique solution. This is referred to as the dummy variable trap. The trap can be avoided by removing either the constant term or one of the offending dummies. The removed dummy then becomes the base category against which the other categories are compared.

ANOVA Models

A regression model in which the dependent variable is quantitative in nature but all the explanatory variables are dummies (qualitative in nature) is called an *Analysis of Variance* (ANOVA) model.

ANOVA Model with One Qualitative Variable

Suppose we want to run a regression to find out if the average annual salary of public school teachers differs among three geographical regions in Country A with 51 states: (1) North (21 states) (2) South (17 states) (3) West (13 states). Say that the simple arithmetic average salaries are as follows: $24,424.14 (North), $22,894 (South), $26,158.62 (West). The arithmetic averages are different, but are they statistically different from each other? To compare the mean values, Analysis of Variance techniques can be used. The regression model can be defined as:

$$Y_i = \alpha_1 + \alpha_2 D_{2i} + \alpha_3 D_{3i} + u_i \text{,}$$

where

Y_i = average annual salary of public school teachers in state i

$D_{2i} = 1$ if the state *i* is in the North Region

$D_{2i} = 0$ otherwise (any region other than North)

$D_{3i} = 1$ if the state *i* is in the South Region

$D_{3i} = 0$ otherwise

In this model, we have only qualitative regressors, taking the value of 1 if the observation belongs to a specific category and 0 if it belongs to any other category. This makes it an ANOVA model.

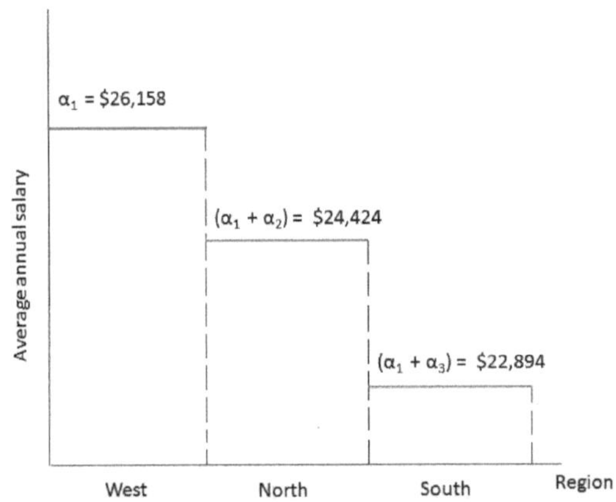

Graph showing the regression results of the ANOVA model example: Average annual salaries of public school teachers in 3 regions of Country A.

Now, taking the expectation of both sides, we obtain the following:

Mean salary of public school teachers in the North Region:

$E(Y_i|D_{2i} = 1, D_{3i} = 0) = \alpha_1 + \alpha_2$

Mean salary of public school teachers in the South Region:

$E(Y_i|D_{2i} = 0, D_{3i} = 1) = \alpha_1 + \alpha_3$

Mean salary of public school teachers in the West Region:

$E(Y_i|D_{2i} = 0, D_{3i} = 0) = \alpha_1$

(The error term does not get included in the expectation values as it is assumed that it satisfies the usual OLS conditions, i.e., $E(U_i) = 0$)

The expected values can be interpreted as follows: The mean salary of public school teachers in the West is equal to the intercept term α_1 in the multiple regression equation and the differential intercept coefficients, α_2 and α_3, explain by how much the mean salaries of teachers in the North and South Regions vary from that of the teachers in the West. Thus, the mean salaries of teachers in the North and South is *compared* against the mean salary of the teachers in the West. Hence, the West Region becomes the base group or the benchmark group,i.e., the group against which the comparisons are made. The omitted category, i.e., the category to which no dummy is assigned, is taken as the base group category.

Using the given data, the result of the regression would be:

$\hat{Y}_i = 26{,}158.62 - 1734.473D_{2i} - 3264.615D_{3i}$

se = (1128.523) (1435.953) (1499.615)

t = (23.1759) (−1.2078) (−2.1776)

p = (0.0000) (0.2330) (0.0349)

$R^2 = 0.0901$

where, se = standard error, *t* = t-statistics, *p* = p value

The regression result can be interpreted as: The mean salary of the teachers in the West (base group) is about \$26,158, the salary of the teachers in the North is lower by about \$1734 (\$26,158.62 – \$1734.473 = \$24.424.14, which is the average salary of the teachers in the North) and that of the teachers in the South is lower by about \$3265 (\$26,158.62 – \$3264.615 = \$22,894, which is the average salary of the teachers in the South).

To find out if the mean salaries of the teachers in the North and South are statistically different from that of the teachers in the West (the comparison category), we have to find out if the slope coefficients of the regression result are statistically significant. For this, we need to consider the *p* values. The estimated slope coefficient for the North is not statistically significant as its *p* value is 23 percent; however, that of the South is statistically significant at the 5% level as its *p* value is only around 3.5 percent. Thus the overall result is that the mean salaries of the teachers in the West and North are not statistically different from each other, but the mean salary of the teachers in the South is statistically lower than that in the West by around \$3265. The model is diagrammatically shown. This model is an ANOVA model with one qualitative variable having 3 categories.

ANOVA Model with Two Qualitative Variables

Suppose we consider an ANOVA model having two qualitative variables, each with two categories: Hourly Wages are to be explained in terms of the qualitative variables Marital Status (Married / Unmarried) and Geographical Region (North / Non-North). Here, Marital Status and Geographical Region are the two explanatory dummy variables.

Say the regression output on the basis of some given data appears as follows:

$$\hat{Y}_i = 8.8148 + 1.0997D_2 - 1.6729D_3$$

where,

Y = hourly wages (in $)

D_2 = marital status, 1 = married, 0 = otherwise

D_3 = geographical region, 1 = North, 0 = otherwise

In this model, a single dummy is assigned to each qualitative variable, one less than the number of categories included in each.

Here, the base group is the omitted category: Unmarried, Non-North region (Unmarried people who do not live in the North region). All comparisons would be made in relation to this base group or omitted category. The mean hourly wage in the base category is about $8.81 (intercept term). In comparison, the mean hourly wage of those who are married is higher by about $1.10 and is equal to about $9.91 ($8.81 + $1.10). In contrast, the mean hourly wage of those who live in the North is lower by about $1.67 and is about $7.14 ($8.81 – $1.67).

Thus, if more than one qualitative variable is included in the regression, it is important to note that the omitted category should be chosen as the benchmark category and all comparisons will be made in relation to that category. The intercept term will show the expectation of the benchmark category and the slope coefficients will show by how much the other categories differ from the benchmark (omitted) category.

ANCOVa Models

A regression model that contains a mixture of both quantitative and qualitative variables is called an *Analysis of Covariance* (ANCOVA) model. ANCOVA models are extensions of ANOVA models. They statistically control for the effects of quantitative explanatory variables (also called covariates or control variables).

To illustrate how qualitative and quantitative regressors are included to form ANCOVA models, suppose we consider the same example used in the ANOVA model with one qualitative variable: average annual salary of public school teachers in three geographical regions of Country A. If we include a quantitative variable, *State Government expenditure on public schools per pupil,* in this regression, we get the following model:

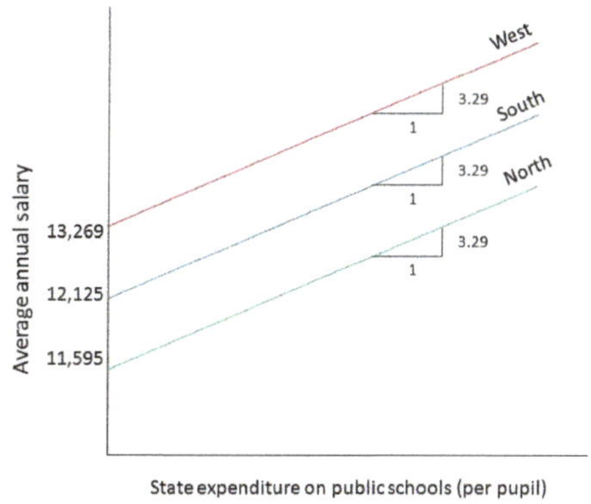

Graph showing the regression results of the ANCOVA model example: Public school teacher's salary (Y) in relation to State expenditure per pupil on public schools.

$$Y_i = \alpha_1 + \alpha_2 D_{2i} + \alpha_3 D_{3i} + \alpha_4 X_i + U_i$$

where,

Y_i = average annual salary of public school teachers in state i

X_i = State expenditure on public schools per pupil

D_{2i} = 1, if the State i is in the North Region

D_{2i} = 0, otherwise

D_{3i} = 1, if the State i is in the South Region

D_{3i} = 0, otherwise

Say the regression output for this model is

$$\hat{Y}_i = 13{,}269.11 - 1673.514D_{2i} - 1144.157D_{3i} + 3.2889X_i$$

The result suggests that, for every $1 increase in State expenditure per pupil on public schools, a public school teacher's average salary goes up by about $3.29. Further, for a state in the North region, the mean salary of the teachers is lower than that of West region by about $1673 and for a state in the South region, the mean salary of teachers is lower than that of the West region by about $1144. Figure above depicts this model diagrammatically. The average salary lines are parallel to each other by the assumption of the model that the coefficient of expenditure does not vary by state. The trade off shown separately in the graph for each category is between the two quantitative variables: public school teachers' salaries (Y) in relation to State expenditure per pupil on public schools (X).

Interactions Among Dummy Variables

Quantitative regressors in regression models often have an interaction among each other. In the same way, qualitative regressors, or dummies, can also have interaction effects between each other, and these interactions can be depicted in the regression model. For example, in a regression involving determination of wages, if two qualitative variables are considered, namely, gender and marital status, there could be an interaction between marital status and gender. These interactions can be shown in the regression equation as illustrated by the example below.

With the two qualitative variables being gender and marital status and with the quantitative explanator being years of education, a regression that is purely linear in the explanators would be

$$Y_i = \beta_1 + \beta_2 D_{2,i} + \beta_3 D_{3,i} + \alpha X_i + U_i$$

where

i denotes the particular individual

Y = Hourly Wages (in $)

X = Years of education

D_2 = 1 if female, 0 otherwise

D_3 = 1 if married, 0 otherwise

This specification does not allow for the possibility that there may be an interaction that occurs between the two qualitative variables, D_2 and D_3. For example, a female who is married may earn wages that differ from those of an unmarried male by an amount that is not the same as the sum of the differentials for solely being female and solely being married. Then the effect of the interacting dummies on the mean of Y is not simply *additive* as in the case of the above specification, but *multiplicative* also, and the determination of wages can be specified as:

$$Y_i = \beta_1 + \beta_2 D_{2,i} + \beta_3 D_{3,i} + \beta_4 (D_{2,i} D_{3,i}) + \alpha X_i + U_i$$

Here,

β_2 = differential effect of being a female

β_3 = differential effect of being married

β_4 = further differential effect of being *both* female *and* married

By this equation, in the absence of a non-zero error the wage of an unmarried male is $\beta_1 + \alpha X_i$, that of an unmarried female is $\beta_1 + \beta_2 + \alpha X_i$, that of being a married male is $\beta_1 + \beta_3 + \alpha X_i$, and that of being a married female is $\beta_1 + \beta_2 + \beta_3 + \beta_4 + \alpha X_i$ (where any of the estimates of the coefficients of the dummies could turn out to be positive, zero, or negative).

Thus, an interaction dummy (product of two dummies) can alter the dependent variable from the value that it gets when the two dummies are considered individually.

However, the use of products of dummy variables to capture interactions can be avoided by using a different scheme for categorizing the data—one that specifies categories in terms of combinations of characteristics. If we let

D_4 = 1 if unmarried female, 0 otherwise

D_5 = 1 if married male, 0 otherwise

D_6 = 1 if married female, 0 otherwise

then it suffices to specify the regression

$$Y_i = \delta_1 + \delta_4 D_{4,i} + \delta_5 D_{5,i} + \delta_6 D_{6,i} + \alpha X_i + U_i.$$

Then with zero shock term the value of the dependent variable is $\delta_1 + \alpha X_i$ for the base category unmarried males, $\delta_1 + \delta_4 + \alpha X_i$ for unmarried females, $\delta_1 + \delta_5 + \alpha X_i$ for married males, and $\delta_1 + \delta_6 + \alpha X_i$ for married females. This specification involves the same number of right-side variables as does the previous specification with an interaction term, and the regression results for the predicted value of the dependent variable contingent on X_i, for any combination of qualitative traits, are identical between this specification and the interaction specification.

Dummy Dependent Variables

What Happens if the Dependent Variable is a Dummy?

A model with a dummy dependent variable (also known as a qualitative dependent variable) is one in which the dependent variable, as influenced by the explanatory variables, is qualitative in nature. Some decisions regarding 'how much' of an act must be performed involve a prior decision making on whether to perform the act or not. For example, the amount of output to produce, the cost to be incurred, etc. involve prior decisions on whether to produce or not, whether to spend or not, etc. Such "prior decisions" become dependent dummies in the regression model.

For example, the decision of a worker to be a part of the labour force becomes a dummy dependent variable. The decision is dichotomous, i.e., the decision has two possible outcomes: yes and no. So the dependent dummy variable Participation would take on the value 1 if participating, 0 if not participating. Some other examples of dichotomous dependent dummies are cited below:

Decision: Choice of Occupation. Dependent Dummy: Supervisory = 1 if supervisor, 0 if not supervisor.

Decision: Affiliation to a Political Party. Dependent Dummy: Affiliation = 1 if affiliated to the party, 0 if not affiliated.

Decision: Retirement. Dependent Dummy: Retired = 1 if retired, 0 if not retired.

When the qualitative dependent dummy variable has more than two values (such as affiliation to many political parties), it becomes a multiresponse or a multinomial or polychotomous model.

Dependent Dummy Variable Models

Analysis of dependent dummy variable models can be done through different methods. One such method is the usual OLS method, which in this context is called the linear probability model. An alternative method is to assume that there is an unobservable continuous latent variable Y^* and that the observed dichotomous variable Y = 1 if $Y^* > 0$, 0 otherwise. This is the underlying concept of the logit and probit models. These models are discussed in brief below.

Linear Probability Model

An ordinary least squares model in which the dependent variable *Y* is a dichotomous dummy, taking the values of 0 and 1, is the linear probability model (LPM). Suppose we consider the following regression:

$$Y_i = \alpha_1 + \alpha_2 X_i + u_i$$

where

X = family income

Y = 1 if a house is owned by the family, 0 if a house is not owned by the family

The model is called the *linear probability model* because, the regression is linear. The conditional mean of Y_i given X_i, written as $\mathbb{E}(Y_i \mid X_i)$, is interpreted as the conditional probability that the event will occur for that value of X_i — that is, $\Pr(Y_i = 1 \mid X_i)$. In this example, $\mathbb{E}(Y_i \mid X_i)$ gives the probability of a house being owned by a family whose income is given by X_i.

Now, using the OLS assumption $E(u_i \mid X_i) = 0$, we get

$$\mathbb{E}(Y_i \mid X_i) = \alpha_1 + \alpha_2 X_i$$

Some problems are inherent in the LPM model:

1. The regression line will not be a well-fitted one and hence measures of significance, such as R^2, will not be reliable.

2. Models that are analyzed using the LPM approach will have heteroscedastic disturbances.

3. The error term will have a non-normal distribution.

4. The LPM may give predicted values of the dependent variable that are greater than 1 or less than 0. This will be difficult to interpret as the predicted values are intended to be probabilities, which must lie between 0 and 1.

5. There might exist a non-linear relationship between the variables of the LPM model, in which case, the linear regression will not fit the data accurately.

Alternatives to LPM

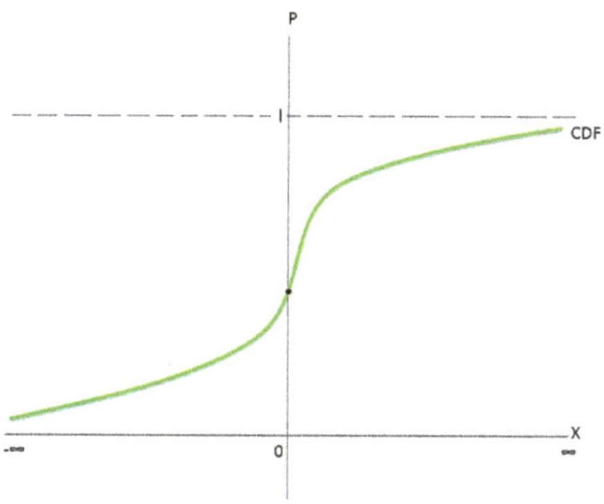

A cumulative distribution function.

To avoid the limitations of the LPM, what is needed is a model that has the feature that as the explanatory variable, X_i, increases, $P_i = E\ (Y_i = 1 \mid X_i)$ should remain within the range between 0 and 1. Thus the relationship between the independent and dependent variables is necessarily non-linear.

For this purpose, a cumulative distribution function (CDF) can be used to estimate the dependent dummy variable regression. Figure above shows an 'S'-shaped curve, which resembles the CDF of a random variable. In this model, the probability is between 0 and 1 and the non-linearity has been captured. The choice of the CDF to be used is now the question.

Two alternative CDFs can be used: the logistic and normal CDFs. The logistic CDF gives rise to the logit model and the normal CDF give rises to the probit model .

Logit Model

The shortcomings of the LPM led to the development of a more refined and improved model called the logit model. In the logit model, the cumulative distribution of the error term in the regression equation is logistic. The regression is more realistic in that it is non-linear.

The logit model is estimated using the maximum likelihood approach. In this model, $P(Y = 1 \mid X)$, which is the probability of the dependent variable taking the value of 1 given the independent variable is:

$$P_i = \frac{1}{1 + e^{-Z_i}} = \frac{e^{Z_i}}{1 + e^{Z_i}}$$

where $z_i = \alpha_1 + \alpha_2 X_i + u_i$.

The model is then expressed in the form of the odds ratio: what is modeled in the logistic regression is the natural logarithm of the odds, the odds being defined as $P/(1-P)$. Taking the natural log of the odds, the logit (L_i) is expressed as

$$L_i = \ln\left(\frac{P_i}{1-P_i}\right) = z_i = \alpha_1 + \alpha_2 X_i.$$

This relationship shows that L_i is linear in relation to X_i, but the probabilities are not linear in terms of X_i.

Probit Model

Another model that was developed to offset the disadvantages of the LPM is the probit model. The probit model uses the same approach to non-linearity as does the logit model; however, it uses the normal CDF instead of the logistic CDF.

Qualitative Response Regression Modelling

It basically represents the involvement of qualitative variable in econometric modelling. We usually we call it dummy variable. Dummy variable is a variable, which can classifying the structure into various subgroups based on qualities or attributes and implicitly allows one to run individual regressions for each group. A dummy variable will take the value 1 or 0 according to whether or not the condition is present or absent for a particular observation. In some cases, it can be presented with the code 1, 2, 3, 4 and alike. For instance, if we like to study the impact of religion on income, the religion will be categorical (qualitative) and in this context, we take the value like 1, 2, 3, etc.

Binary Choice Model

We start our study of qualitative response models by first considering the binary response regression model. The outcome (or response, or endpoint) values 0, 1 can represent "success" and "failure". Occurs often in the biopharmaceutical field; dose-response studies, bioassays, clinical trials. Industrial applications include failure analysis, fatigue testing, reliability testing. For example, functional electrical testing on a semiconductor can yield: "success" in which case the device works; "failure" due to a short, an open, or some other failure mode

$$y_i = \beta_0 + \sum_{j=1}^{k} \beta_j x_{ij} + \varepsilon_i = x_i'\beta + \varepsilon_i \begin{cases} i = 1, 2, \ldots, n \\ y_i = 0 \text{ or } 1 \end{cases}$$

The response y_i is a Bernoulli random variable and that follows the below conditions:

$$P(y_i = 1) = \pi_i \text{ with } 0 \leq \pi_i \leq 1$$
$$P(y_i = 0) = 1 - \pi_i$$
$$E(y_i) = \mu_i = x_i'\beta = \pi_i$$
$$\text{Var}(y_i) = \sigma_{y_i}^2 = \pi_i(1 - \pi_i)$$

- The error terms take on only two values, so they can't possibly be normally distributed
- The variance of the observations is a function of the mean.
- A linear response function could result in predicted values that fall outside the 0, 1 range, and this is impossible.

The Logit Model

In the logit model the dependent variable is the log of the odds ratio, which is a linear function of the regressors. The probability function that underlies the logit model is the logistic distribution. If the data is available in grouped form, we can use the OLS to estimate the parameters of the logit model, provided we take into account explicitly the heteroscedastic nature of the error term. If the data are available at the individual or micro level, non linear in parameter estimation procedures are called for. There is a lot of empirical evidence that the response function should be nonlinear; an "S" shape is quite logical.

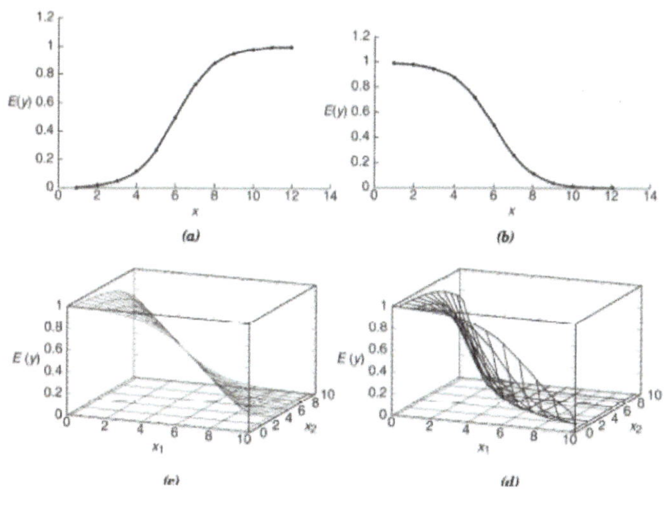

$$\text{Examples of the logistic response function:}$$
$$(a)E(y)=1/\left(1+e^{-6.0+1.0x}\right)$$
$$(b)E(y)=1/\left(1+e^{-6.0+1.0x}\right)$$
$$(c)E(y)=1/\left(1+e^{-5.0+0.65x_1+0.4x_2}\right)$$
$$(d)E(y)=1/\left(1+e^{-5.0+0.65x_1+0.4x_2+0.15x_1x_2}\right)$$

The usual LOGT model is presented as follows:

$$E(y)=\frac{\exp(x'\beta)}{1+\exp(x'\beta)}=\frac{1}{1+\exp(-x'\beta)}$$

After simplification, the LOGIT model can be presented in this format:

$$\text{Log}\left[p/(1-p)\right]=\beta_0+\beta_1X_1+\beta_2X_2+u$$

or else, we can write

$$\text{Log}\left[p/(1-p)\right]=\sum\beta_k x_k$$

The LOGIT model is related to the odds for a binary outcome. The LOGIT model has the following features:

- As p goes from 0 to 1, L or LOGIT goes from - infinity to + infinity that is although the probabilities lie between 0 and 1 the LOGIT are not so bounded.
- The logit model is not subject to problems due to heteroscedastic or non-normal error distributions.
- The logit of the outcome tends to have a linear relationship with the explanatory variables.

The Probit Model

The structure PROBIT model is very similar to LOGIT model. The difference lies on its functional form. We use normal distribution function in PROBIT instead of logistic function in LOGIT. The PROBIT uses as the outcome variable the t-score associated with a given p, where

$$-F(p)=t=\sum\beta_k x_k$$

And the functional relationship between t and p is the equation for the normal curve that is as follows

$$E(p) = \int_{-\infty}^{\sum \beta_k x_k} \frac{1}{\sqrt{2\pi}} \exp\left(-\frac{t^2}{2}\right) dt$$

Coming to estimation procedure, it is very similar to LOGIT model. For comparative point of view, the estimated results and the findings are very similar. However, the following differences can be noted.

- In a LOGIT model, β_0 and β_1 coefficient refers to the log of an odds ratio. In a PROBIT model, β_0 and β_1 coefficient refers to the change in z-score per unit change in x.
- Alternately, in a PROBIT model, β_0 and β_1 coefficient refers to the change in probability units per unit change in x.
- The chief difference between logit and probit model is that the logistic model has a flatter tail that is the normal or probit curves approach the axis faster than the LOGIT model.
- Quantitatively LOGIT and PROBIT models give similar results but the estimates of the parameters of the two models are not directly comparable.

Logistic Regression

In statistics, logistic regression, or logit regression, or logit model is a regression model where the dependent variable (DV) is categorical. This article covers the case of a binary dependent variable—that is, where it can take only two values, "0" and "1", which represent outcomes such as pass/fail, win/lose, alive/dead or healthy/sick. Cases where the dependent variable has more than two outcome categories may be analysed in multinomial logistic regression, or, if the multiple categories are ordered, in ordinal logistic regression. In the terminology of economics, logistic regression is an example of a qualitative response/discrete choice model.

Logistic regression was developed by statistician David Cox in 1958. The binary logistic model is used to estimate the probability of a binary response based on one or more predictor (or independent) variables (features). It allows one to say that the presence of a risk factor increases the probability of a given outcome by a specific percentage.

Fields and Example Applications

Logistic regression is used in various fields, including machine learning, most medical fields, and social sciences. For example, the Trauma and Injury Severity Score (TRISS), which is widely used to predict mortality in injured patients, was originally developed by Boyd et al. using logistic regression. Many other medical scales used to assess severity of a patient have been developed using logistic regression. Logistic regression may be used to predict whether a patient has a given disease (e.g. diabetes; coronary heart disease), based on observed characteristics of the patient (age, sex, body mass index, results of various blood tests, etc.). Another example might be to predict whether an American voter will vote Democratic or Republican, based on age, income, sex, race, state of residence, votes in previous elections, etc. The technique can also be used in engineering, especially for predicting the probability of failure of a given process, system or product. It is also used in marketing applications such as prediction of a customer's propensity to purchase a product or halt a subscription, etc. In economics it can be used to predict the likelihood of a person's choosing to be in the labor force, and a business application would be to predict the likelihood of a homeowner defaulting on a mortgage. Conditional random fields, an extension of logistic regression to sequential data, are used in natural language processing.

Example: Probability of Passing an Exam Versus Hours of Study

Suppose we wish to answer the following question:

A group of 20 students spend between 0 and 6 hours studying for an exam. How does the number of hours spent studying affect the probability that the student will pass the exam?

The reason for using logistic regression for this problem is that the dependent variable pass/fail represented by "1" and "0" are not cardinal numbers. If the problem was changed so that pass/fail was replaced with the grade 0–100 (cardinal numbers), then simple regression analysis could be used.

The table shows the number of hours each student spent studying, and whether they passed (1) or failed (0).

Hours	0.50	0.75	1.00	1.25	1.50	1.75	1.75	2.00	2.25	2.50	2.75	3.00
Pass	0	0	0	0	0	0	1	0	1	0	1	0

Hours	3.25	3.50	4.00	4.25	4.50	4.75	5.00	5.50
Pass	1	0	1	1	1	1	1	1

The graph shows the probability of passing the exam versus the number of hours studying, with the logistic regression curve fitted to the data.

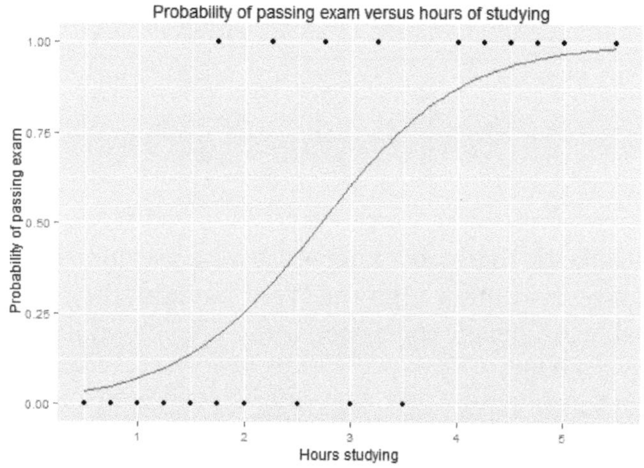

Graph of a logistic regression curve showing probability of passing an exam versus hours studying

The logistic regression analysis gives the following output.

	Coefficient	Std.Error	z-value	P-value (Wald)
Intercept	−4.0777	1.7610	−2.316	0.0206
Hours	1.5046	0.6287	2.393	0.0167

The output indicates that hours studying is significantly associated with the probability of passing the exam ($p = 0.0167$, Wald test). The output also provides the coefficients for $\text{Intercept} = -4.0777$ and $\text{Hours} = 1.5046$. These coefficients are entered in the logistic regression equation to estimate the probability of passing the exam:

$$\text{Probability of passing exam} = \frac{1}{1 + \exp\left(-\left(1.5046 \cdot \text{Hours} - 4.0777\right)\right)}$$

For example, for a student who studies 2 hours, entering the value $\text{Hours} = 2$ in the equation gives the estimated probability of passing the exam of 0.26:

$$\text{Probability of passing exam} = \frac{1}{1 + \exp\left(-\left(1.5046 \cdot 2 - 4.0777\right)\right)} = 0.26$$

Similarly, for a student who studies 4 hours, the estimated probability of passing the exam is 0.87:

$$\text{Probability of passing exam} = \frac{1}{1 + \exp\left(-\left(1.5046 \cdot 4 - 4.0777\right)\right)} = 0.87$$

This table shows the probability of passing the exam for several values of hours studying.

Hours of study	Probability of passing exam
1	0.07
2	0.26
3	0.61
4	0.87
5	0.97

The output from the logistic regression analysis gives a p-value of $p = 0.0167$, which is based on the Wald z-score. Rather than the Wald method, the recommended method to calculate the p-value for logistic regression is the Likelihood Ratio Test (LRT), which for this data gives $\text{p} = 0.0006$.

Some Discussion

Logistic regression can be binomial, ordinal or multinomial. Binomial or binary logistic regression deals with situations in which the observed outcome for a dependent variable can have only two possible types, "0" and "1" (which may represent, for example, "dead" vs. "alive" or "win" vs. "loss"). Multinomial logistic regression deals with situations where the outcome can have three or more possible types (e.g., "disease A" vs. "disease B" vs. "disease C") that are not ordered. Ordinal logistic regression deals with dependent variables that are ordered. In binary logistic regression, the outcome is usually coded as "0" or "1", as this leads to the most straightforward interpretation. If a particular observed outcome for the dependent variable is the noteworthy possible outcome (referred to as a "success" or a "case") it is usually coded as "1" and the contrary outcome (referred to as a "failure" or a "noncase") as "0". Logistic regression is used to predict the odds of being a case based on the values of the independent variables (predictors). The odds are defined as the probability that a particular outcome is a case divided by the probability that it is a noncase.

Like other forms of regression analysis, logistic regression makes use of one or more predictor variables that may be either continuous or categorical. Unlike ordinary linear regression, however, logistic regression is used for predicting binary dependent variables (treating the dependent variable as the outcome of a Bernoulli trial) rather than a continuous outcome. Given this difference, the assumptions of linear regression are violated. In particular, the residuals cannot be normally distributed. In addition, linear regression may make nonsensical predictions for a binary dependent variable. What is needed is a way to convert a binary variable into a continuous one that can take on any real value (negative or positive). To do that logistic regression first takes the odds of the event happening for different levels of each independent variable, then takes the ratio of those odds (which is continuous but cannot be negative) and then takes the logarithm of that ratio. This is referred to as logit or log-odds) to create a continuous criterion as a transformed version of the dependent variable.

Thus the logit transformation is referred to as the *link function* in logistic regression—although the dependent variable in logistic regression is binomial, the logit is the continuous criterion upon which linear regression is conducted.

The logit of success is then fitted to the predictors using linear regression analysis. The predicted value of the logit is converted back into predicted odds via the inverse of the natural logarithm, namely the exponential function. Thus, although the observed dependent variable in logistic regression is a zero-or-one variable, the logistic regression estimates the odds, as a continuous variable, that the dependent variable is a success (a case). In some applications the odds are all that is needed. In others, a specific yes-or-no prediction is needed for whether the dependent variable is or is not a case; this categorical prediction can be based on the computed odds of a success, with predicted odds above some chosen cutoff value being translated into a prediction of a success.

Logistic Regression vs. Other Approaches

Logistic regression measures the relationship between the categorical dependent variable and one or more independent variables by estimating probabilities using a logistic function, which is the cumulative logistic distribution. Thus, it treats the same set of problems as probit regression using similar techniques, with the latter using a cumulative normal distribution curve instead. Equivalently, in the latent variable interpretations of these two methods, the first assumes a standard logistic distribution of errors and the second a standard normal distribution of errors.

Logistic regression can be seen as a special case of the generalized linear model and thus analogous to linear regression. The model of logistic regression, however, is based on quite different assumptions (about the relationship between dependent and independent variables) from those of linear regression. In particular the key differences between these two models can be seen in the following two features of logistic regression. First, the conditional distribution $y \mid x$ is a Bernoulli distribution rather than a Gaussian distribution, because the dependent variable is binary. Second, the predicted values are probabilities and are therefore restricted to (0,1) through the logistic distribution function because logistic regression predicts the probability of particular outcomes.

Logistic regression is an alternative to Fisher's 1936 method, linear discriminant analysis. If the assumptions of linear discriminant analysis hold, the conditioning can be reversed to produce logistic regression. The converse is not true, however, because logistic regression does not require the multivariate normal assumption of discriminant analysis.

Latent Variable Interpretation

The logistic regression can be understood simply as finding the β parameters that best fit:

$$y = \begin{cases} 1 & \beta_0 + \beta_1 x + \varepsilon > 0 \\ 0 & \text{else} \end{cases}$$

where ε is an error distributed by the standard logistic distribution. (If the standard normal distribution is used instead, it is a probit regression.)

The associated latent variable is $y' = \beta_0 + \beta_1 x + \varepsilon$. The error term ε is not observed, and so the y' is also an unobservable, hence termed "latent". (The observed data are values of y and x.) Unlike ordinary regression, however, the β parameters cannot be expressed by any direct formula of the y and x values in the observed data. Instead they are to be found by an iterative search process, usually implemented by a software program, that finds the maximum of a complicated "likelihood expression" that is a function of all of the observed y and x values. The estimation approach is explained below.

Logistic Function, Odds, Odds Ratio, and Logit

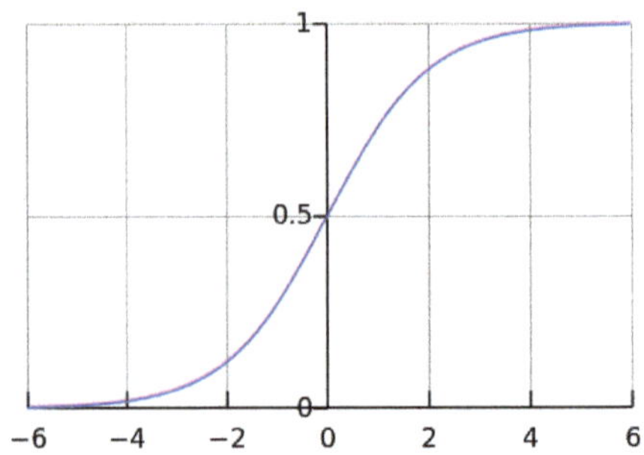

The standard logistic function $\sigma(t)$; note that $\sigma(t) \in (0,1)$ for all t.

Definition of the Logistic Function

An explanation of logistic regression can begin with an explanation of the standard logistic function. The logistic function is useful because it can take any real input t, ($t \in \mathbb{R}$), whereas the output always takes values between zero and one and hence is interpretable as a probability. The logistic function $\sigma(t)$ is defined as follows:

$$\sigma(t) = \frac{e^t}{e^t + 1} = \frac{1}{1 + e^{-t}}$$

A graph of the logistic function on the *t*-interval (-6,6) is shown in the figure above.

Let us assume that t is a linear function of a single explanatory variable x (the case where t is a *linear combination* of multiple explanatory variables is treated similarly). We can then express t as follows:

$$t = \beta_0 + \beta_1 x$$

And the logistic function can now be written as:

$$F(x) = \frac{1}{1+e^{-(\beta_0+\beta_1 x)}}$$

Note that F(x) is interpreted as the probability of the dependent variable equaling a "success" or "case" rather than a failure or non-case. It's clear that the response variables Y_i are not identically distributed: $P(Y_i = 1 \mid X)$ differs from one data point X_i to another, though they are independent given design matrix X and shared with parameters β.

Definition of the Inverse of the Logistic Function

We can now define the inverse of the logistic function, g, the logit (log odds):

$$g(F(x)) = \ln\left(\frac{F(x)}{1-F(x)}\right) = \beta_0 + \beta_1 x,$$

and equivalently, after exponentiating both sides:

$$\frac{F(x)}{1-F(x)} = e^{\beta_0+\beta_1 x}.$$

Interpretation of these Terms

In the above equations, the terms are as follows:

- is the logit function. The equation for g(F(x)) illustrates that the logit (i.e., log-odds or natural logarithm of the odds) is equivalent to the linear regression expression.
- ln denotes the natural logarithm.
- F(x) is the probability that the dependent variable equals a case, given some linear combination of the predictors. The formula for F(x) illustrates that the probability of the dependent variable equaling a case is equal to the value of the logistic function of the linear regression expression. This is important in that it shows that the value of the linear regression expression can vary from negative to positive infinity and yet, after transformation, the resulting expression for the probability F(x) ranges between 0 and 1.
- β_0 is the intercept from the linear regression equation (the value of the criterion when the predictor is equal to zero).
- $\beta_1 x$ is the regression coefficient multiplied by some value of the predictor.
- base e denotes the exponential function.

Definition of the Odds

The odds of the dependent variable equaling a case (given some linear combination x of the predictors) is equivalent to the exponential function of the linear regression expression. This illustrates how the logit serves as a link function between the probability and the linear regression expression. Given that the logit ranges between negative and positive infinity, it provides an adequate criterion upon which to conduct linear regression and the logit is easily converted back into the odds.

So we define odds of the dependent variable equaling a case (given some linear combination x of the predictors) as follows:

$$\text{odds} = e^{\beta_0 + \beta_1 x}.$$

The Odds Ratio

For a continuous independent variable the odds ratio can be defined as:

$$\text{OR} = \frac{\text{odds}(x+1)}{\text{odds}(x)} = \frac{\left(\frac{F(x+1)}{1-F(x+1)}\right)}{\left(\frac{F(x)}{1-F(x)}\right)} = \frac{e^{\beta_0+\beta_1(x+1)}}{e^{\beta_0+\beta_1 x}} = e^{\beta_1}$$

This exponential relationship provides an interpretation for β_1: The odds multiply by e^{β_1} for every 1-unit increase in x.

For a binary independent variable the odds ratio is defined as $\frac{ad}{bc}$ where a, b, c and d are cells in a 2×2 contingency table.

Multiple Explanatory Variables

If there are multiple explanatory variables, the above expression $\beta_0 + \beta_1 x$ can be revised to $\beta_0 + \beta_1 x_1 + \beta_2 x_2 + \cdots + \beta_m x_m$. Then when this is used in the equation relating the logged odds of a success to the values of the predictors, the linear regression will be a multiple regression with m explanators; the parameters β_j for all j = 0, 1, 2, ..., m are all estimated.

Model Fitting

Estimation

Because the model can be expressed as a generalized linear model, for $0 < p < 1$, ordinary least squares can suffice, with R-squared as the measure of goodness of fit in the fitting space. When $p = 0$ or 1, more complex methods are required.

"Rule of Ten"

A widely-used rule of thumb states that logistic regression models give stable values for the explanatory variables if based on a minimum of about 10 events per explanatory variable (EPV); where *event* denotes the cases belonging to the less frequent category in the dependent variable. Thus a study designed to use k explanatory variables for an event (eg myocardial infarction) expected to occur in a proportion p of participants in the study will require a total of $10k/p$ participants. However, there is considerable debate about the reliability of this rule, which is based on simulation studies and lacks a secure theoretical underpinning. According to some authors the rule is over conservative, some circumstances; with the authors stating "If we (somewhat subjectively) regard confidence interval coverage less than 93 percent, type I error greater than 7 percent, or relative bias greater than 15 percent as problematic, our results indicate that problems are fairly frequent with 2–4 EPV, uncommon with 5–9 EPV, and still observed with 10–16 EPV. Cox models appear to be slightly more susceptible than logistic. The worst instances of each problem were not severe with 5–9 EPV and usually comparable to those with 10–16 EPV".

Maximum Likelihood Estimation

The regression coefficients are usually estimated using maximum likelihood estimation. Unlike linear regression with normally distributed residuals, it is not possible to find a closed-form expression for the coefficient values that maximize the likelihood function, so that an iterative process must be used instead; for example Newton's method. This process begins with a tentative solution, revises it slightly to see if it can be improved, and repeats this revision until no more improvement is made, at which point the process is said to have converged.

In some instances the model may not reach convergence. Nonconvergence of a model indicates that the coefficients are not meaningful because the iterative process was unable to find appropriate solutions. A failure to converge may occur for a number of reasons: having a large ratio of predictors to cases, multicollinearity, sparseness, or complete separation.

- Having a large ratio of variables to cases results in an overly conservative Wald statistic (discussed below) and can lead to nonconvergence.
- Multicollinearity refers to unacceptably high correlations between predictors. As multicollinearity increases, coefficients remain unbiased but standard errors increase and the likelihood of model convergence decreases. To detect multicollinearity amongst the predictors, one can conduct a linear regression analysis with the predictors of interest for the sole purpose of examining the tolerance statistic used to assess whether multicollinearity is unacceptably high.

- Sparseness in the data refers to having a large proportion of empty cells (cells with zero counts). Zero cell counts are particularly problematic with categorical predictors. With continuous predictors, the model can infer values for the zero cell counts, but this is not the case with categorical predictors. The model will not converge with zero cell counts for categorical predictors because the natural logarithm of zero is an undefined value, so that final solution to the model cannot be reached. To remedy this problem, researchers may collapse categories in a theoretically meaningful way or add a constant to all cells.

- Another numerical problem that may lead to a lack of convergence is complete separation, which refers to the instance in which the predictors perfectly predict the criterion – all cases are accurately classified. In such instances, one should reexamine the data, as there is likely some kind of error.

Iteratively Reweighted Least Squares (IRLS)

Binary logistic regression ($y=0$ or $y=1$) can, for example, be calculated using *iteratively reweighted least squares* (IRLS), which is equivalent to minimizing the Log-likelihood of a Bernoulli distributed process using Newton's method. If the problem is written in vector matrix form, with parameters $w^T=[\beta_0,\beta_1,\beta_2,\ldots]$, explanatory variables $x(i)=[1,x_1(i),x_2(i),\ldots]^T$ and expected value of the Bernoulli distribution $\mu(i)=\frac{1}{1+e^{-w^T x(i)}}$, the parameters w can be found using the following iterative algorithm:

$$w_{k+1}=\left(X^T S_k X\right)^{-1} X^T\left(S_k X w_k + y - \mu_k\right)$$

where $S=\operatorname{diag}(\mu(i)(1-\mu(i)))$ is a diagonal weighting matrix, $\mu=[\mu(1),\mu(2),\ldots]$ the vector of expected values,

$$X=\begin{bmatrix} 1 & x_1(1) & x_2(1) & \ldots \\ 1 & x_1(2) & x_2(2) & \ldots \\ \vdots & \vdots & \vdots & \end{bmatrix}$$

the regressor matrix and $y(i)=[y(1),y(2),\ldots]^T$ the vector of response variables. More details can be found e.g. here

Evaluating Goodness of Fit

Discrimination in linear regression models is generally measured using R^2. Since this has no direct analog in logistic regression, various methods including the following can be used instead.

Deviance and Likelihood Ratio Tests

In linear regression analysis, one is concerned with partitioning variance via the sum of squares calculations – variance in the criterion is essentially divided into variance accounted for by the predictors and residual variance. In logistic regression analysis, deviance is used in lieu of sum of squares calculations. Deviance is analogous to the sum of squares calculations in linear regression and is a measure of the lack of fit to the data in a logistic regression model. When a "saturated" model is available (a model with a theoretically perfect fit), deviance is calculated by comparing a given model with the saturated model. This computation gives the likelihood-ratio test:

$$D = -2\ln\frac{\text{likelihood of the fitted model}}{\text{likelihood of the saturated model}}.$$

In the above equation *D* represents the deviance and ln represents the natural logarithm. The log of this likelihood ratio (the ratio of the fitted model to the saturated model) will produce a negative value, hence the need for a negative sign. *D* can be shown to follow an approximate chi-squared distribution. Smaller values indicate better fit as the fitted model deviates less from the saturated model. When assessed upon a chi-square distribution, nonsignificant chi-square values indicate very little unexplained variance and thus, good model fit. Conversely, a significant chi-square value indicates that a significant amount of the variance is unexplained.

When the saturated model is not available (a common case), deviance is calculated simply as −2·(log likelihood of the fitted model), and the reference to the saturated model's log likelihood can be removed from all that follows without harm.

Two measures of deviance are particularly important in logistic regression: null deviance and model deviance. The null deviance represents the difference between a model with only the intercept (which means "no predictors") and the saturated model. The model deviance represents the difference between a model with at least one predictor and the saturated model. In this respect, the null model provides a baseline upon which to compare predictor models. Given that deviance is a measure of the difference between a given model and the saturated model, smaller values indicate better fit. Thus, to assess the contribution of a predictor or set of predictors, one can subtract the model deviance from the null deviance and assess the difference on a χ^2_{s-p}, chi-square distribution with degrees of freedom equal to the difference in the number of parameters estimated.

Let

$$D_{\text{null}} = -2\ln\frac{\text{likelihood of null model}}{\text{likelihood of the saturated model}}$$

$$D_{\text{fitted}} = -2\ln\frac{\text{likelihood of fitted model}}{\text{likelihood of the saturated model}}.$$

Then the difference of both is:

$$D_{null} - D_{fitted} = -2\left(\ln \frac{\text{likelihood of null model}}{\text{likelihood of the saturated model}} - \ln \frac{\text{likelihood of fitted model}}{\text{likelihood of the saturated model}} \right)$$

$$= -2 \ln \frac{\left(\frac{\text{likelihood of null model}}{\text{likelihood of the saturated model}} \right)}{\left(\frac{\text{likelihood of fitted model}}{\text{likelihood of the saturated model}} \right)}$$

$$= -2 \ln \frac{\text{likelihood of the null model}}{\text{likelihood of fitted model}}.$$

If the model deviance is significantly smaller than the null deviance then one can conclude that the predictor or set of predictors significantly improved model fit. This is analogous to the *F*-test used in linear regression analysis to assess the significance of prediction.

Pseudo-R^2s

In linear regression the squared multiple correlation, R^2 is used to assess goodness of fit as it represents the proportion of variance in the criterion that is explained by the predictors. In logistic regression analysis, there is no agreed upon analogous measure, but there are several competing measures each with limitations.

Four of the most commonly used indices and one less commonly used one are examined on this page:

- Likelihood ratio R^2_L
- Cox and Snell R^2_{CS}
- Nagelkerke R^2_N
- McFadden R^2_{McF}
- Tjur R^2_T

R^2_L is given by

$$R_L^2 = \frac{D_{null} - D_{fitted}}{D_{null}}.$$

This is the most analogous index to the squared multiple correlation in linear regression. It represents the proportional reduction in the deviance wherein the deviance is treated as a measure of variation analogous but not identical to the variance in linear regression analysis. One limitation of the likelihood ratio R^2 is that it is not monotonically related to the odds ratio, meaning that it does not necessarily increase as the odds ratio increases and does not necessarily decrease as the odds ratio decreases.

R^2_{CS} is an alternative index of goodness of fit related to the R^2 value from linear regression. It is given by:

$$R^2_{CS} = 1 - \left(\frac{L_M}{L_0}\right)^{2/n}.$$

where L_M and L_0 are the likelihoods for the model being fitted and the null model, respectively. The Cox and Snell index is problematic as its maximum value is $1 - L_0^{2/n}$. The highest this upper bound can be is 0.75, but it can easily be as low as 0.48 when the marginal proportion of cases is small.

R^2_N provides a correction to the Cox and Snell R^2 so that the maximum value is equal to 1. Nevertheless, the Cox and Snell and likelihood ratio R^2s show greater agreement with each other than either does with the Nagelkerke R^2. Of course, this might not be the case for values exceeding .75 as the Cox and Snell index is capped at this value. The likelihood ratio R^2 is often preferred to the alternatives as it is most analogous to R^2 in linear regression, is independent of the base rate (both Cox and Snell and Nagelkerke R^2s increase as the proportion of cases increase from 0 to .5) and varies between 0 and 1.

R^2_{McF} is defined as

$$R^2_{McF} = 1 - \frac{\ln(L_M)}{\ln(L_0)},$$

and is preferred over R^2_{CS} by Allison. The two expressions R^2_{McF} and R^2_{CS} are then related respectively by,

$$R^2_{CS} = 1 - \left(\frac{1}{L_0}\right)^{\frac{2(R^2_{McF})}{n}}$$

$$R^2_{McF} = -\frac{n}{2} \cdot \frac{\ln(1 - R^2_{CS})}{\ln(L_0)}$$

However, Allison now prefers R^2_T which is a relatively new measure developed by Tjur. It can be calculated in two steps:

1. For each level of the dependent variable, find the mean of the predicted probabilities of an event.

2. Take the absolute value of the difference between these means

A word of caution is in order when interpreting pseudo-R^2 statistics. The reason these indices of fit are referred to as *pseudo* R^2 is that they do not represent the proportionate reduction in error as the R^2 in linear regression does. Linear regression assumes homoscedasticity, that the error variance is the same for all values of the criterion. Logistic regression will always be heteroscedastic – the error variances differ for each value of the predicted score. For each value of the predicted score there would be a different value of the proportionate reduction in error. Therefore, it is inappropriate to think of R^2 as a proportionate reduction in error in a universal sense in logistic regression.

Hosmer–Lemeshow Test

The Hosmer–Lemeshow test uses a test statistic that asymptotically follows a χ^2 distribution to assess whether or not the observed event rates match expected event rates in subgroups of the model population. This test is considered to be obsolete by some statisticians because of its dependence on arbitrary binning of predicted probabilities and relative low power.

Coefficients

After fitting the model, it is likely that researchers will want to examine the contribution of individual predictors. To do so, they will want to examine the regression coefficients. In linear regression, the regression coefficients represent the change in the criterion for each unit change in the predictor. In logistic regression, however, the regression coefficients represent the change in the logit for each unit change in the predictor. Given that the logit is not intuitive, researchers are likely to focus on a predictor's effect on the exponential function of the regression coefficient – the odds ratio. In linear regression, the significance of a regression coefficient is assessed by computing a *t* test. In logistic regression, there are several different tests designed to assess the significance of an individual predictor, most notably the likelihood ratio test and the Wald statistic.

Likelihood Ratio Test

The likelihood-ratio test discussed above to assess model fit is also the recommended procedure to assess the contribution of individual "predictors" to a given model. In the case of a single predictor model, one simply compares the deviance of the predictor model with that of the null model on a chi-square distribution with a single degree of freedom. If the predictor model has a significantly smaller deviance (c.f chi-square using the difference in degrees of freedom of the two models), then one can conclude that there is a significant association between the "predictor" and the outcome. Although some common statistical packages (e.g. SPSS) do provide likelihood ratio test statistics, without this computationally intensive test it would be more difficult to assess the contribution of individual predictors in the multiple logistic regression case. To assess the contribution of individual predictors one can enter the predictors hierarchically, comparing each new model with the previous to determine the contribution of each predictor. There is some debate among statisticians about the appropriateness of so-called "stepwise" procedures. The fear is that they may not preserve nominal statistical properties and may become misleading.

Wald Statistic

Alternatively, when assessing the contribution of individual predictors in a given model, one may examine the significance of the Wald statistic. The Wald statistic, analogous to the *t*-test in linear regression, is used to assess the significance of coefficients. The Wald statistic is the ratio of the square of the regression coefficient to the square of the standard error of the coefficient and is asymptotically distributed as a chi-square distribution.

$$W_j = \frac{\beta_j^2}{SE_{\beta_j}^2}$$

Although several statistical packages (e.g., SPSS, SAS) report the Wald statistic to assess the contribution of individual predictors, the Wald statistic has limitations. When the regression coefficient is large, the standard error of the regression coefficient also tends to be large increasing the probability of Type-II error. The Wald statistic also tends to be biased when data are sparse.

Case-control Sampling

Suppose cases are rare. Then we might wish to sample them more frequently than their prevalence in the population. For example, suppose there is a disease that affects 1 person in 10,000 and to collect our data we need to do a complete physical. It may be too expensive to do thousands of physicals of healthy people in order to obtain data for only a few diseased individuals. Thus, we may evaluate more diseased individuals, perhaps all of the rare outcomes. This is also retrospective sampling, or equivalently it is called unbalanced data. As a rule of thumb, sampling controls at a rate of five times the number of cases will produce sufficient control data.

Logistic regression is unique in that it may be estimated on unbalanced data, rather than randomly sampled data, and still yield correct coefficient estimates of the effects of each independent variable on the outcome. That is to say, if we form a logistic model from such data, if the model is correct in the general population, the β_j parameters are all correct except for β_0. We can correct β_0 if we know the true prevalence as follows:

$$\widehat{\beta_0^*} = \widehat{\beta_0} + \log\frac{\pi}{1-\pi} - \log\frac{\tilde{\pi}}{1-\tilde{\pi}}$$

where is the true prevalence and $\tilde{\pi}$ is the prevalence in the sample.

Formal mathematical specification

There are various equivalent specifications of logistic regression, which fit into different types of more general models. These different specifications allow for different sorts of useful generalizations.

Setup

The basic setup of logistic regression is the same as for standard linear regression.

It is assumed that we have a series of N observed data points. Each data point i consists of a set of m explanatory variables $x_{1,i} \ldots x_{m,i}$ (also called independent variables, predictor variables, input variables, features, or attributes), and an associated binary-valued outcome variable Y_i (also known as a dependent variable, response variable, output variable, outcome variable or class variable), i.e. it can assume only the two possible values 0 (often meaning "no" or "failure") or 1 (often meaning "yes" or "success"). The goal of logistic regression is to explain the relationship between the explanatory variables and the outcome, so that an outcome can be predicted for a new set of explanatory variables.

Some examples:

- The observed outcomes are the presence or absence of a given disease (e.g. diabetes) in a set of patients, and the explanatory variables might be characteristics of the patients thought to be pertinent (sex, race, age, blood pressure, body-mass index, etc.).
- The observed outcomes are the votes (e.g. Democratic or Republican) of a set of people in an election, and the explanatory variables are the demographic characteristics of each person (e.g. sex, race, age, income, etc.). In such a case, one of the two outcomes is arbitrarily coded as 1, and the other as 0.

As in linear regression, the outcome variables Y_i are assumed to depend on the explanatory variables $x_{1,i} \ldots x_{m,i}$.

Explanatory Variables

As shown above in the above examples, the explanatory variables may be of any type: real-valued, binary, categorical, etc. The main distinction is between continuous variables (such as income, age and blood pressure) and discrete variables (such as sex or race). Discrete variables referring to more than two possible choices are typically coded using dummy variables (or indicator variables), that is, separate explanatory variables taking the value 0 or 1 are created for each possible value of the discrete variable, with a 1 meaning "variable does have the given value" and a 0 meaning "variable does not have that value". For example, a four-way discrete variable of blood type with the possible values "A, B, AB, O" can be converted to four separate two-way dummy variables, "is-A, is-B, is-AB, is-O", where only one of them has the value 1 and all the rest have the value 0. This allows for separate regression coefficients to be matched for each possible value of the discrete variable. (In a case like this, only three of the four dummy variables are independent of each other, in the sense that once the values of three of the variables are known, the fourth is automatically determined. Thus, it is necessary to encode only three of the four possibilities as dummy variables. This also means that when all four possibilities are encoded, the overall model is not identifiable in the absence of additional constraints such as a regularization constraint. Theoretically, this could cause problems, but in reality almost all logistic regression models are fitted with regularization constraints.)

Outcome Variables

Formally, the outcomes Y_i are described as being Bernoulli-distributed data, where each outcome is determined by an unobserved probability p_i that is specific to the outcome at hand, but related to the explanatory variables. This can be expressed in any of the following equivalent forms:

$$Y_i \mid x_{1,i}, \ldots, x_{m,i} \sim \text{Bernoulli}(p_i)$$

$$\mathbb{E}[Y_i \mid x_{1,i}, \ldots, x_{m,i}] = p_i$$

$$\Pr(Y_i = y \mid x_{1,i}, \ldots, x_{m,i}) = \begin{cases} p_i & \text{if } y = 1 \\ 1 - p_i & \text{if } y = 0 \end{cases}$$

$$\Pr(Y_i = y \mid x_{1,i}, \ldots, x_{m,i}) = p_i^y (1 - p_i)^{(1-y)}$$

The meanings of these four lines are:

1. The first line expresses the probability distribution of each Y_i: Conditioned on the explanatory variables, it follows a Bernoulli distribution with parameters p_i, the probability of the outcome of 1 for trial *i*. As noted above, each separate trial has its own probability of success, just as each trial has its own explanatory variables. The probability of success p_i is not observed, only the outcome of an individual Bernoulli trial using that probability.

2. The second line expresses the fact that the expected value of each Y_i is equal to the probability of success p_i, which is a general property of the Bernoulli distribution. In other words, if we run a large number of Bernoulli trials using the same probability of success p_i, then take the average of all the 1 and 0 outcomes, then the result would be close to p_i. This is because doing an average this way simply computes the proportion of successes seen, which we expect to converge to the underlying probability of success.

3. The third line writes out the probability mass function of the Bernoulli distribution, specifying the probability of seeing each of the two possible outcomes.

4. The fourth line is another way of writing the probability mass function, which avoids having to write separate cases and is more convenient for certain types of calculations. This relies on the fact that Y_i can take only the value 0 or 1. In each case, one of the exponents will be 1, "choosing" the value under it, while the other is 0, "canceling out" the value under it. Hence, the outcome is either p_i or $1 - p_i$, as in the previous line.

Linear Predictor Function

The basic idea of logistic regression is to use the mechanism already developed for linear regression by modeling the probability p_i using a linear predictor function, i.e. a linear combination of the explanatory variables and a set of regression coefficients that are specific to the model at hand but the same for all trials. The linear predictor function $f(i)$ for a particular data point i is written as:

$$f(i) = \beta_0 + \beta_1 x_{1,i} + \cdots + \beta_m x_{m,i},$$

where $\beta_0, \ldots, \beta_m$ are regression coefficients indicating the relative effect of a particular explanatory variable on the outcome.

The model is usually put into a more compact form as follows:

- The regression coefficients $\beta_0, \beta_1, \ldots, \beta_m$ are grouped into a single vector β of size $m + 1$.
- For each data point i, an additional explanatory pseudo-variable $x_{0,i}$ is added, with a fixed value of 1, corresponding to the intercept coefficient β_0.
- The resulting explanatory variables $x_{0,i}, x_{1,i}, \ldots, x_{m,i}$ are then grouped into a single vector X_i of size $m + 1$.

This makes it possible to write the linear predictor function as follows:

$$f(i) = \beta \cdot X_i,$$

using the notation for a dot product between two vectors.

As a Generalized Linear Model

The particular model used by logistic regression, which distinguishes it from standard linear regression and from other types of regression analysis used for binary-valued outcomes, is the way the probability of a particular outcome is linked to the linear predictor function:

$$\text{logit}(\mathbb{E}[Y_i \mid x_{1,i}, \ldots, x_{m,i}]) = \text{logit}(p_i) = \ln\left(\frac{p_i}{1-p_i}\right) = \beta_0 + \beta_1 x_{1,i} + \cdots + \beta_m x_{m,i}$$

Written using the more compact notation described above, this is:

$$\operatorname{logit}(\mathbb{E}[Y_i \mid X_i]) = \operatorname{logit}(p_i) = \ln\left(\frac{p_i}{1-p_i}\right) = \beta \cdot X_i$$

This formulation expresses logistic regression as a type of generalized linear model, which predicts variables with various types of probability distributions by fitting a linear predictor function of the above form to some sort of arbitrary transformation of the expected value of the variable.

The intuition for transforming using the logit function (the natural log of the odds) was explained above. It also has the practical effect of converting the probability (which is bounded to be between 0 and 1) to a variable that ranges over $(-\infty, +\infty)$ — thereby matching the potential range of the linear prediction function on the right side of the equation.

Note that both the probabilities p_i and the regression coefficients are unobserved, and the means of determining them is not part of the model itself. They are typically determined by some sort of optimization procedure, e.g. maximum likelihood estimation, that finds values that best fit the observed data (i.e. that give the most accurate predictions for the data already observed), usually subject to regularization conditions that seek to exclude unlikely values, e.g. extremely large values for any of the regression coefficients. The use of a regularization condition is equivalent to doing maximum a posteriori (MAP) estimation, an extension of maximum likelihood. (Regularization is most commonly done using a squared regularizing function, which is equivalent to placing a zero-mean Gaussian prior distribution on the coefficients, but other regularizers are also possible.) Whether or not regularization is used, it is usually not possible to find a closed-form solution; instead, an iterative numerical method must be used, such as iteratively reweighted least squares (IRLS) or, more commonly these days, a quasi-Newton method such as the L-BFGS method.

The interpretation of the β_j parameter estimates is as the additive effect on the log of the odds for a unit change in the *j*th explanatory variable. In the case of a dichotomous explanatory variable, for instance gender, e^{β} is the estimate of the odds of having the outcome for, say, males compared with females.

An equivalent formula uses the inverse of the logit function, which is the logistic function, i.e.:

$$\mathbb{E}[Y_i \mid X_i] = p_i = \operatorname{logit}^{-1}(\beta \cdot X_i) = \frac{1}{1+e^{-\beta \cdot X_i}}$$

The formula can also be written as a probability distribution (specifically, using a probability mass function):

$$\Pr(Y_i = y \mid X_i) = p_i^{\,y}(1-p_i)^{1-y} = \left(\frac{e^{\beta\cdot X_i}}{1+e^{\beta\cdot X_i}}\right)^{y}\left(1-\frac{e^{\beta\cdot X_i}}{1+e^{\beta\cdot X_i}}\right)^{1-y} = \frac{e^{\beta\cdot X_i\cdot y}}{1+e^{\beta\cdot X_i}}$$

As a Latent-variable Model

The above model has an equivalent formulation as a latent-variable model. This formulation is common in the theory of discrete choice models, and makes it easier to extend to certain more complicated models with multiple, correlated choices, as well as to compare logistic regression to the closely related probit model.

Imagine that, for each trial i, there is a continuous latent variable Y_i^* (i.e. an unobserved random variable) that is distributed as follows:

$$Y_i^* = \beta \cdot X_i + \varepsilon$$

where

$$\varepsilon \sim \text{Logistic}(0,1)$$

i.e. the latent variable can be written directly in terms of the linear predictor function and an additive random error variable that is distributed according to a standard logistic distribution.

Then Y_i can be viewed as an indicator for whether this latent variable is positive:

$$Y_i = \begin{cases} 1 & \text{if } Y_i^* > 0 \ \text{ i.e. } -\varepsilon < \beta \cdot X_i, \\ 0 & \text{otherwise.} \end{cases}$$

The choice of modeling the error variable specifically with a standard logistic distribution, rather than a general logistic distribution with the location and scale set to arbitrary values, seems restrictive, but in fact it is not. It must be kept in mind that we can choose the regression coefficients ourselves, and very often can use them to offset changes in the parameters of the error variable's distribution. For example, a logistic error-variable distribution with a non-zero location parameter μ (which sets the mean) is equivalent to a distribution with a zero location parameter, where μ has been added to the intercept coefficient. Both situations produce the same value for Y_i^* regardless of settings of explanatory variables. Similarly, an arbitrary scale parameter s is equivalent to setting the scale parameter to 1 and then dividing all regression coefficients by s. In the latter case, the resulting value of Y_i^* will be smaller by a factor of s than in the former case, for all sets of explanatory variables – but critically, it will always remain on the same side of 0, and hence lead to the same Y_i choice.

(Note that this predicts that the irrelevancy of the scale parameter may not carry over into more complex models where more than two choices are available.)

It turns out that this formulation is exactly equivalent to the preceding one, phrased in terms of the generalized linear model and without any latent variables. This can be shown as follows, using the fact that the cumulative distribution function (CDF) of the standard logistic distribution is the logistic function, which is the inverse of the logit function, i.e.

$$\Pr(\varepsilon < x) = \operatorname{logit}^{-1}(x)$$

Then:

$$\begin{aligned}
&\Pr(Y_i = 1 \mid X_i) = \Pr(Y_i^* > 0 \mid X_i) \\
&= \Pr(\beta \cdot X_i + \varepsilon > 0) \\
&= \Pr(\varepsilon > -\beta \cdot X_i) \\
&= \Pr(\varepsilon < \beta \cdot X_i) \qquad \text{(because the logistic distribution is symmetric)} \\
&= \operatorname{logit}^{-1}(\beta \cdot X_i) \\
&= p_i
\end{aligned}$$

This formulation—which is standard in discrete choice models—makes clear the relationship between logistic regression (the "logit model") and the probit model, which uses an error variable distributed according to a standard normal distribution instead of a standard logistic distribution. Both the logistic and normal distributions are symmetric with a basic unimodal, "bell curve" shape. The only difference is that the logistic distribution has somewhat heavier tails, which means that it is less sensitive to outlying data (and hence somewhat more robust to model mis-specifications or erroneous data).

Two-way Latent-variable Model

Yet another formulation uses two separate latent variables:

$$Y_i^{0*} = \beta_0 \cdot X_i + \varepsilon_0$$
$$Y_i^{1*} = \beta_1 \cdot X_i + \varepsilon_1$$

where

$$\varepsilon_0 \sim EV_1(0,1)$$
$$\varepsilon_1 \sim EV_1(0,1)$$

where $EV_1(0,1)$ is a standard type-1 extreme value distribution: i.e.

$$\Pr(\varepsilon_0 = x) = \Pr(\varepsilon_1 = x) = e^{-x} e^{-e^{-x}}$$

Then

$$Y_i = \begin{cases} 1 & \text{if } Y_i^{1*} > Y_i^{0*}, \\ 0 & \text{otherwise.} \end{cases}$$

This model has a separate latent variable and a separate set of regression coefficients for each possible outcome of the dependent variable. The reason for this separation is that it makes it easy to extend logistic regression to multi-outcome categorical variables, as in the multinomial logit model. In such a model, it is natural to model each possible outcome using a different set of regression coefficients. It is also possible to motivate each of the separate latent variables as the theoretical utility associated with making the associated choice, and thus motivate logistic regression in terms of utility theory. (In terms of utility theory, a rational actor always chooses the choice with the greatest associated utility.) This is the approach taken by economists when formulating discrete choice models, because it both provides a theoretically strong foundation and facilitates intuitions about the model, which in turn makes it easy to consider various sorts of extensions.

The choice of the type-1 extreme value distribution seems fairly arbitrary, but it makes the mathematics work out, and it may be possible to justify its use through rational choice theory.

It turns out that this model is equivalent to the previous model, although this seems non-obvious, since there are now two sets of regression coefficients and error variables, and the error variables have a different distribution. In fact, this model reduces directly to the previous one with the following substitutions:

$$\beta = \beta_1 - \beta_0$$

$$\varepsilon = \varepsilon_1 - \varepsilon_0$$

An intuition for this comes from the fact that, since we choose based on the maximum of two values, only their difference matters, not the exact values — and this effectively removes one degree of freedom. Another critical fact is that the difference of two type-1 extreme-value-distributed variables is a logistic distribution, i.e. $\varepsilon = \varepsilon_1 - \varepsilon_0 \sim \text{Logistic}(0,1)$. We can demonstrate the equivalent as follows:

$$
\begin{aligned}
\Pr(Y_i = 1 \mid X_i) &= \Pr\left(Y_i^{1*} > Y_i^{0*} \mid X_i\right) \\
&= \Pr\left(Y_i^{1*} - Y_i^{0*} > 0 \mid X_i\right) \\
&= \Pr\left(\beta_1 \cdot X_i + \varepsilon_1 - (\beta_0 \cdot X_i + \varepsilon_0) > 0\right) \\
&= \Pr\left((\beta_1 \cdot X_i - \beta_0 \cdot X_i) + (\varepsilon_1 - \varepsilon_0) > 0\right) \\
&= \Pr((\beta_1 - \beta_0) \cdot X_i + (\varepsilon_1 - \varepsilon_0) > 0) \\
&= \Pr((\beta_1 - \beta_0) \cdot X_i + \varepsilon > 0) \quad \text{(substitute } \varepsilon \text{ as above)} \\
&= \Pr(\beta \cdot X_i + \varepsilon > 0) \quad \text{(substitute } \beta \text{ as above)} \\
&= \Pr(\varepsilon > -\beta \cdot X_i) \quad \text{(now, same as above model)} \\
&= \Pr(\varepsilon < \beta \cdot X_i) \\
&= \operatorname{logit}^{-1}(\beta \cdot X_i) \\
&= p_i
\end{aligned}
$$

Example

As an example, consider a province-level election where the choice is between a right-of-center party, a left-of-center party, and a secessionist party (e.g. the Parti Québécois, which wants Quebec to secede from Canada). We would then use three latent variables, one for each choice. Then, in accordance with utility theory, we can then interpret the latent variables as expressing the utility that results from making each of the choices. We can also interpret the regression coefficients as indicating the strength that the associated factor (i.e. explanatory variable) has in contributing to the utility — or more correctly, the amount by which a unit change in an explanatory variable changes the utility of a given choice. A voter might expect that the right-of-center party would lower taxes, especially on rich people. This would give low-income people no benefit, i.e. no change in utility (since they usually don't pay taxes); would cause moderate benefit (i.e. somewhat more money, or moderate utility increase) for middle-incoming people; and would cause significant benefits for high-income people. On the other hand, the left-of-center party might be expected to raise taxes and offset it with increased welfare and other assistance for the lower and middle classes. This would cause significant positive benefit to low-income people, perhaps weak benefit to middle-income people, and significant negative benefit to high-income people. Finally, the secessionist party would take no direct actions on the economy, but simply secede. A low-income or middle-income voter might expect basically no clear utility gain or loss from this, but a high-income voter might expect negative utility, since he/she is likely to own companies, which will have a harder time doing business in such an environment and probably lose money.

These intuitions can be expressed as follows:

Estimated strength of regression coefficient for different outcomes (party choices) and different values of explanatory variables			
	Center-right	**Center-left**	**Secessionist**
High-income	strong +	strong –	strong –
Middle-income	moderate +	weak +	none
Low-income	none	strong +	none

This clearly shows that

1. Separate sets of regression coefficients need to exist for each choice. When phrased in terms of utility, this can be seen very easily. Different choices have different effects on net utility; furthermore, the effects vary in complex ways that depend on the characteristics of each individual, so there need to be separate sets of coefficients for each characteristic, not simply a single extra per-choice characteristic.

2. Even though income is a continuous variable, its effect on utility is too complex for it to be treated as a single variable. Either it needs to be directly split up into ranges, or higher powers of income need to be added so that polynomial regression on income is effectively done.

As a "Log-linear" Model

Yet another formulation combines the two-way latent variable formulation above with the original formulation higher up without latent variables, and in the process provides a link to one of the standard formulations of the multinomial logit.

Here, instead of writing the logit of the probabilities p_i as a linear predictor, we separate the linear predictor into two, one for each of the two outcomes:

$$\ln \Pr(Y_i = 0) = \beta_0 \cdot X_i - \ln Z$$
$$\ln \Pr(Y_i = 1) = \beta_1 \cdot X_i - \ln Z$$

Note that two separate sets of regression coefficients have been introduced, just as in the two-way latent variable model, and the two equations appear a form that writes the logarithm of the associated probability as a linear predictor, with an extra term $-\ln Z$ at the end. This term, as it turns out, serves as the normalizing factor ensuring that the result is a distribution. This can be seen by exponentiating both sides:

$$\Pr(Y_i = 0) = \frac{1}{Z} e^{\beta_0 \cdot X_i}$$

$$\Pr(Y_i = 1) = \frac{1}{Z} e^{\beta_1 \cdot X_i}$$

In this form it is clear that the purpose of Z is to ensure that the resulting distribution over Y_i is in fact a probability distribution, i.e. it sums to 1. This means that Z is simply the sum of all un-normalized probabilities, and by dividing each probability by Z, the probabilities become "normalized". That is:

$$Z = e^{\beta_0 \cdot X_i} + e^{\beta_1 \cdot X_i}$$

and the resulting equations are

$$\Pr(Y_i = 0) = \frac{e^{\beta_0 \cdot X_i}}{e^{\beta_0 \cdot X_i} + e^{\beta_1 \cdot X_i}}$$

$$\Pr(Y_i = 1) = \frac{e^{\beta_1 \cdot X_i}}{e^{\beta_0 \cdot X_i} + e^{\beta_1 \cdot X_i}}.$$

Or generally:

$$\Pr(Y_i = c) = \frac{e^{\beta_c \cdot X_i}}{\sum_h e^{\beta_h \cdot X_i}}$$

This shows clearly how to generalize this formulation to more than two outcomes, as in multinomial logit. Note that this general formulation is exactly the Softmax function as in

$$\Pr(Y_i = c) = \operatorname{soft\,max}(c, \beta_0 \cdot X_i, \beta_1 \cdot X_i, \ldots).$$

In order to prove that this is equivalent to the previous model, note that the above model is overspecified, in that $\Pr(Y_i = 0)$ and $\Pr(Y_i = 1)$ cannot be independently specified: rather $\Pr(Y_i = 0) + \Pr(Y_i = 1) = 1$ so knowing one automatically determines the other. As a result, the model is nonidentifiable, in that multiple combinations of β_0 and β_1 will produce the same probabilities for all possible explanatory variables. In fact, it can be seen that adding any constant vector to both of them will produce the same probabilities:

$$\Pr(Y_i = 1) = \frac{e^{(\beta_1 + C) \cdot X_i}}{e^{(\beta_0 + C) \cdot X_i} + e^{(\beta_1 + C) \cdot X_i}}$$

$$= \frac{e^{\beta_1 \cdot X_i} e^{C \cdot X_i}}{e^{\beta_0 \cdot X_i} e^{C \cdot X_i} + e^{\beta_1 \cdot X_i} e^{C \cdot X_i}}$$

$$= \frac{e^{C \cdot X_i} e^{\beta_1 \cdot X_i}}{e^{C \cdot X_i} (e^{\beta_0 \cdot X_i} + e^{\beta_1 \cdot X_i})}$$

$$= \frac{e^{\beta_1 \cdot X_i}}{e^{\beta_0 \cdot X_i} + e^{\beta_1 \cdot X_i}}.$$

As a result, we can simplify matters, and restore identifiability, by picking an arbitrary value for one of the two vectors. We choose to set $\beta_0 = 0$. Then,

$$e^{\beta_0 \cdot X_i} = e^{0 \cdot X_i} = 1$$

and so

$$\Pr(Y_i = 1) = \frac{e^{\beta_1 \cdot X_i}}{1 + e^{\beta_1 \cdot X_i}} = \frac{1}{1 + e^{-\beta_1 \cdot X_i}} = p_i$$

which shows that this formulation is indeed equivalent to the previous formulation. (As in the two-way latent variable formulation, any settings where $\beta = \beta_1 - \beta_0$ will produce equivalent results.)

Note that most treatments of the multinomial logit model start out either by extending the "log-linear" formulation presented here or the two-way latent variable formulation presented above, since both clearly show the way that the model could be extended to multi-way outcomes. In general, the presentation with latent variables is more common in econometrics and political science, where discrete choice models and utility theory reign, while the "log-linear" formulation here is more common in computer science, e.g. machine learning and natural language processing.

As a Single-layer Perceptron

The model has an equivalent formulation

$$p_i = \frac{1}{1 + e^{-(\beta_0 + \beta_1 x_{1,i} + \cdots + \beta_k x_{k,i})}}.$$

This functional form is commonly called a single-layer perceptron or single-layer artificial neural network. A single-layer neural network computes a continuous output instead of a step function. The derivative of p_i with respect to $X = (x_1, \ldots, x_k)$ is computed from the general form:

$$y = \frac{1}{1 + e^{-f(X)}}$$

where $f(X)$ is an analytic function in X. With this choice, the single-layer neural network is identical to the logistic regression model. This function has a continuous derivative, which allows it to be used in backpropagation. This function is also preferred because its derivative is easily calculated:

$$\frac{dy}{dX} = y(1 - y)\frac{df}{dX}.$$

In terms of Binomial Data

A closely related model assumes that each i is associated not with a single Bernoulli trial but with n_i independent identically distributed trials, where the observation Y_i is the number of successes observed (the sum of the individual Bernoulli-distributed random variables), and hence follows a binomial distribution:

$$Y_i \sim \text{Bin}(n_i, p_i), \text{ for } i = 1, \ldots, n$$

An example of this distribution is the fraction of seeds (p_i) that germinate after n_i are planted.

In terms of expected values, this model is expressed as follows:

$$p_i = \mathbb{E}\left[\frac{Y_i}{n_i} \middle| X_i\right],$$

so that

$$\operatorname{logit}\left(\mathbb{E}\left[\frac{Y_i}{n_i} \middle| X_i\right]\right) = \operatorname{logit}(p_i) = \ln\left(\frac{p_i}{1-p_i}\right) = \beta \cdot X_i,$$

Or equivalently:

$$\Pr(Y_i = y \mid X_i) = \binom{n_i}{y} p_i^y (1-p_i)^{n_i - y} = \binom{n_i}{y}\left(\frac{1}{1+e^{-\beta \cdot X_i}}\right)^y \left(1 - \frac{1}{1+e^{-\beta \cdot X_i}}\right)^{n_i - y}.$$

This model can be fit using the same sorts of methods as the above more basic model.

Bayesian

In a Bayesian statistics context, prior distributions are normally placed on the regression coefficients, usually in the form of Gaussian distributions. There is no conjugate prior of the likelihood function in logistic regression. When Bayesian inference was performed analytically, this made the posterior distribution difficult to calculate except in very low dimensions. Now, though, automatic software such as OpenBUGS, JAGS and Stan allow these posteriors to be computed using simulation, so lack of conjugacy is not a concern. However, when the sample size or the number of parameters is large, full Bayesian simulation can be slow, and people often use approximate methods such as variational Bayes and expectation propagation.

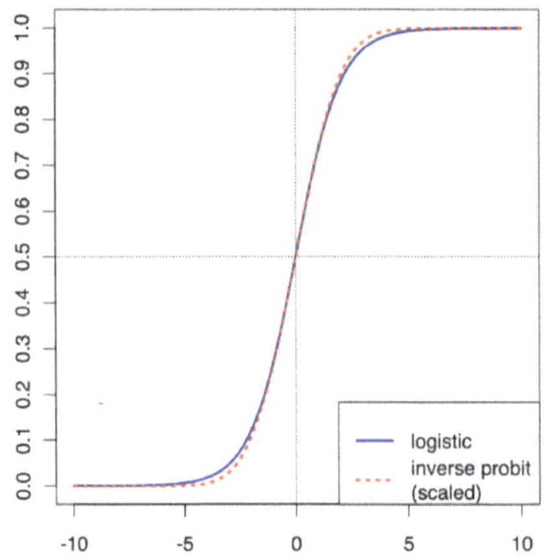

Comparison of logistic function with a scaled inverse probit function (i.e. the CDF of the normal distribution), comparing $\sigma(x)$ vs. $\Phi(\sqrt{\frac{\pi}{8}}x)$, which makes the slopes the same at the origin. This shows the heavier tails of the logistic distribution.

Extensions

There are large numbers of extensions:

- Multinomial logistic regression (or multinomial logit) handles the case of a multi-way categorical dependent variable (with unordered values, also called "classification"). Note that the general case of having dependent variables with more than two values is termed *polytomous regression.*
- Ordered logistic regression (or ordered logit) handles ordinal dependent variables (ordered values).
- Mixed logit is an extension of multinomial logit that allows for correlations among the choices of the dependent variable.
- An extension of the logistic model to sets of interdependent variables is the conditional random field.
- Conditional logistic regression handles matched or stratified data when the strata are small. It is mostly used in the analysis of observational studies.

Software

Most statistical software can do binary logistic regression.

- SAS
  - PROC LOGISTIC for basic logistic regression.
  - PROC CATMOD when all the variables are categorical.

  - PROC GLIMMIX for multilevel model logistic regression.
- R
  - glm in the stats package (using family = binomial)
  - GLMNET package for an efficient implementation regularized logistic regression
  - lmer for mixed effects logistic regression
  - arm package for bayesian logistic regression
- python
  - Part of the linear module in sklearn
  - Full example of logistic regression in the Theano tutorial
  - Bayesian Logistic Regression with ARD prior code, tutorial
  - Variational Bayes Logistic Regression with ARD prior code , tutorial
  - Bayesian Logistic Regression code, tutorial
- NCSS
  - Logistic Regression in NCSS

Notably, Microsoft Excel's statistics extension package does not include it.

Probit Model

In statistics, a probit model is a type of regression where the dependent variable can only take two values, for example married or not married. The word is a portmanteau, coming from *probability* + *unit*. The purpose of the model is to estimate the probability that an observation with particular characteristics will fall into a specific one of the categories; Moreover, classifying observations based on their predicted probabilities is a type of binary classification model.

A probit model is a popular specification for an ordinal or a binary response model. As such it treats the same set of problems as does logistic regression using similar techniques. The probit model, which employs a probit link function, is most often estimated using the standard maximum likelihood procedure, such an estimation being called a probit regression.

Probit models were introduced by Chester Bliss in 1934; a fast method for computing maximum likelihood estimates for them was proposed by Ronald Fisher as an appendix to Bliss' work in 1935.

Conceptual Framework

Suppose a response variable *Y* is *binary*, that is it can have only two possible outcomes which we will denote as 1 and 0. For example *Y* may represent presence/absence of a certain condition, success/failure of some device, answer yes/no on a survey, etc. We also have a vector of regressors *X*, which are assumed to influence the outcome *Y*. Specifically, we assume that the model takes the form

$$\Pr(Y = 1 \mid X) = \Phi(X^T \beta),$$

where Pr denotes probability, and Φ is the Cumulative Distribution Function (CDF) of the standard normal distribution. The parameters β are typically estimated by maximum likelihood.

It is possible to motivate the probit model as a latent variable model. Suppose there exists an auxiliary random variable

$$Y^* = X^T \beta + \varepsilon,$$

where $\varepsilon \sim N(0, 1)$. Then *Y* can be viewed as an indicator for whether this latent variable is positive:

$$Y = \begin{cases} 1 & Y^* > 0 \\ 0 & \text{otherwise} \end{cases} = \begin{cases} 1 & -\varepsilon < X^T \beta, \\ 0 & \text{otherwise.} \end{cases}$$

The use of the standard normal distribution causes no loss of generality compared with using an arbitrary mean and standard deviation because adding a fixed amount to the mean can be compensated by subtracting the same amount from the intercept, and multiplying the standard deviation by a fixed amount can be compensated by multiplying the weights by the same amount.

To see that the two models are equivalent, note that

$$\begin{aligned}
&\Pr(Y = 1 \mid X) \\
&= \Pr(Y^* > 0) \\
&= \Pr(X^T \beta + \varepsilon > 0) \\
&= \Pr(\varepsilon > -X^T \beta) \\
&= \Pr(\varepsilon < X^T \beta) \qquad \text{by symmetry of the normal distribution} \\
&= \Phi(X^T \beta)
\end{aligned}$$

Model Estimation

Maximum Likelihood Estimation

Suppose data set $\{y_i, x_i\}_{i=1}^n$ contains *n* independent statistical units corresponding to the model above. Then their joint log-likelihood function is

$$\ln \mathcal{L}(\beta) = \sum_{i=1}^{n} \left(y_i \ln \Phi(x_{i'}\beta) + (1 - y_i) \ln\left(1 - \Phi(x_{i'}\beta)\right) \right)$$

The estimator $\hat{\beta}$ which maximizes this function will be consistent, asymptotically normal and efficient provided that E[*XX'*] exists and is not singular. It can be shown that this log-likelihood function is globally concave in *β*, and therefore standard numerical algorithms for optimization will converge rapidly to the unique maximum.

Asymptotic distribution for $\hat{\beta}$ is given by

$$\sqrt{n}(\hat{\beta} - \beta) \xrightarrow{d} \mathcal{N}(0, \Omega^{-1}),$$

where

$$\Omega = E\left[\frac{\varphi^2(X'\beta)}{\Phi(X'\beta)(1 - \Phi(X'\beta))} XX'\right], \qquad \hat{\Omega} = \frac{1}{n} \sum_{i=1}^{n} \frac{\varphi^2(x_i'\hat{\beta})}{\Phi(x_i'\hat{\beta})(1 - \Phi(x_i'\hat{\beta}))} x_i x_i'$$

and *φ* = *Φ*› is the Probability Density Function (PDF) of standard normal distribution.

Berkson's Minimum Chi-square Method

This method can be applied only when there are many observations of response variable y_i having the same value of the vector of regressors x_i (such situation may be referred to as "many observations per cell"). More specifically, the model can be formulated as follows.

Suppose among *n* observations $\{y_i, x_i\}_{i=1}^n$ there are only *T* distinct values of the regressors, which can be denoted as $\{x_{(1)}, \ldots, x_{(T)}\}$. Let n_t be the number of observations with $x_i = x_{(t)}$, and r_t the number of such observations with $y_i = 1$. We assume that there are indeed "many" observations per each "cell": for each $t, \lim_{n \to \infty} n_t / n = c_t > 0$.

Denote

$$\hat{p}_t = r_t / n_t$$

$$\hat{\sigma}_t^2 = \frac{1}{n_t} \frac{\hat{p}_t(1 - \hat{p}_t)}{\varphi^2\left(\Phi^{-1}(\hat{p}_t)\right)}$$

Then Berkson's minimum chi-square estimator is a generalized least squares estimator in a regression of $\Phi^{-1}(\hat{p}_t)$ on $x_{(t)}$ with weights $\hat{\sigma}_t^{-2}$:

$$\hat{\beta} = \Big(\sum_{t=1}^{T} \hat{\sigma}_t^{-2} x_{(t)} x'_{(t)}\Big)^{-1} \sum_{t=1}^{T} \hat{\sigma}_t^{-2} x_{(t)} \Phi^{-1}(\hat{p}_t)$$

It can be shown that this estimator is consistent (as $n \to \infty$ and T fixed), asymptotically normal and efficient. Its advantage is the presence of a closed-form formula for the estimator. However, it is only meaningful to carry out this analysis when individual observations are not available, only their aggregated counts r_t, n_t, and $x_{(t)}$ (for example in the analysis of voting behavior).

Gibbs Sampling

Gibbs sampling of a probit model is possible because regression models typically use normal prior distributions over the weights, and this distribution is conjugate with the normal distribution of the errors (and hence of the latent variables Y^*). The model can be described as

$$\begin{aligned} \beta &\sim \mathcal{N}(b_0, B_0) \\ y_i^* \mid x_i, \beta &\sim \mathcal{N}(x_i'\beta, 1) \\ y_i &= \begin{cases} 1 & \text{if } y_i^* > 0 \\ 0 & \text{otherwise} \end{cases} \end{aligned}$$

From this, we can determine the full conditional densities needed:

$$\begin{aligned} & B = (B_0^{-1} + X'X)^{-1} \\ & \beta \mid y^* \sim \mathcal{N}(B(B_0^{-1} b_0 + X'y^*), B) \\ & y_i^* \mid y_i = 0, x_i, \beta \sim \mathcal{N}(x'_i\beta, 1)[y_i^* < 0] \\ & y_i^* \mid y_i = 1, x_i, \beta \sim \mathcal{N}(x'_i\beta, 1)[y_i^* \geq 0] \end{aligned}$$

The result for β is given in Bayesian linear regression, although specified with different notation.

The only trickiness is in the last two equations. The notation $[y_i^* < 0]$ is the Iverson bracket, sometimes written $\mathcal{I}(y_i^* < 0)$ or similar. It indicates that the distribution must be truncated within the given range, and rescaled appropriately. In this particular case, a truncated normal distribution arises. Sampling from this distribution depends on how much is truncated. If a large fraction of the original mass remains, sampling can be easily done with rejection sampling—simply sample a number from the non-truncated distribution, and reject it if it falls outside the restriction imposed by the truncation. If sampling from only a small fraction of the original mass, however (e.g. if sampling from one of the tails of the normal distribution—for example if $x_i'\beta$ is around 3 or more, and a negative sample is desired), then this will be inefficient and it becomes necessary to fall back on other sampling algorithms. General sampling from the truncated normal can be achieved using approximations to the normal CDF and the probit function, and R has a function rtnorm() for generating truncated-normal samples.

Model Evaluation

The suitability of an estimated binary model can be evaluated by counting the number of true observations equaling 1, and the number equaling zero, for which the model assigns a correct predicted classification by treating any estimated probability above 1/2 (or, below 1/2), as an assignment of a prediction of 1 (or, of 0).

Simultaneous Equation Model

Simultaneous equation models are a type of statistical model in the form of a set of linear simultaneous equations. They are often used in econometrics.

Structural and Reduced Form

Suppose there are m regression equations of the form

$$y_{it} = y_{-i,t}'\gamma_i + x_{it}'\beta_i + u_{it}, \quad i = 1,\ldots,m,$$

where i is the equation number, and $t = 1, \ldots, T$ is the observation index. In these equations x_{it} is the $k_i \times 1$ vector of exogenous variables, y_{it} is the dependent variable, $y_{-i,t}$ is the $n_i \times 1$ vector of all other endogenous variables which enter the ith equation on the right-hand side, and u_{it} are the error terms. The "$-i$" notation indicates that the vector $y_{-i,t}$ may contain any of the y's except for y_{it} (since it is already present on the left-hand side). The regression coefficients β_i and γ_i are of dimensions $k_i \times 1$ and $n_i \times 1$ correspondingly. Vertically stacking the T observations corresponding to the ith equation, we can write each equation in vector form as

$$y_i = Y_{-i}\gamma_i + X_i\beta_i + u_i, \quad i = 1,\ldots,m,$$

where y_i and u_i are $T \times 1$ vectors, X_i is a $T \times k_i$ matrix of exogenous regressors, and Y_{-i} is a $T \times n_i$ matrix of endogenous regressors on the right-hand side of the ith equation. Finally, we can move all endogenous variables to the left-hand side and write the m equations jointly in vector form as

$$Y\Gamma = XB + U.$$

This representation is known as the structural form. In this equation $Y = [y_1\ y_2\ \ldots\ y_m]$ is the $T\times m$ matrix of dependent variables. Each of the matrices Y_{-i} is in fact an n_i-columned submatrix of this Y. The $m\times m$ matrix Γ, which describes the relation between the dependent variables, has a complicated structure. It has ones on the diagonal, and all other elements of each column i are either the components of the vector $-\gamma_i$ or zeros, depending on which columns of Y were included in the matrix Y_{-i}. The $T\times k$ matrix X contains all exogenous regressors from all equations, but without repetitions (that is, matrix X should be of full rank). Thus, each X_i is a k_i-columned submatrix of X. Matrix Β has size $k\times m$, and each of its columns consists of the components of vectors β_i and zeros, depending on which of the regressors from X were included or excluded from X_i. Finally, $U = [u_1\ u_2\ \ldots\ u_m]$ is a $T\times m$ matrix of the error terms.

Postmultiplying the structural equation by Γ^{-1}, the system can be written in the reduced form as

$$Y = XB\Gamma^{-1} + U\Gamma^{-1} = X\Pi + V.$$

This is already a simple general linear model, and it can be estimated for example by ordinary least squares. Unfortunately, the task of decomposing the estimated matrix $\hat{\Pi}$ into the individual factors Β and Γ^{-1} is quite complicated, and therefore the reduced form is more suitable for prediction but not inference.

Assumptions

Firstly, the rank of the matrix X of exogenous regressors must be equal to k, both in finite samples and in the limit as $T \to \infty$ (this later requirement means that in the limit the expression $\frac{1}{T}X'X$ should converge to a nondegenerate $k\times k$ matrix). Matrix Γ is also assumed to be non-degenerate.

Secondly, error terms are assumed to be serially independent and identically distributed. That is, if the tth row of matrix U is denoted by $u_{(t)}$, then the sequence of vectors $\{u_{(t)}\}$ should be iid, with zero mean and some covariance matrix Σ (which is unknown). In particular, this implies that $E[U] = 0$, and $E[U'U] = T\Sigma$.

Lastly, the identification conditions require that the number of unknowns in this system of equations should not exceed the number of equations. More specifically, the *order condition* requires that for each equation $k_i + n_i \leq k$, which can be phrased as "the number of excluded exogenous variables is greater or equal to the number of included endogenous variables". The *rank condition* of identifiability is that $\text{rank}(\Pi_{io}) = n_i$, where Π_{io} is a $(k-k_i)\times n_i$ matrix which is obtained from Π by crossing out those columns which correspond to the excluded endogenous variables, and those rows which correspond to the included exogenous variables.

Estimation

Two-stages Least Squares (2SLS)

The simplest and the most common estimation method for the simultaneous equations model is the so-called two-stage least squares method, developed independently by Theil (1953) and Basmann (1957). It is an equation-by-equation technique, where the endogenous regressors on the right-hand side of each equation are being instrumented with the regressors X from all other equations. The method is called "two-stage" because it conducts estimation in two steps:

Step 1: Regress Y_{-i} on X and obtain the predicted values $\hat{Y}_{-i}$;

Step 2: Estimate γ_i, β_i by the ordinary least squares regression of y_i on $\hat{Y}_{-i}$ and X_i.

If the ith equation in the model is written as

$$y_i = \begin{pmatrix} Y_{-i} & X_i \end{pmatrix} \begin{pmatrix} \gamma_i \\ \beta_i \end{pmatrix} + u_i \equiv Z_i \delta_i + u_i,$$

where Z_i is a $T \times (n_i + k_i)$ matrix of both endogenous and exogenous regressors in the ith equation, and δ_i is an $(n_i + k_i)$-dimensional vector of regression coefficients, then the 2SLS estimator of δ_i will be given by

$$\hat{\delta}_i = \left(\hat{Z}_i' \hat{Z}_i\right)^{-1} \hat{Z}_i' y_i = \left(Z_i' P Z_i\right)^{-1} Z_i' P y_i,$$

where $P = X(X'X)^{-1}X'$ is the projection matrix onto the linear space spanned by the exogenous regressors X.

Indirect Least Squares

Indirect least squares is an approach in econometrics where the coefficients in a simultaneous equations model are estimated from the reduced form model using ordinary least squares. For this, the structural system of equations is transformed into the reduced form first. Once the coefficients are estimated the model is put back into the structural form.

Limited Information Maximum Likelihood (LIML)

The "limited information" maximum likelihood method was suggested by Anderson & Rubin (1949). It is used when one is interested in estimating a single structural equation at a time (hence its name of limited information), say for observation i:

$$y_i = Y_{-i}\gamma_i + X_i\beta_i + u_i \equiv Z_i\delta_i + u_i$$

The structural equations for the remaining endogenous variables Y_{-i} are not specified, and they are given in their reduced form:

$$Y_{-i} = X\Pi + U_{-i}$$

Notation in this context is different than for the simple IV case. One has:

- Y_{-i} : The endogenous variable(s).
- X_{-i} : The exogenous variable(s)
- X : The instrument(s) (often denoted Z)

The explicit formula for the LIML is:

$$\hat{\delta}_i = \left(Z_i'(I - \lambda M)Z_i\right)^{-1} Z_i'(I - \lambda M)y_i,$$

where $M = I - X(X'X)^{-1}X'$, and λ is the smallest characteristic root of the matrix:

$$\left(\begin{bmatrix} y_i \\ Y_{-i} \end{bmatrix} M_i [y_i \quad Y_{-i}]\right)\left(\begin{bmatrix} y_i \\ Y_{-i} \end{bmatrix} M [y_i \quad Y_{-i}]\right)^{-1}$$

where, in a similar way, $M_i = I - X_i(X_i'X_i)^{-1}X_i'$.

In other words, λ is the smallest solution of the generalized eigenvalue problem:

$$\left|[y_i \quad Y_{-i}]' M_i [y_i \quad Y_{-i}] - \lambda [y_i \quad Y_{-i}]' M [y_i \quad Y_{-i}]\right| = 0$$

K Class Estimators

The LIML is a special case of the K-class estimators:

$$\hat{\delta} = \left(Z'(I - \kappa M)Z\right)^{-1} Z'(I - \kappa M)y,$$

with:

- $\delta = [\beta_i \quad \gamma_i]$
- $Z = [X_i \quad Y_{-i}]$

Several estimators belong to this class:

- $\kappa=0$: OLS
- $\kappa=1$: 2SLS. Note indeed that in this case, $I - \kappa M = I - M = P$ the usual projection matrix of the 2SLS
- $\kappa=\lambda$: LIML

- $\kappa=\lambda - \alpha\,(n-K)$: Fuller (1977) estimator. Here K represents the number of instruments, n the sample size, and α a positive constant to specify. A value of $\alpha=1$ will yield an estimator that is approximately unbiased.

Three-stage Least Squares (3SLS)

The three-stage least squares estimator was introduced by Zellner & Theil (1962). It can be seen as a special case of multi-equation GMM where the set of instrumental variables is common to all equations. If all regressors are in fact predetermined, then 3SLS reduces to seemingly unrelated regressions (SUR). Thus it may also be seen as a combination of two-stage least squares (2SLS) with SUR.

Using Cross-equation Restrictions to Achieve Identification

In simultaneous equations models, the most common method to achieve identification is by imposing within-equation parameter restrictions. Yet, identification is also possible using cross equation restrictions.

To illustrate how cross equation restrictions can be used for identification, consider the following example from Wooldridge

$$y_1 = \gamma_{12} y_2 + \delta_{11} z_1 + \delta_{12} z_2 + \delta_{13} z_3 + u_1$$

$$y_2 = \gamma_{21} y_1 + \delta_{21} z_1 + \delta_{22} z_2 + u_2$$

where z's are uncorrelated with u's and y's are endogenous variables. Without further restrictions, the first equation is not identified because there is no excluded exogenous variable. The second equation is just identified if $\delta_{13}\neq 0$, which is assumed to be true for the rest of discussion.

Now we impose the cross equation restriction of $\delta_{12}=\delta_{22}$. Since the second equation is identified, we can treat δ_12 as known for the purpose of identification. Then, the first equation becomes:

$$y_1 - \delta_{12} z_2 = \gamma_{12} y_2 + \delta_{11} z_1 + \delta_{13} z_3 + u_1$$

Then, we can use (z_1,z_2,z_3) as instruments to estimate the coefficients in the above equation since there are one endogenous variable (y_2) and one excluded exogenous variable (z_2) on the right hand side. Therefore, cross equation restrictions in place of within-equation restrictions can achieve identification.

Applications in Social Science

Across fields and disciplines simultaneous equation models are applied to various observational phenomena. These equations are applied when phenomena are assumed to be reciprocally causal. The classic example is supply and demand in economics. In other disciplines there are examples such as candidate evaluations and party identification or public opinion and social policy in political science; road investment and travel demand in geography; and educational attainment and parenthood entry in sociology or demography. The simultaneous equation model requires a theory of reciprocal causality that includes special features if the causal effects are to be estimated as simultaneous feedback as opposed to one-sided 'blocks' of an equation where a researcher is interested in the causal effect of X on Y while holding the causal effect of Y on X constant, or when the researcher knows the exact amount of time it takes for each causal effect to take place, i.e., the length of the causal lags. Instead of lagged effects, simultaneous feedback means estimating the simultaneous and perpetual impact of X and Y on each other. This requires a theory that causal effects are simultaneous in time, or so complex that they appear to behave simultaneously; a common example are the moods of roommates. To estimate simultaneous feedback models a theory of equilibrium is also necessary. That X and Y are in relatively steady states or are part of a system (society, market, classroom) that is in a relatively stable state.

It is a system that describes the joint dependence of variables. Regression modeling has two structures: Single equation modelling; structural equation modelling.

Single Equation Modelling

- One dependent variable with one or more independent variables;
- It is a case of multiple regression analysis;
- One way causality is allowed.

Structural Equation Modelling

- Joint dependence of variables;
- All are interdependent;
- Identification is required for estimation process;
- Two ways causality is allowed.

The above two cases can be analyzed by this model:

In case of the single equation models where we dealt with only unidirectional cause and effect relationship, in simultaneous equation models we lump together a set of variables that can be solved simultaneously by the remaining set of variables. Simple market model: consists of demand equation, supply equation and equilibrium condition

$$\text{Supply equation:} \qquad Q^s = g(p) \text{ with } \frac{\partial Q^s}{\partial p} > 0$$

$$\text{Demand equation:} \qquad Q^d = f(p) \text{ with } \frac{\partial Q^d}{\partial p} > 0$$

$$\text{Equilibrium Condition:} \qquad Q^s = Q^d = Q$$

A linear version of this model specified for an agricultural commodity is:

$$Q_t^s = \alpha_1 + \alpha_2 P_t + \alpha_3 R_t + u_{1t}$$
$$Q_t^d = \beta_1 + \beta_2 P_t + \beta_3 Y_t + u_{2t}$$
$$Q^s = Q^d = Q$$

- Q_s is the supply equation and Q_d is the demand equation and the third equation is the equilibrium equation.
- Q_s,Q_d are the endogenous variables while let R and Y be the exogenous variables

Features of Simultaneous Equation Models

- There is more than one equation in the system
- Variables are classified into two groups: endogenous and exogenous
- Parameters cannot be estimated in a particular equation without knowing the information about other equations.
- The direct OLS is not feasible to estimate the parameters.

Different Types of Simultaneous Equation Models

Structural Equation Models

Structural equation models (SEMs), also called simultaneous equation models, are multivariate (i.e., multiple equation) regression models. Unlike the more traditional multivariate linear model, however, the response variable in one regression equation in an SEM may appear as a predictor in another equation; indeed, variables in an SEM may influence one-another reciprocally, either directly or through other variables as intermediaries. These structural equations are meant to represent causal relationships among the variables in the model.

Reduced Form Models

In statistics, and particularly in econometrics, the reduced form of a system of equations is the result of solving the system for the endogenous variables. This gives the latter as a function of the exogenous variables, if any. In econometrics, "structural form" models begin from deductive theories of the economy, while "reduced form" models begin by identifying particular relationships between variables.

Let Y and X be random vectors. Y is the vector of the variables to be explained (endogenous variables) by a statistical model and X is the vector of explanatory (exogenous) variables. In addition let be a vector of error terms.

Then the general expression of a structural form is,

$$f(Y,X,e)=0$$

Where, f is a function, possibly from vectors to vectors in the case of a multiple-equation model. The reduced form of this model is given by, $Y=g(X,\varepsilon)$ with g as function.

Recursive Models

A model is recursive if its structural equations are can be ordered in such a way that the first includes only predetermined variables in the right hand side and the second consists of predetermined variables and the endogenous variable on the right hand side. This system of equations can be estimated by OLS which will yield unbiased and consistent estimates.

Various Issues Under Simultaneous Equation System

Endogenous Variable

A variable included in the model is said to endogenous if it determines the model and is also determined by it. When there are two or more than two such variables, there is a feedback among these variables and hence they are jointly-determined by the system of equations. Consequently the error terms and the endogenous variables are always assumed to be correlated. Statistically it means that endogenous variables are stochastic variables and their distribution can be derived from that of the error component.

Exogenous Variable

A variable included in the model is said to exogenous if it determines the model and is not determined by it. Consequently the error terms and the exogenous variables are always assumed to be independent of each other or uncorrelated. Statistically it means that exogenous variables are non-stochastic variables. Lagged dependent variables are also exogenous variables and also referred to as predetermined variables.

Major Problems

Simultaneous equation has two most important issues; Problem of identification and problem of estimation

Problems of Identification

A model is identifiable if coefficients of all its equations can be uniquely determined from those of its reduced form model. Even if coefficients of some of its equations cannot be determined uniquely, still the model is not identifiable. An equation in a model is said to be over identified if the information in the regression function is more than sufficient to determine the structural coefficients uniquely. Any equation which is not identifiable is said to be under identified. Alternatively, an equation in a model is said to be under identified if the information in the RF is not sufficient to determine the structural coefficients uniquely.

Assessing Identification Problems

There are three possible ways of identification:

- Over-identified model
- Under-identified model
- Exactly- identified model

It can be noted that a simultaneous equation system is consistent, if it satisfies the followings:

1. Model must be uniquely in statistical form
2. All equations are identified one
3. No of equations is equal to no of parameters
4. All parameters are indentified

There are two approaches to assess the identification of the equations/ model. They are

- Order condition for identification
- Rank condition for identification

Order Condition for Identification

It is a necessary condition for the identification problem. The test is s based on the number of exogenous variables to be excluded in each equation to make that equation identifiable. For an equation to be identified the total number of variables excluded from it must be equal to or greater than the number of endogenous variables in the model less one. It can also define that "for an equation to be identified the total number of variables excluded from it but included in other equations must be at least as great as the number of equations in the system less one."

To interpret the same, let us define the followings:

M = Total number of endogenous variables in the system of equations

m = Number of endogenous variables in the equation under consideration

K = Total number of exogenous variables in the system of equations

k = Number of exogenous variables in the equation under consideration

Now, the identification of the models can be tracked by the following conditions:

$$K - M \geq G - 1$$

Order Condition for Identification problem:

- An equation in the model is under identified if $K - M < G - 1$
- An equation in the is under identified if $K - M = G - 1$
- An equation in the model is over identified if $K - M > G - 1$
- Sometimes the order condition fails to give proper identification so we use the rank condition.
- First use the rank condition to find out if the equation is identified or not. If the equation is identified, then use the order condition to check if it is exactly identified or over identified.

Rank Condition for Identification Problem

It is a sufficient condition for the identification problem. The structure defines like this. "In a system of G equations, any particular equation is identified, if it is possible to construct at least one non-zero determinant of order (G-1) from the coefficients of the variables excluded from the particular equation but included in other equation of the model."

The followings steps to be taken to do the same:

1. Write all the parameters of the model in the separate table. That is matrix of structural parameters.
2. Strike all the rows of coefficients of that equation to be identified.
3. Strike all the columns of non-zero coefficients.

4. Set the determinant of the order (G-1) from the left items.
5. At least one determinants of order (G-1) should have positive value.

Advantages Associated with Identification Problem

- It solves multicolinearity
- It gives an indication of various alternatives to solve simultaneous equation system
- It gives a structure of structural modelling vs. reduced from of the modelling

Problems of Estimation

In the simultaneous equation systems, OLS cannot be used directly to have the estimate the parameters and use the model for prediction and forecasting. On the contrary, we have several alternatives methods to solve the simultaneous equations system. These include:

1. Indirect Least Squares (ILS)
2. Two Stages Least Squares Method (2SLS)
3. Three Stages Least Squares Method (3 SLS)
4. Limited Information Maximum Likelihood Method (LIMLM)
5. Full Information Maximum Likelihood Method (FIMLM)

The Sample Problems

$$y_1 = 3y_2 - 2x_1 + x_2 + u_1$$
$$y_2 = y_3 + x_3 + u_2$$
$$y_3 = y_1 - y_2 - 2x_3 + u_3$$

$$-y_1 + 3y_2 + 0y_3 - 2x_1 + x_2 + 0x_3 + u_1 = 0$$
$$0y_1 - y_2 + y_3 + 0x_1 + 0x_2 + x_3 + u_2 = 0$$
$$y_1 - y_2 - y_3 + 0x_1 + 0x_2 - 2x_3 + u_3 = 0$$

y_1	y_2	y_3	x_1	x_2	x_3
−1	3	0	−2	1	0
0	−1	1	0	0	1
1	−1	−1	0	0	−2

Equation 1

Order Condition:

K=6; M=4; G=3

(K-M) = 6-4=2

(G-1) = 3-1=2

Exactly identified

Rank condition:

$$\begin{matrix} -1 & 3 & 0 & -2 & 1 & 0 \\ 0 & -1 & 1 & 0 & 0 & 1 \\ 1 & -1 & -1 & 0 & 0 & -2 \end{matrix}$$

$$\begin{vmatrix} 1 & 1 \\ -1 & -2 \end{vmatrix}$$

As this is non-zero, equation 1 is exactly identified.

Equation 2: Order Condition:

K=6; M=3; G=3

(K-M) = 6-3=3

(G-1) = 3-1=2

Over-identified

Rank condition:

$$\begin{matrix} -1 & 3 & 0 & -2 & 1 & 0 \\ 0 & -1 & 1 & 0 & 0 & 1 \\ 1 & -1 & -1 & 0 & 0 & -2 \end{matrix}$$

$$\begin{matrix} -1 & -2 & 1 \\ 1 & 0 & 0 \end{matrix}$$

$$\begin{vmatrix} -1 & -2 \\ 1 & 0 \end{vmatrix}$$

As this is non-zero, equation 2 is exactly identified.

Equation 3

Order Condition:

K=6; M=4; G=3

(K-M) = 6-4=2

(G-1) = 3-1=2

Exactly identified

Rank condition:

$$\begin{matrix} -1 & 3 & 0 & -2 & 1 & 0 \\ 0 & -1 & 1 & 0 & 0 & 1 \\ 1 & -1 & -1 & 0 & 0 & -2 \end{matrix}$$

$$\begin{vmatrix} 2 & 1 \\ 0 & 0 \end{vmatrix}$$

As this is zero, equation 3 is not identified.

Establishing Identification from the Reduced Form

Order Condition

$$(K-M) \geq (G-1)$$

Rank condition

G^* = number of endogenous variables contained in a particular equation.

An equation containing G^* =endogenous variables is identified if it is possible to construct at least one non-zero determinant of order G^*-1 from the reduced form coefficients of the exogenous variables excluded from that particular equation.

$$\begin{aligned} y_1 &= 3y_2 - 2x_1 + x_2 + u_1 \\ y_2 &= y_3 + x_3 + u_2 \\ y_3 &= y_1 - y_2 - 2x_3 + u_3 \end{aligned}$$

The reduced form for this model is:

$$\begin{aligned} y_1 &= 4x_1 - 2x_2 + 3x_3 \\ y_2 &= 2x_1 - x_2 + x_3 \\ y_3 &= 2x_1 - x_2 \end{aligned}$$

Equation 1

Order Condition:

K=6; M=4;G=3

(K-M) = 6-4=2

(G-1) = 3-1=2

Exactly identified

Rank condition:

Excluded endogenous: y_3

Included exogenous: x_1, x_2

$$\begin{matrix} 4 & -2 & 3 \\ 2 & -1 & 1 \\ 2 & -1 & 0 \\ 3 & & \\ 1 & & \end{matrix}$$

$$G^* = 2, \left(G^* - 1\right) = 1$$

As both 3 and 1 are non-zero, equation 1 is exactly identified.

Equation 2

Order Condition:

K=6; M=3; G=3

(K-M) = 6-3=3

(G-1) = 3-1=2

Over-identified

Rank condition:

Excluded endogenous: y_1

Included exogenous: x_3

$$\begin{matrix} 4 & -2 & 3 \\ 2 & -1 & 1 \\ 2 & -1 & 0 \end{matrix}$$

$$\begin{matrix} 2 & -1 \\ 2 & -1 \end{matrix}$$

$$G^* = 2, \left(G^* - 1\right) = 1$$

As both 2 and -1 are non-zero, equation 2 is over-identified.

Equation 3

Order Condition:

K=6; M=4; G=3

(K-M) = 6-4=2

(G-1) = 3-1=2

Exactly identified

Rank condition:

Excluded endogenous: None

Included exogenous: x_3

$$\begin{matrix} 4 & -2 & 3 \\ 2 & -1 & 1 \\ 2 & -1 & 0 \end{matrix}$$

$$\begin{matrix} 4 & -2 \\ 2 & -1 \\ 2 & -1 \end{matrix}$$

$$G^* = 3, \left(G^* - 1\right) = 2$$

$$\begin{vmatrix} 4 & -2 \\ 2 & -1 \end{vmatrix} = 0$$

$$\begin{vmatrix} 2 & -1 \\ 2 & -1 \end{vmatrix} = 0$$

Structural Equation Modeling

It is a system that describes the joint dependence of variables. Regression modeling has two structures: Single equation modelling; structural equation modelling (SEM). The SEM is similar to simultaneous equation system, but the only difference is its path model, which is connected through measured variables and latent variables.

Single Equation Modelling

- One dependent variable with one or more independent variables;
- It is a case of multiple regression analysis;
- One way causality is allowed.

Structural Equation Modelling

- Joint dependence of variables;
- All are interdependent;
- Identification is required for estimation process;
- Two ways causality is allowed.

But in SEM, we expect two-way causality in many cases.

The Pre-requisite of Structural Equation Modelling

The basis of structural equation modelling is based on the issues of two variables: measured and latent.

- Measured variable
  - Observed variables, indicators or manifest variables in an SEM design
  - Predictors and outcomes
  - Squares in the diagram
- Latent Variable
  - Un-observable variable in the model, factor, construct
  - Construct derived from measured variables in the measurement model
  - Circles in the diagram
- Error or E

- Variance left over after prediction of a measured variable

- Disturbance or D
  - Variance left over after prediction of a factor
- Exogenous Variable
  - Variable that predicts other variables Giver/ IV
- Endogenous Variables Receiver/DV
  - A variable that is predicted by another variable
  - A predicted variable is endogenous even if it in turn predicts another variable
- Measurement Model
  - The part of the model that relates indicators to latent factors
  - The measurement model is the factor analytic part of SEM
- Structural model
  - This is the part of the model that relates variable or factors to one another (as in regression, prediction)

This is the regression part of the SEM

- Direct Effect
  - Regression coefficients of direct prediction
- Indirect Effect
  - Mediating effect of x_1 on y through x_2
- Confirmatory Factor Analysis
- Covariance Structure
  - Relationships based on variance and covariance
- Mean Structure
  - Includes means (intercepts) into the model
- Single-headed arrow →
  - This is prediction

  - Regression coefficient or factor loading
- Double headed arrow ↔
  - This is correlation
- Missing Paths
  - Hypothesized absence of relationship

The Basic Framework

- Variance- covariance structure
- Path analysis
- Regression analysis
- Confirmatory factor analysis
- Path analysis
- Structural regression models
- Latent change analysis

This can be analyzed as follows:

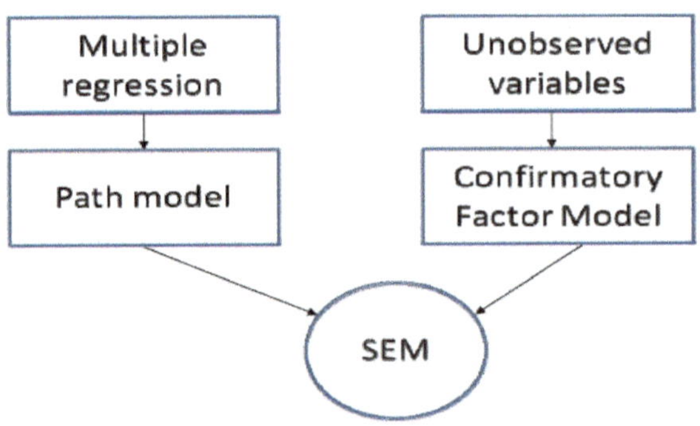

Multiple Regressions

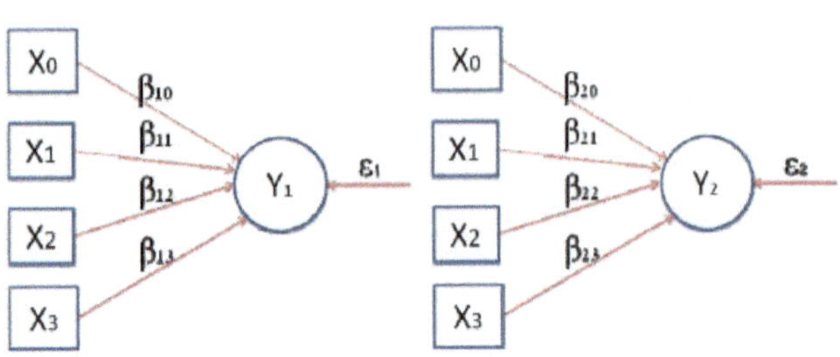

Multivariate Regression

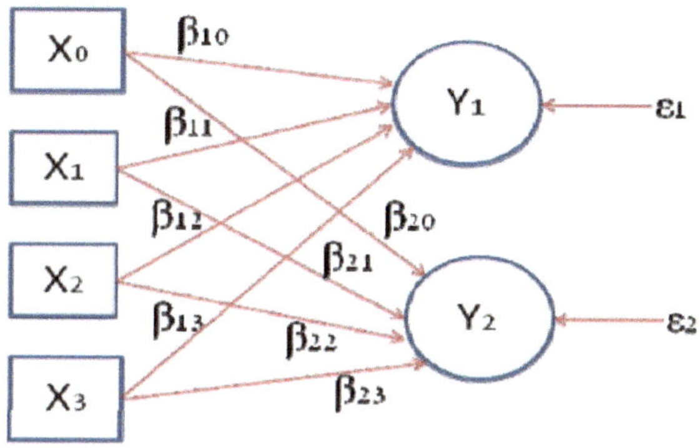

Path Model

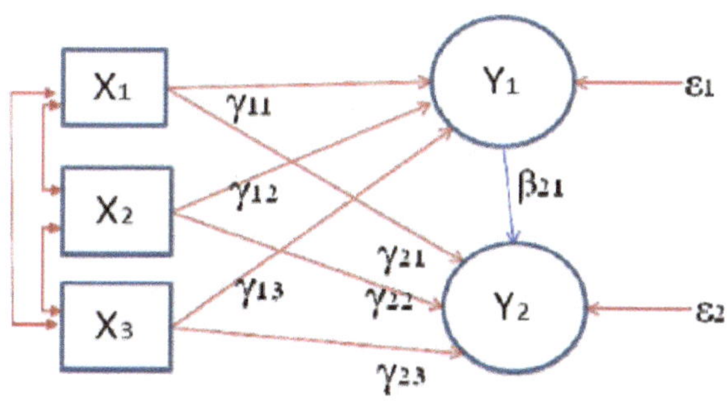

Factor Analysis

There are two approaches of factor analysis: Confirmatory factor analysis and exploratory factor analysis. But we use here the confirmatory factor analysis. This is best feasible for structural equation modelling (SEM)

Confirmatory Factor Model

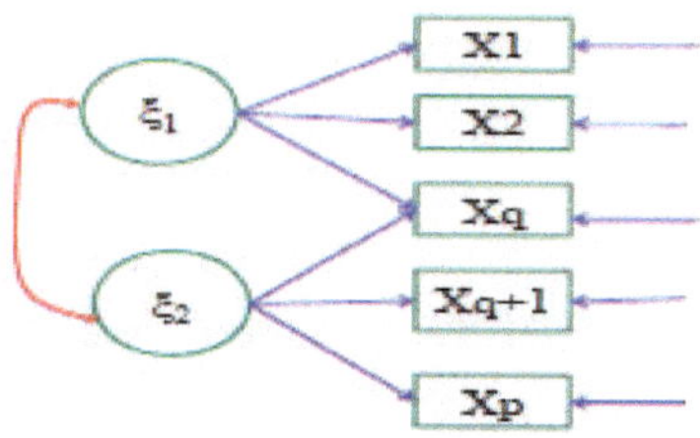

The need of factor analysis (FA) is as follows:

1. Dimension Reduction: 80 characteristics of retail shops and their services what consumers wanted to be changed. The owner wants to reduce them into fewer dimensions. The consultant collected data from consumers and then did factor analysis.

2. Variable Reduction: On the basis of grouping variables, 20 variables 3 factors may emerge.

3. Test Items into Factors: Twenty items proposed to measure ethical leadership in our study reduced into two factors- empowerment, motive and character.

The general purpose of FA is to find out a way of condensing /summarizing the information contained in a number of original variables into a smaller set of new, composite dimensions or factors with a minimum loss of information –that is, to search for and define the fundamental constructs or dimensions assumed to underlie the original variables.

1. Identify the structure of relationship among variables or respondents. R FA analyses a set of variables to identify the dimensions that are latent. Q FA analyses a large no individuals into distinct groups.
2. Identify the representative variables.
3. Create a new set of variables much smaller in number for subsequent analysis.

The Designing of Factor Analysis

- Correlation among Variables (R)/ Respondents (Q).
- Correlation matrix.
- FA (similarity of individuals on variance structure) and Cluster analysis (distance among respondents scores).

Variable Selection and Measurement Issues

Metric measurement of variables and some variables may be nonmetric or dummy. If all variables are dummy types, then it is a Boolean FA. It can be noted that the reasonable number of variables per factor, generally five or more.

Sample Size

Sample size needs to be > 100 or larger. 5 or 10 times observations X number of variables to be analysed. If there are 30 items in a scale, there needs to be 150 or 300 respondents to apply FA. Cases per Variable= 5 or 10 minimum. More cases will minimize the over fitting to the data.

Assumptions in FA

Correlation in substantial number of cases is > >.30, or partial correlation low. DV, IV mixed in FA is inadequate. Male and female mixed. Separate analysis for each group FA.

Deriving Factors and Assessing Overall Fit

Method of extracting factors (common factor analysis vs. component analysis/principal component analysis) and number of factors selected to represent the underlying structure in the data. Common factor analysis extracts factors specifying what the variables share in common. Component analysis/principal component analysis specifies the minimum number of factors.

Total Variance= Common + specific + error

Criteria for the Number of Factors to be extracted

1. Latent root criterion
2. A priori criterion; Percentage of variance extracted =60%, Screen test criterion, latent root: 1

Interpreting Factors

Factor loadings are correlation of each variable and the factor. Factor rotation: for interpretation. The reference axes of the factors are turned about the origin until some other position has been reached. Orthogonal 90°

Criterion for Significance of Loadings

350= .30, 250=. 35, 200=.40,

150=. 45, 100=.55, 85=.60, etc.

The Flowchart of SEM

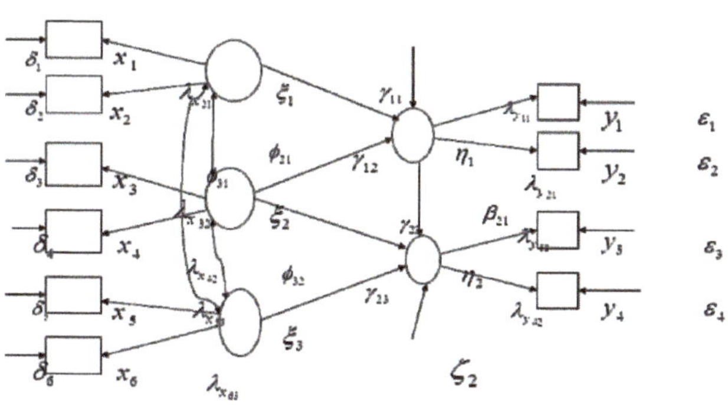

The stages of SEM

Stage 1: Developing a Theoretically Based Model

Stage 2: Constructing a Path Diagram of Causal Relationships

- Elements of a Path Diagram
- Examples of Path Diagrams
- Basic Terminology

Stage 3: Converting the Path Diagram into a Set of Structural Equations and Specifying the Measurement Model

- Structural Model
- Measurement Model

- Correspondence to Factor Analysis
- Specifying the Measurement Model
- Determining the Number of Indicators
- Accounting For Construct Reliability
  - Empirically Estimating Reliabilities
  - Specifying the Reliabilities
    - » Single-item Measures
    - » Use of Validated Scales or Measures
    - » Two-stage Analysis
    - » Methods of Specifying the Reliability

Stage 4: Choosing the Input Matrix Type and Estimating the Proposed Model

- Inputting Data

- Assumptions
- Covariance versus Correlations
- Sample Size
  - Model Estimation
- Estimation Technique
- Estimation Processes
- Computer Programs

Stage 5: Assessing the Identification of the Structural Model

Stage 6: Evaluating Goodness-of-Fit Criteria

- Offending Estimates
- Overall Model Fit
- Measurement Model Fit
    - Composite Reliability
    - Variance Extracted
- Structural Model Fit
- Comparison of Competing or Nested Models

The Details are Summarizing in the Following Flow Charts

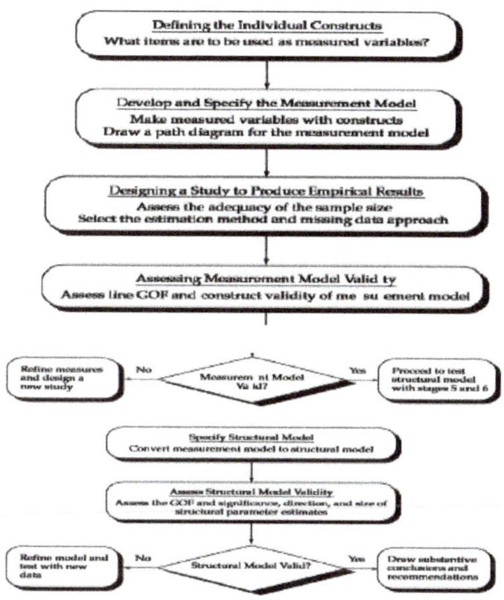

References

- Armstrong, J. Scott (2012). "Illusions in Regression Analysis". International Journal of Forecasting (forthcoming). 28 (3): 689. doi:10.1016/j.ijforecast.2012.02.001
- Mogull, Robert G. (2004). Second-Semester Applied Statistics. Kendall/Hunt Publishing Company. p. 59. ISBN 0-7575-1181-3
- Waegeman, Willem; De Baets, Bernard; Boullart, Luc (2008). "ROC analysis in ordinal regression learning". Pattern Recognition Letters. 29: 1–9. doi:10.1016/j.patrec.2007.07.019
- Yule, G. Udny (1897). "On the Theory of Correlation". Journal of the Royal Statistical Society. Blackwell Publishing. 60 (4): 812–54. JSTOR 2979746. doi:10.2307/2979746
- Ronald A. Fisher (1954). Statistical Methods for Research Workers (Twelfth ed.). Edinburgh: Oliver and Boyd. ISBN 0-05-002170-2

- Galton, Francis (1989). "Kinship and Correlation (reprinted 1989)". Statistical Science. Institute of Mathematical Statistics. 4 (2): 80–86. JSTOR 2245330. doi:10.1214/ss/1177012581
- Fisher, R.A. (1922). "The goodness of fit of regression formulae, and the distribution of regression coefficients". Journal of the Royal Statistical Society. Blackwell Publishing. 85 (4): 597–612. JSTOR 2341124. doi:10.2307/2341124
- Fotheringham, A. Stewart; Brunsdon, Chris; Charlton, Martin (2002). Geographically weighted regression: the analysis of spatially varying relationships (Reprint ed.). Chichester, England: John Wiley. ISBN 978-0-471-49616-8
- Pearson, Karl; Yule, G.U.; Blanchard, Norman; Lee,Alice (1903). "The Law of Ancestral Heredity". Biometrika. Biometrika Trust. 2 (2): 211–236. JSTOR 2331683. doi:10.1093/biomet/2.2.211
- Tofallis, C. (2009). "Least Squares Percentage Regression". Journal of Modern Applied Statistical Methods. 7: 526–534. SSRN 1406472. doi:10.2139/ssrn.1406472
- Chiang, C.L, (2003) Statistical methods of analysis, World Scientific. ISBN 981-238-310-7 - page 274 section 9.7.4 "interpolation vs extrapolation"
- Aldrich, John (2005). "Fisher and Regression". Statistical Science. 20 (4): 401–417. JSTOR 20061201. doi:10.1214/088342305000000331
- For a detailed discussion, see Van Den Poel, D.; Larivière, B. (2004). "Customer attrition analysis for financial services using proportional hazard models". European Journal of Operational Research. 157: 196. doi:10.1016/S0377-2217(03)00069-9
- Good, P. I.; Hardin, J. W. (2009). Common Errors in Statistics (And How to Avoid Them) (3rd ed.). Hoboken, New Jersey: Wiley. p. 211. ISBN 978-0-470-45798-6
- Fotheringham, AS; Wong, DWS (1 January 1991). "The modifiable areal unit problem in multivariate statistical analysis". Environment and Planning A. 23 (7): 1025–1044. doi:10.1068/a231025
- Kock, N.; Lynn, G. S. (2012). "Lateral collinearity and misleading results in variance-based SEM: An illustration and recommendations" (PDF). Journal of the Association for Information Systems. 13 (7): 546–580
- Belsley, David (1991). Conditioning Diagnostics: Collinearity and Weak Data in Regression. New York: Wiley. ISBN 0-471-52889-7
- O'Brien, R. M. (2007). "A Caution Regarding Rules of Thumb for Variance Inflation Factors". Quality & Quantity. 41 (5): 673. doi:10.1007/s11135-006-9018-6
- Suits, Daniel B. (1957). "Use of Dummy Variables in Regression Equations". Journal of the American Statistical Association. 52 (280): 548–551. JSTOR 2281705. doi:10.1080/01621459.1957.10501412
- Chatterjee, S.; Hadi, A. S.; Price, B. (2000). Regression Analysis by Example (Third ed.). John Wiley and Sons. ISBN 0-471-31946-5

Permissions

All chapters in this book are published with permission under the Creative Commons Attribution Share Alike License or equivalent. Every chapter published in this book has been scrutinized by our experts. Their significance has been extensively debated. The topics covered herein carry significant information for a comprehensive understanding. They may even be implemented as practical applications or may be referred to as a beginning point for further studies.

We would like to thank the editorial team for lending their expertise to make the book truly unique. They have played a crucial role in the development of this book. Without their invaluable contributions this book wouldn't have been possible. They have made vital efforts to compile up to date information on the varied aspects of this subject to make this book a valuable addition to the collection of many professionals and students.

This book was conceptualized with the vision of imparting up-to-date and integrated information in this field. To ensure the same, a matchless editorial board was set up. Every individual on the board went through rigorous rounds of assessment to prove their worth. After which they invested a large part of their time researching and compiling the most relevant data for our readers.

The editorial board has been involved in producing this book since its inception. They have spent rigorous hours researching and exploring the diverse topics which have resulted in the successful publishing of this book. They have passed on their knowledge of decades through this book. To expedite this challenging task, the publisher supported the team at every step. A small team of assistant editors was also appointed to further simplify the editing procedure and attain best results for the readers.

Apart from the editorial board, the designing team has also invested a significant amount of their time in understanding the subject and creating the most relevant covers. They scrutinized every image to scout for the most suitable representation of the subject and create an appropriate cover for the book.

The publishing team has been an ardent support to the editorial, designing and production team. Their endless efforts to recruit the best for this project, has resulted in the accomplishment of this book. They are a veteran in the field of academics and their pool of knowledge is as vast as their experience in printing. Their expertise and guidance has proved useful at every step. Their uncompromising quality standards have made this book an exceptional effort. Their encouragement from time to time has been an inspiration for everyone.

The publisher and the editorial board hope that this book will prove to be a valuable piece of knowledge for students, practitioners and scholars across the globe.

Index